Leitmotiv and Drama

Wagner, Brecht, and the
Limits of 'Epic' Theatre

HILDA MELDRUM BROWN

CLARENDON PRESS · OXFORD

1991

Oxford University Press, Walton Street, Oxford OX2 6DP
Oxford New York Toronto
Delhi Bombay Calcutta Madras Karachi
Petaling Jaya Singapore Hong Kong Tokyo
Nairobi Dar es Salaam Cape Town
Melbourne Auckland
and associated companies in
Berlin Ibadan

Oxford is a trade mark of Oxford University Press

Published in the United States
by Oxford University Press, New York

British Library Cataloguing in Publication Data
Data available

Library of Congress Cataloging in Publication Data
Brown, H. M. (Hilda Meldrum)
Leitmotiv and drama: Wagner, Brecht, and the limits of 'Epic'
theatre/Hilda Meldrum Brown.
Includes bibliographical references and index.
1. Brecht, Bertolt, 1898–1956—Technique. 2. Wagner, Richard,
1813–1883—Criticism and interpretation. 3. Leitmotiv. 4 Drama—
History and criticism. I. Title.
PT2603.R397Z58113 1991
832'.912—dc20
ISBN 0–19—816227–8

Typeset by Cambrian Typesetters, Frimley, Surrey
Printed in Great Britain by
Bookcraft (Bath) Ltd
Midsomer Norton, Avon

M. J. et P. J. B.
collegis fautoribus diligentissimis adiutoribus

Acknowledgements

It is a pleasure for the author to acknowledge the help and support of a number of institutions, colleagues, and friends. The British Academy and the German Academic Exchange Service provided generous grants which enabled most of the groundwork for this study to be done in Germany, in the stimulating surroundings in Regensburg and Bonn provided by Prof. Dr Hans Joachim Kreutzer and Prof. Dr Peter Pütz respectively. To the latter colleagues I owe a special debt of gratitude. Colleagues in Oxford, St Andrews, and Cambridge gave generously of their time, support, and expertise: conspicuously Margaret Jacobs, Peter Branscombe, Francis Lamport, and Raymond Lucas, all of whom read sections of the typescript at various stages in its evolution and made invaluable suggestions. Derrick Puffett tried to set me on the right musical path, but must bear no responsibility for the result. Peter Branscombe, Ronald Speirs, and John Deathridge read the final draft and made numerous suggestions for its improvement, most of which I hope they will find to have been incorporated. Jill Hughes, Assistant Librarian of the Taylorian, gave valuable assistance. Lisa Johnson showed potential talent as a copy-editor, and my husband was a tower of strength, especially on the word-processing front. Any remaining errors and other inadequacies are mine alone.

The author gratefully acknowledges permission to reproduce copyright material as follows:
Methuen and John Willett (translator), Bertolt Brecht, *Collected Plays*, vol. 5: i, *Life of Galileo* (London, 1980).
Methuen and Frank Jones (translator), *Saint Joan of the Stockyards* (London, 1976).
Suhrkamp Verlag, Frankfurt-on-Main: permission to quote from *GKA*, and *GW*.
Wilhelm Fink Verlag, Stuttgart, Manfred Pfister, *Das Drama* (for permission to use the diagram on p. 8).

Contents

Abbreviations

GKA   Bertolt Brecht, *Große kommentierte Berliner und Frank-furter Ausgabe* (30 vols., Berlin and Frankfurt-on-Main, 1988 ff.).

GSD   R. Wagner, *Gesammelte Schriften und Dichtungen* (12 vols., Leipzig, 1871–1911).

GW   Bertolt Brecht, *Gesammelte Werke*, ed. Suhrkamp-Verlag in collaboration with E. Hauptmann (Werkausgabe Edition Suhrkamp, 20 vols., Frankfurt-on-Main, 1967).

Note on Terminology

The term 'motiv' is used as a contraction of 'leitmotiv' and is to be distinguished from 'motif', which generally signifies mere thematic repetition without visual, metaphorical, or symbolic overtones. I have taken the liberty of anglicizing the plural form of 'motiv' for present purposes. Other terms such as 'Grundmotiv' and 'Nebenmotiv' are treated as German words.

Note on Translations

Translations for *Baal, Das Badener Lehrstück vom Einverständnis*, and the theoretical works of Brecht and Wagner are my own. Those for *Die Heilige Johanna* and *Leben des Galilei* are by Frank Jones and J. Willett respectively. I am grateful to the Bertolt Brecht Estate for permission to use those Brecht translations which are my own. These translations are © Stefan S. Brecht 1991.

I

General Introduction:
The Theoretical Background

Brecht and the Break with Tradition

The present study arises out of a sense of dissatisfaction with recent and contemporary dramatic theory and a conviction that the gap between leading theoretical approaches and the evidence presented to the reader and spectator in the form of a specific corpus of dramatic texts, at least as far as the German tradition is concerned, has been growing uncomfortably wide. It is evident, and must surely give rise to scepticism, that so many theorists are obsessed with what they see as the unique position of twentieth-century drama, pointing to developments—especially in the formal and technical spheres—which have carried it far beyond its origins. The modern drama, it is claimed, has made a complete break with tradition: innovation and experiment on a hitherto unprecedented scale have produced structures (it is not even clear that they should be termed 'dramas') which would be scarcely recognizable to the dramatists belonging to the great German tradition of the late eighteenth and early nineteenth centuries: that of Lessing, Schiller, Kleist, Grillparzer, and Hebbel. All notions of the carefully crafted, compact dramatic form, so succinctly analysed by Gustav Freytag,[1] have been abandoned and new criteria—over which there is still a large measure of disagreement—developed, in order to meet the new challenges of interpretation and assessment. Agreement appears to reign on one thing, however, and it is a matter of some importance to our theme; it is that the most profound and influential figure in both the theoretical and the practical spheres is that great and provocative anti-traditionalist, Bertolt Brecht. However, recent evidence also suggests that, despite all his protestations to the contrary, Brecht's roots, no less than those of

[1] Gustav Freytag, *Die Technik des Dramas* (Darmstadt, 1965 (reprint of 1922 13th edn.)).

others, lie deep in past traditions—biblical and literary, for instance—and that the salient difference lies only in the complexity of his relationship to these. This, together with the fact that Brecht himself is now firmly established as a 'twentieth-century classic', seems to me to indicate that the time is ripe for a stock-taking of some of the theoretical and practical foundations of his dramatic *œuvre*. It is especially opportune to reappraise and reassess a number of assumptions which have become common currency and which deserve a more critical scrutiny than they have often received. The claims for the uniqueness of Brechtian dramatic practice and Brechtian theory during this period, for instance, should not simply be left at the level of incontrovertible statement, if only because, as can be shown, they tend to be extremely selective and beg many important issues which cannot be ignored. While in no way being unmindful or unappreciative of the many exciting innovations that have taken place in twentieth-century drama, many of them attributable to Brecht's influence, we must carefully consider whether or not the case for discontinuity has been overstated.

Perspectivism

It must not be inferred from the above that the motivation for this study is wholly, or even substantially, negative in character. For the means by which I propose to conduct the reassessment will bring together a number of seemingly disparate theoretical concerns which have so far been treated in piecemeal fashion.[2] These all relate to what I shall call 'perspectivism'—the diverse means, that is, which the dramatist has at his disposal to bring together central issues or direct the reader's or spectator's attention away from the particularities of text, situation, characters, etc. to a more reflective, analytical, or contemplative level of reaction and understanding. It is my belief that there is an underlying principle at work here on which all drama (however defined) is based; this explains why such striking similarities can be discovered between, say, what could be described as a theory of perspective via choric means as advocated by Schiller in his essay 'Über den Gebrauch des Chors' and Brecht's

---

[2] See esp. discussion of examples of 'Episierung' (epicizing) in drama by various theorists to which attention is drawn below, p. 10 and p. 14.

variation on this particular theme in his theoretical works. It so happens that both these theories represent clear and straightforward examples of the operation of authorial perspective (in what I shall later term the *disjunctive* mode, a form, that is, which is *detached from* and may even appear to be set *in contrast to* the continuum of dramatic action). But it is a major part of my thesis to demonstrate that the underlying phenomenon which I have described is far from assuming the form of a set of prescriptive, exemplary, or didactic statements on the part of the author of a kind which will open up to reader or spectator once and for all the 'meaning' of a dramatic work. As we shall see, 'perspectives', even when they assume the disjunctive form, may express ambiguous formulations; they may include the dimension of paradox; they may, even, bring into question the very possibility of a certainty or fixity of meaning and interpretation. Furthermore—and this is a part of my thesis which I believe to be inadequately understood by students of drama—they may also, particularly in the *integrated* form most familiar to us in image-patterns, exist within a quasi-hierarchical structure or network of perspectival devices which fan out over a drama, interacting to form dominant, authoritative, or 'overarching' viewpoints; these, when taken together, resemble in function the more straightforward type of disjunctive commentary, such as is supplied most clearly through the agency of a chorus or a Brechtian 'singer'.

To illustrate the principle of perspective which I have in mind more clearly and to explain its often insufficiently appreciated dual mode of operation (i.e. the *disjunctive* and the *integrated*) it is useful to note the range of possibilities open to the dramatist. Familiar devices such as prologues, epilogues, *ad spectatores* addresses to the audience clearly fall into similar categories to the choric devices favoured by Brecht and Schiller; interpolated songs ('Liedeinlagen'), on the other hand, present a more complex aspect: in the hands of Brecht, and to a lesser extent Büchner, they may appear to stand in a contradictory relationship to text and dramatic situation, to be without textual moorings, so to speak, and therefore disjunctive; in the hands of Goethe, (cf. *Urfaust*), however, the reverse may seem to apply. Many theorists (e.g. Klotz, Szondi)[3] would have us believe that this formal distinction is of

[3] Volker Klotz, *Geschlossene und offene Form im Drama* (8th edn. Munich, 1976); Peter Szondi, *Theorie des modernen Dramas* (4th edn., Frankfurt, 1967);

fundamental importance. It is part of my thesis to demonstrate that this is not the case. A similar difficulty arises with a device which was especially favoured by dramatists of the Naturalist movement: the 'Bote aus der Fremde'.[4] In so far as such figures tend to introduce broader horizons of judgement into groupings of characters from often claustrophobically narrow milieux, whose outlooks are parochial, their function *vis-à-vis* the other characters and within the terms of the plot and action ('Inhalt') appears sharply contrastive. And yet, at the same time such 'Boten' may well be important characters in their own right (Anna Mahr in Hauptmann's *Einsame Menschen* is a case in point). To which mode, the integrated or the disjunctive, are they therefore to be assigned? Or can their character roles be harmoniously combined with their contribution to opening up wider, general vistas or perspectives upon a particular action?

Leitmotiv and Perspective

Less ambiguous in their structural status, because they are more obviously integrated into the text, are devices such as imagery and symbolism in drama. Largely because of the lack of attention they have bestowed upon the hierarchical and interconnecting leitmotiv networks which such imagery may assume and to which I referred above, few theorists[5] would recognize these as contributing to the generalizing, universalizing process and would therefore disclaim that they bear any relationship to those other examples of 'perspective' enumerated above. And yet, when one reviews a variety of masterpieces of the German dramatic tradition, there are striking instances where a careful analysis will demonstrate that a complex form of perspectival commentary is achieved by the operation of such devices. Pertinent examples could be cited from German twentieth-century drama too: the leitmotivic 'Gericht' symbolism in Hauptmann's *Die Weber*; the circus and the picture

English trans. by Michael Hayes: *The Theory of the Modern Drama* (Minneapolis, 1987)).

[4] See Szondi, *Theorie des Dramas*, 60; also Bruno Markwardt, *Geschichte der deutschen Poetik* (Berlin, 1967), 564 ff.

[5] There are a few notable exceptions (e.g. Emil Staiger and Volker Klotz), as I shall discuss below.

imagery in Wedekind's *Lulu*; the symbolic use of stage-setting in, for example, Georg Kaiser's use of the tapestry depicting the building of the harbour of Calais in *Die Bürger von Calais*. And the celebrated twentieth-century practitioner of disjunctive perspective, *par excellence*, Bertolt Brecht, is, as my later chapters will reveal, second to none in his exploitation of leitmotiv networks, both at the integrated and the disjunctive levels. The generalizing function of symbolism is familiar enough in German drama of the eighteenth and nineteenth centuries and is used extensively by authors like Goethe, Kleist, and Grillparzer. What has to be demonstrated is that, unlike the other, more obvious disjunctive commenting devices, it nearly always assumes the dynamic, highly structured shape and appearance of the form that it inhabits: drama. What I mean by this is that images acquire cross-referential meaning across the entire work and can even be seen to operate within a hierarchical structure in which different degrees of 'authority' obtain, so far as its status as 'commentary' for the spectator or reader is concerned. I shall be returning to this point at a later stage.

Polarization of Drama and 'Epic'

There is another, even more substantial explanation for the continuing tendency to polarize such tendencies as integrated and disjunctive perspective in twentieth-century drama. This is the tacit assumption by leading twentieth-century theorists that such polarization derives from the sharply antithetical relationship in which the two major genres of drama and narrative prose stand to one another. Such an antithesis can be traced back to Aristotle and, also, nearer in time, to the Classical Goethe and Schiller, who set out their joint ideas in a celebrated short essay entitled 'Über epische und dramatische Dichtung', defining the respective roles of the poet as that of the rhapsodist ('der Rhapsode') and that of the mime ('der Mime').[6] It may be useful briefly to examine the views of contemporary literary theorists such as the semioticians (including

---

[6] Goethe, *Werke*, ed. Erich Trunz (9th edn., Hamburg, 1981), xii. *Schriften zur Kunst und Literatur*, 249–51. See also *Der Briefwechsel zwischen Schiller und Goethe*, 1794–1797 (Munich, 1984), letters from Goethe to Schiller of 23 and 27 Dec. 1797 and from Schiller to Goethe 26 and 29 Dec. 1797.

Elam, Ubersfeld, Pavis),[7] communications theorists (whose theories are perhaps more fully summarized and extended by Manfred Pfister),[8] and also a generation of influential German pre-Structuralist writers (of which Szondi, Grimm, and Klotz can stand as the most typical representatives). A still earlier school of thought, closer to the generation of Brecht, is appropriately represented by Alfred Döblin. It will be observed that this list makes no claim to completeness, nor is it relevant to the main concerns of this study that it should be so. My principle of selection is simply to engage with what seem to me to be the most influential and interesting theories which have direct bearing on the operation of perspective in drama and, where possible, to suggest ways in which certain lines of argument may be drawn together.

While a tendency may be observed in contemporary literary theory to give disproportionate attention to genres other than the drama (a particularly strong bias being shown towards narrative forms, see Barthes, Lacan, etc.), semioticians have recently demonstrated their concern to make good this deficiency, showing a particular interest in the structure of dialogue and exhibiting what may strike us, perhaps, as a naïve belief that the structural units (morphemes, phonemes, etc.) proposed in linguistic theory can serve equally well as a model for dramatic structures. Elam's minute dissection of the segments of dialogue in the first 79 lines of *Hamlet* reveals just how uphill the going is and how wide the discrepancy between theoretical models and dramatic practice remains. Semioticians like Elam uphold unquestioningly the sharp distinction between dramatic and narrative fiction which can, of course, be traced back to Aristotle's differentiation of representational modes according to diegesis (narrative description) and mimesis (direct imitation). Elam's consequential emphasis on 'actualization' and 'deixis' (meaning literally 'pointing to') as distinctive elements in drama, as well as justifying a preoccupation with dialogue rather than with the descriptive functions of dramatic language, leads to a drastic subordination of what we have defined above as examples of disjunctive perspective (e.g. prologues,

---

[7] See Keir Elam, *The Semiotics of Theatre and Drama* (London and New York, 1980); Anne Ubersfeld, *Lire le thèâtre 2* (Paris, 1981); Patrice Pavis, *Voix et images de la scène: Essais de sémiologie thèâtrale* (Lille, 1982).

[8] Manfred Pfister, *Das Drama*, (3rd edn., Munich, 1982). English trans. *Theory and Analysis of Drama* (Cambridge, 1988).

epilogues, and *ad spectatores* addresses) to the level of 'meta-dramatic' or 'metatheatrical' features. Despite this, and despite the assumptions which the semiotician shares with the Structuralists that the purposeful organization of structure which we associate with great works of art can in no way be identified with the author himself,[9] Elam does not fail to record the importance of devices such as 'framing' or 'theatrical foregrounding' in drama, which look suspiciously like examples of 'perspective' according to my definition above. It is clear from this that an interpretation of drama based exclusively on what is regarded as its most distinctive feature, dialogue, cannot satisfy any semiotician whose attention is focused on theatrical and dramatic practicalities.

It is intriguing to observe how an identical tendency to 'explain away' the somewhat embarrassing appearance of perspectival devices in drama can be seen in the impressively detailed book of Manfred Pfister which provides the fullest and most convincing synthesis to date of the various strands of communications theory. Once more devices such as choric commentary, prologues, epilogues, etc. are noted; once more they are relegated to a subordinate role and designated as examples of subsidiary or 'Nebentext' because they do not conform to the demands of a 'model'—the model in question, though radically different from that of the linguisticians, is one to which I shall return, as I believe it to be of much greater practical usefulness for a study of dramatic perspective than theirs. But it still rests squarely on the unchallenged assumption of a polarity between the respective genres of narrative and drama, and the perspectival devices which are fully acknowledged and of which an impressive array of examples from world literature are cited (they even include imagery, which is especially interesting for our purpose) are identified as belonging strictly to the 'epic' mode of narrative and consequently are regarded as alien intruders into the realm of drama. Here, then, the generic link between perspective and the epic or narrative mode is made fully explicit by the communications theorist, a point which the semioticians had

---

[9] The elimination of the author and of authorial perspective is a commonplace of Structuralist theory and is identified with the 'decentering of the subject'. See A. Jefferson, 'Structuralism and Post-Structuralism', *Modern Literary Theory* (2nd edn., London, 1987), 98. Note that Elam identifies different levels of structure and interpretation, e.g. 'high-order action', 'deep structure', and surface structure': *The Semiotics of Theatre and Drama*, 16–17 and 126.

tended to gloss over in their eagerness to analyse linguistic patterns in dialogue.

It is, perhaps, understandable that a theory which is as concerned as communications theory is to analyse minutely the mechanism of the two-way process of transmission of 'information' in a literary work from author and text to receiver (albeit via responses which are reduced to non-literary terms, such as 'codes' or 'signals') should have to take so fully into account such important 'signals' as perspectival devices, even while theoretically acknowledging that they do not exist! For the same reason, Pfister's views diverge from the semioticians' and the linguisticians' when he admits that what is neutrally termed the 'Steuerungsprozeß' ('steering or regulating process') to which such devices contribute is not one which can be altogether divorced from the guiding intelligence of an authorial or artistic presence. Because of the aforementioned assumption of a complete polarity of genres, this presence is seen, in Pfister's communications model, to operate in a much more complex fashion in narrative fiction than it does in drama.

Clear diagrams are used to express the processes of communication and reception in narrative fiction and drama respectively (see Fig. 1). Interlocking rectangles are designated 'inner' and 'mediating' communications system respectively ('inneres' and 'vermittelndes Kommunikationssystem').[10]

(*a*) Narrative Texte

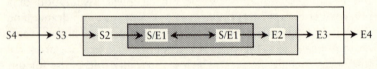

(*b*) Dramatische Texte

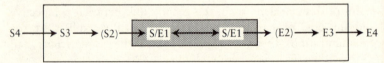

S = 'Sender' (transmitter)
E = 'Empfänger' (receiver)

FIG. 1. Pfister's models for narrative prose and drama

[10] Pfister, *Das Drama*, 20–1.

The smallest inner area (S/E 1) relates to the level of inter-textual communication, as, for example, in exchanges of dialogue between characters; the adjoining second area (S 2) operates most clearly via an identifiable figure such as a narrator, 'das epische oder auktoriale ich' (the epic or authorial 'I') who, in the rebarbative jargon of communications theory, also appears as 'den im Werk formulierten fiktiven Erzähler als vermittelnde Erzählfunktion' (the fictional narrator whose role in the work is that of narrative mediation). Beyond these levels comes a third, the external 'communications system' (S 3), which itself contains and encloses the two inner and mediating layers. Nearest to the 'mediating' level comes the author as he appears in the literary framework of the text (i.e. as an implicit rather than an explicit presence: 'den im Text implizierten "idealen" Autor als Subjekt des Werkganzen' (the 'ideal' author implied in the text as the subject of the whole work). Finally—and at this point we step right outside the confines of the fictional text itself—there is the 'empirical author'. Pfister's rectangular boxes thus present the authorial 'input' as passing through a series of phases (such a two-dimensional diagram cannot, of course, clearly indicate simultaneity as well as sequentiality, which is a limitation): via, that is, the 'implied, ideal author' to the mediating narrator figure, and thence to the heart of the work, the characters and their interactions. The process of reception (E) then follows a similar series of stages: from the innermost textual levels (E 1) information flows via the fictitious receiver (E 2) (i.e. still within the text) to the 'ideal' receiver (E 3), 'den im Text implizierten "idealen" Rezipienten des Werkganzen' (the implied 'ideal' receiver of the whole work), and finally to the 'empirical' receiver (E 4) (this category includes the reader and audience to whom the work is directed at the time of writing, but also others, as yet unknown, of whom the author could not possibly have been aware).

One reason why it is useful to consider Pfister's models in some detail is that his extreme polarization of narrative and dramatic forms points up, as I see it, paradoxically and unintentionally, the artificiality of disallowing any strategic, perspectival, or 'narratorial' function within the communications process which is deemed appropriate to drama. Influenced by a priori assumptions concerning the antithetical relationship of the two genres, Pfister can only permit of three stages in the processes of reception and transmission in drama as against the four which he had identified for narrative prose fiction. The entire 'mediating' system, in fact, disappears from his scheme, leaving the 'inner' and 'outer' systems in stark confrontation. The many forms of 'Nebentext' (subsidiary text) in drama which, as I already indicated, he himself describes and which he has to explain away as an atypical 'epicizing' or as 'alternative', 'compensatory' forms of communication might quite comfortably be fitted into the very 'mediating' system which he has so convincingly established for his narrative model. This is as clear an example as one can find of how rigidity in formulating theoretical principles can be starkly at variance with the practical evidence. One of the greatest merits of Pfister's book, it seems to me, is the rich and impressive diversity of examples which he has assembled; the pity is that he is unwilling to sacrifice the theoretical 'purity' of his model to the challenge of the very evidence he has amassed.

The Notion of Genre Purity

The amazing consistency with which present-day theorists of drama cling to the notion of genre purity may well, in the case of German exponents, stem from the respect in which the writings of one particular authority, Peter Szondi, are held. For one can observe how even what may appear to be the most dogmatic and unsubstantiated assertions made by Szondi on this topic seem until recently to have carried with them a consensus of unquestioning agreement which would be hard to find in any other area of dramatic enquiry. In the course of his examination of drama Szondi's enthusiasm at times reflects almost the fanaticism of the scientist who has isolated a pure substance: 'Das Drama ist absolut. Um reiner Bezug, das heißt: dramatisch sein zu können, muß es von allem Äußerlichen abgelöst sein. Es kennt nichts außer sich' (drama is Absolute. To be entirely relational, i.e. dramatic, it must be divested of all extraneous elements and to have no knowledge of anything outside itself).[11] Szondi's thinking here owes nothing, of course, to linguistic or communications theory but rests rather on a neo-Hegelian dialectical opposition of 'subject' and 'object',

---

[11] Szondi, *Theorie des Dramas*, 15.

Content and Form: 'Die Ganzheit des Dramas . . . ist dialektischen Ursprungs. Sie entsteht nicht dank dem ins Werk hineinragenden epischen Ich, sondern durch die je und je geleistete und wieder ihrerseits zerstörte Aufhebung der zwischenmenschlichen Dialektik, die im Dialog Sprache wird' (drama as an entity . . . is dialectical in origin. It comes into being not by the forceful intrusion into the work of the epic 'I', but by the interpersonal dialectic being constantly attained and then disrupted, a process which in the dialogue becomes speech).[12] It follows that any signs of extraneous or genre-alien elements appearing in drama—and these will, of course, be especially relevant to perspectival or 'epic'/narratorial devices—must be regarded as deviant. Such aberrations being richly evident, as Szondi notes, in modern drama from Ibsen and the Naturalists to Brecht, he is led to diagnose that unique or 'crisis' position of twentieth-century drama as a genre, to which I alluded earlier. In fact, such is the purity of the 'model' being applied here that Szondi's survey must needs exclude as 'absolute drama' not only the works of Classical Antiquity, the Middle Ages, and the Baroque 'Welttheater' but also all of Shakespeare's histories (and apparently all historical drama). This does not leave very much to set as a yardstick against the 'impure' form of modern drama and must surely detract from the credibility of Szondi's diagnosis of crisis and catastrophe in modern drama, as, according to his dialectical reasoning, Content strains against Form. Even the respectful Pfister seems to find the gulf between theory and practice rather uncomfortable at this point: 'Diese Absolutheit des Dramas, von der Peter Szondi spricht, ist freilich nicht wirklich gegeben, sondern eine Fiktion' (the absolute autonomy of drama to which Szondi refers does not, of course, really exist. It is fictional).[13] However, as we have seen, he himself is not prepared to challenge its foundations and perpetuates the notion of antithesis of genres, extolling what he regards as Szondi's 'progressive' tendencies, when

[12] Ibid., 18–19.
[13] Pfister, *Das Drama*, 22. Note too the less than respectful critique by W. Kirchesch, 'Zu Szondis "Theorie des modernen Dramas" ' in *Das Verhältnis von Handlung und Dramaturgie: Fragwürdige Theorien zum modernen Drama*, diss. (Munich, 1962), 15: 'Szondi setzt absolut: dies ist gewiß auch eine Methode (sicher nicht die beste)' (Szondi posits an Absolute: that, too, is certainly a method (clearly not the best)). Jochen Schulte-Sasse, in an ambitious analysis of the philosophical foundations of Szondi's theorists, points to 'unevenness' in the argumentation and inconsistency in the exposition of the concept of Absolute Drama. See Szondi, *Theory of Modern Drama*, Foreword, p. ix.

compared to the 'deductive-normative' approaches of other theoretical purists (which for him are represented by Aristotle, Hegel,
and Emil Staiger).

It goes without saying that Szondi's extreme postulates and
dialectically based polarization of genres will not permit of any
complexity in the reception process between the reader or spectator
of a dramatic work and the text itself: 'Das Verhältnis Zuschauer–
Drama kennt nur vollkommene Trennung und vollkommene
Identität, nicht aber Eindringen des Zuschauers ins Drama oder
Angesprochenwerden des Zuschauers durch das Drama' (the
relationship between the spectator and the drama is characterized
by either a complete separation or a complete identification and
nothing else, certainly not by the spectator's intrusion into the
drama nor by his being verbally assailed by it).[14] This cavalier
approach to matters of 'reception' is a major criticism which has
been levelled against him, particularly by certain leading semioticians.[15] For Szondi, therefore, the notion of 'perspective' is even
less relevant to the true purposes of drama than it is for Pfister. On
the other hand, the dialectical relationship which he establishes
between Form and Content, while, as has been pointed out, lacking
clarity in matters of definition, is an attractive feature to others,[16]
some of whom profess to wish to give due weight to both the
immanent and the historical aspects of textual analysis. This
possibly explains the high regard in which Szondi's theories are
held by them. They too, of course, accept as uncritically as does
Szondi the thesis that dramatic form in the traditional sense has
disappeared entirely in modern drama, and work, as he does, from
the premiss of a basic opposition, or even polarity, between the
genres.

The prolific and also influential German dramatic theorist
Reinhold Grimm has shown a much greater willingness to

[14] Szondi, *Theorie des Dramas*, 16.

[15] e.g. Pavis, *Voix et images*, 66. 'Or, cette enquête sur le public et sa condition de
réception font défaut dans le livre de Szondi, ce qui s'explique sans doute par sa
volonté d'examiner les contradictions entre forme dramatique et contenu social,
seulement à l'intérieur des œuvres, sans faire entrer en jeu la constitution du public et
la relativité de ses différentes lectures possibles' (this enquiry into the audience and
its conditions of reception are absent in Szondi's book. That is undoubtedly
explained by his desire to examine the contradictions between dramatic form and
social content entirely from within the works, without bringing into play the
audience's make-up and the relativity of its different possible readings).

[16] See *Theory of Modern Drama*, pp. ix–xvi.

accommodate the practical evidence of dramatic texts to his particular theories than Szondi, which is perhaps not all that surprising in a critic whose work is firmly rooted in the more traditional pattern of close and sensitive textual analysis, a merit which Szondi's *Theorie des modernen Dramas* patently lacks and which his entire approach disdains. What is especially valuable about Grimm's essay (1963)[17] on changing structure in drama is his willingness to penetrate beyond the merely contrastive patterns of dramatic structure. Grimm uses the terms 'pyramid' and 'carousel' to describe the two extreme poles of dramatic action, these being identified, respectively, as a strict, architectural structure à la Freytag, on the one hand, and a distinct, virtually self-contained action (or actions) which rotate around a central pivot to which they are only loosely connected, on the other. But while this might appear to be perpetuating the Szondian model of antithesis and dialectic, Grimm emphatically denies an exclusive association of the second category, the 'carousel', with modern drama, maintaining that both forms have always existed, and demonstrating that, in the case of Gerhart Hauptmann, for example, they are equally well represented in his works. '[es] festigt sich der Eindruck immer mehr, als gebe es grundsätzlich und von allem Anfang an zwei strukturell verschiedene Dramentypen, die *gleichberechtigt nebeneinander bestehen*' (increasingly, the impression is gaining ground that there are essentially and primarily two types of drama which differ structurally and which *exist alongside one another on equal terms*) (my italics).[18] What is especially interesting here is Grimm's emancipation from the all-pervading opposition of 'drama' and 'narrative' or 'epic' forms which we have been following and the admissability in his scheme of 'epic' elements as essential, not as intrusive features in drama. His fondness for the schematic in characterizing dramatic structure may, it is true, sometimes carry him away. His attempt, for example, to trace the tendency of certain dramas towards the 'carousel' form to an inner structural dialectic seems particularly strained: 'Die Pyramide zerfällt, eben weil sie Pyramide wurde' (the pyramid collapses precisely because it became a pyramid).[19] His reluctance to take issue with the questionable features of Szondi's arguments is rather

---

[17] Reinhold Grimm, 'Pyramide und Karusell: Zum Strukturwandel im Drama', in *Nach dem Naturalismus: Essays zur modernen Dramatik* (Kronberg, 1978), 3–27.
[18] Ibid. 20. [19] Ibid. 21.

disappointing. But the treatment of drama as a continuum and the avoidance of what can be described as the 'modern fallacy' of regarding decent developments in dramatic practice as unique and without any kind of parallel or antecedent is constructive. If more attention had been paid to the implications it might have been possible before now to view such issues as perspectivism in drama as intrinsic rather than extraneous, 'metatextual' features.

Unfortunately the same value cannot be attached to another, even more influential theorist, Volker Klotz, whose focus in his book *Geschlossene und offene Form im Drama* (8th edition, 1976) is more firmly fixed on the superficial aspects of dramatic form, and whose categories of 'closed' and 'open' structure, although they are appreciatively linked by Grimm to his own categories of 'pyramid' and 'carousel', are, in fact, set in far too sharply antithetical a relationship and are too overstated and contrived in the selection of examples to be convincing. After a period of almost universal uncritical acceptance, it is interesting to find that dissatisfaction is increasingly being expressed with this theory,[20] though it will take a long time before Klotz's over-simplified categories—which have penetrated into secondary school syllabuses—are abandoned completely. There are some particular points in Klotz's analysis with which I shall be taking issue in later chapters and one or two others with which I shall concur.

The Theory of Alfred Döblin

We have now briefly examined a goodly sprinkling of leading theories which share as their common ground the assumption of an opposition, antithesis, or polarization between the genres of drama and narrative prose. This theoretical opposition has been steadfastly maintained despite (or even because of?) the persistent array of evidence pointing to the process of what is generally described as the 'epicizing' of drama in the twentieth century and we have noted the sundry attempts which have been made to find explanations for the phenomenon, ranging from the philosophical and historical (Szondi's neo-Hegelian dialectic of Form and Content) to the aesthetic (Grimm's dialectic within the Form itself), the Structuralist

---

[20] See John Guthrie, *Lenz and Büchner: Studies in Dramatic Form* (Frankfurt-on-Main, 1984).

(the semioticians), and that relating to Communications Theory. While exhibiting among themselves a great diversity and range of ideas, these theories all share an approach via the *model*, or 'ideal type', whereby specific examples of modern drama are set against an abstract construct (to which, of course, in practice they seldom conform perfectly).

Bertolt Brecht's theory of 'epic' theatre can, of course, be seen to presuppose a similar oppositional standpoint as well as an a priori model. Brecht's position both as theorist and practitioner is extremely complex and will form the basis for later chapters of this book. For the purposes of this introductory survey it is, however, useful to include the theories of a contemporary of Brecht's, with whom he has often been said to share much common ground but who, instead of emphasizing, as do the above-mentioned writers, the differences between the genres, is concerned to illustrate their similarities and areas of overlap, which he regards as both desirable and natural. This is the eminent novelist (who, incidentally, also wrote dramas) Alfred Döblin, who sets out these views in an essay of 1929, entitled 'Der Bau des epischen Werks,[21] a piece which stands out for its readability and sagacity, and which has even caught the attention recently of the influential Structuralist critic Tzvetan Todorov.[22] Writing at a point when Brecht's 'epic theatre' was just becoming known and established, Döblin was especially concerned about what he saw as an undesirable tendency towards the polarization of genres in contemporary literary practice: report-based narrative fiction on the one hand and dialogue-based drama on the other. Moreover, he specifically deplored in both these instances the obliteration of any authorial presence. For Döblin both narrative prose and drama are representational forms (he uses the term 'Darstellung' rather than the more portentous 'mimesis') and the fact that one relates to past, the other to present, events is neither here nor there: 'Alle Darstellung ist gegenwärtig, sie mag formal erfolgen, wie sie will' (all representation is immediate, whatever the formal sequence intended).[23] It is complete dogma, he

---

[21] A. Döblin, *Aufsätze zur Literatur* (Freiburg im Breisgau, 1963), 103–32.

[22] Tzvetan Todorov, 'Le Retour de l'Épique', in *Festschrift R. Wellek*, Part 1 (Berne, Frankfurt, New York, 1984), 609 ff. An earlier critic, Käthe Hamburger, *Das Verhältnis der dramatischen zur epischen Fiktion*, in *Die Logik der Dichtung* (2nd edn., Stuttgart, 1968), 157, draws drama and narrative together under the umbrella of 'mimesis'.

[23] Döblin, 'Der Bau des epischen Werks', *Aufsätze*, 112.

argues, to propose that drama operates exclusively via dialogue: both drama and narrative/epic—and lyric, too, for that matter—should incorporate elements of other genres as well, particularly important in all these cases being the authorial perspectives which will raise the 'iron curtain' that has been erected between stage and audience, reader and author:

Wie das Theater von heute erstarrt ist im Dialog der Personen oben—und die Wohltat der Betrachtung, des lyrischen oder spottenden Eingriffs der freien wechselnden Kunstaktion, auch der direkten Rede an uns wird versagt, wir werden nicht hinreichend beteiligt an dem, was oben vorgeht—genau so steht es im Epischen (it is the same with the epic mode as it is with the theatre: it is nowadays ossified in the dialogue of the characters up there above us and we are deprived of the benefit of reflection, of any lyrical or satirical interruption to the free flow of the action, even to the direct speech. We are not sufficiently involved in what is taking place up there).[24]

Döblin's interest in perspectival stance in drama is especially striking and he notes appreciatively such 'epic' devices as the chorus, the Shakespearian *ad spectatores* address, and—possibly with his eye already on developments in the stage-work of both Piscator and Brecht—he senses that cinematographic interpolations can be expected to move modern drama even further in this direction. However, while drawing the two genres more closely together, Döblin is not trying to blur all distinctions between them; he insists, for example, on the need for an appropriate choice of genre to suit the subject-matter, arguing that Cervantes' *Don Quixote* is inconceivable in terms of dramatic representation because of the proliferation of events, and the 'breadth' of the material determining the choice of genre (this assumption that Content determines Form would certainly not find favour with many of our contemporary Structuralists). Equally, Döblin decries novels that try to be dramas—what he terms 'Pseudoepik': 'aus der meisten heutigen Romanen läßt sich so etwas wie ein Drama destillieren' (something resembling a drama can be distilled from most present-day novels).[25] Thus the genres retain for Döblin their distinct qualities.

It is worth looking more closely at what Döblin understands by

---

[24] Döblin, 'Der Bau des epischen Werks', *Aufsätze*, 113.
[25] Ibid. 125.

authorial perspective over and above the technical devices mentioned above which contribute towards what is often termed the 'Steuerungsprozeß' (regulating process). For he does not see such interventions—in drama or in prose—as serving purely aesthetic functions, and he specifically dissociates himself from, for instance, the Schillerian and Schlegelian conception of choric perspective as representing the 'ideal spectator' who can raise the issues presented in drama to the level of the general and universal. For that dimension Döblin substitutes, rather speculatively, a more historically conditioned and politically coloured 'universal', namely the social collective, or 'Volk', for whom he believes the author is acting as a mouthpiece to articulate their intuitive perceptions: 'der Autor trägt . . . das Volk in sich' (the author carries the people within himself).[26]

While the socio-political dimension which Döblin seeks to attach to the principle of authorial perspective in drama and narrative prose may now seem time-bound, his identification of the principle itself, which derives from his closer juxtaposition of the two genres, is no less valid. Viewed in a broader historical context, the relationship between the genres seems to have been subject to many pendulum swings: it is a commonplace that the eighteenth century (cf. Lessing's *Laokoon* and *Hamburgische Dramaturgie*) emphasized not only sharp differences between the visual and the verbal arts but also reaffirmed the Aristotelian divide within the latter, while showing an almost overwhelming preoccupation with the genre of tragedy (which is associated exclusively with drama). The Romantics, as is equally well known, confounded these Classical divisions (cf. Tieck's dramas with their mixture of epic and lyric features). It is surely not fanciful to suppose that the present-day insistence, in theory at least, on strict purity of genre will yield eventually to a view more akin to Döblin's. My purpose is to try to loosen the ground a little. Principally, I would hope to do so by approaching some of the dramas written by arguably the most significant dramatist of the twentieth century, Bertolt Brecht, which patently do not conform in practical terms to the tenets of genre purity, with criteria which seem more appropriate to their particular character than those we have so far been offered.

---

[26] Ibid. 120.

Implicit and Explicit Perspective

As I have indicated above, I believe this purpose may best be served
by demonstrating that a common function exists between many
external or explicit perspectival techniques in drama and certain
implicit ones. This, I am sure, is a controversial assertion, since
though the former category is already well recognized by students
of dramatic theory, the latter has scarcely attracted any independent
attention. As an important bridge to its understanding I shall call
upon the theoretical ideas of Richard Wagner on music drama for
reasons which will be explained in greater detail below. The various
implicit devices used to provide general perspectives will be
represented by imagery and will feature leitmotiv as the major
technique, though occasionally the form in which this is presented
will include such things as stage-directions. But no attempt will be
made to analyse the various technical devices specifically associated
with theoretical production (*mise-en-scène*, gesture, mime, acting
techniques, etc.), nor the diverse devices employed by theatre
directors themselves, who, arguably, represent an important
element, independent of the author, in the 'Steuerungsprozeß' itelf.
Such aspects have, in Brecht's case, been amply examined by others,
but in any case I believe that these aspects, though fascinating for
the student of drama, are comparatively ephemeral, while the
dramatic text stands for all time and for all generations as the
creation of a single author, however much such a view may have
been undermined by contemporary theorists. That is why the gulf
between theatre studies and drama studies remains so wide.

It is true that the semioticians, with their highly developed
interest in 'signs' and 'signals', are increasingly turning their
attention to matters such as stage-production.[27] They, and the
Structuralists in general, are inclined to see confirmation here for
their view of the diminished importance of the author (and, by
implication, authorial perspective) in drama. But the logic of a
position which raises the status of the practitioners of an art form at
the expense of its creators seems very questionable to me. This is
not to say that the former may not bring to light possibilities of
which the latter were not consciously aware. But I shall hope to

---

[27] See esp. the two illuminating studies by Anne Ubersfeld, *Lire le théâtre* (Paris,
1977) and *Lire le théâtre 2* (Paris, 1981).

demonstrate that more of these possibilities may be revealed *through the text itself* than has often been appreciated.

The Strategic Role of Leitmotiv

It might be thought that difficulty will be experienced in drawing lines between implicit perspectival devices and other dramatic techniques, equally implicit (e.g. characterization, direct and indirect), which have hitherto formed the mainstay of dramatic interpretation. Concentration on Brecht's drama, which deliberately eschews a traditional form of characterization, may, however, make the process of delimiting and identifying the principle less hazardous. It will be important to build on the slender but deep-laid foundations which are to be discovered in the form of pointers thrown out by such theorists as Volker Klotz and, more especially, Emil Staiger, for both of these writers are sensitive to the particular ways in which dramatic structures tend to be organized. Klotz, for example, has invented the term 'metaphorical bracketing' to describe the co-ordinating role played in some dramas by repeated image-patterns. He describes such points, in which the threads of the action are drawn together in one general focus, as 'vanishing-points'; he himself uses the word 'perspective' to describe their function: 'Es ist der Fluchtpunkt, in dem die vielerlei Perspektiven des Dramas sich koordinieren' (it is the vanishing-point in which the numerous perspectives in drama are co-ordinated).[28] Oddly, Klotz associates the device exclusively with the 'open' dramatic form, where he sees it providing a compensatory mechanism for the looseness of structure, in stark contrast to the clear, generalized statements which are found in the 'closed' form typical, say, of Goethe's *Iphigenie*. Manfred Pfister takes over Klotz's term (and also the associated term 'metaphorical bracketing' ('metaphorische Verklammerung') used by Klotz, and perpetuates Klotz's allocation of the device to 'open' structure.[29] This is extremely debatable, as can easily be demonstrated by referring to the central, generalizing role of such elaborate image-patterns in a drama like Kleist's *Penthesilea*, which, according to Klotz's highly questionable typology, comes under the heading of 'closed' structure.

[28] Klotz, *Geschlossene und offene Form*, 119.
[29] Pfister, *Das Drama*, 218.

More profound in its response to the dynamic nature of dramatic structure is the contribution of the great Swiss theorist Emil Staiger, who, in the celebrated *Grundbegriffe der Poetik* (1946), employs, in his chapter on 'Das Dramatische' (a basic concept, or 'Grundbegriff' which may, but does not necessarily, coincide with the genre of drama), the term 'Zwischenbilanz' to describe the way in which summarizing utterances are placed strategically within dramatic texts:

Zwischenbilanzen finden sich aber auch innerhalb der Akte. So fassen die Helden und Gegenspieler gelegentlich ihre Meinung, ihren Willen in einer Sentenz zusammen . . . Dieselbe Bedeutung können bildhaft einprägsame Vorgänge gewinnen . . . Es ist bei diesen Bildern und Vorgängen wesentlich, daß sie etwas bedeuten' (but interim surveys can also be found within the acts. The protagonists and antagonists occasionally sum up their opinions or their resolve in one sententia . . . The same meaning can be achieved by episodes that are easily remembered in visual terms. With such images and episodes it is vital that they signify something).[30]

Staiger's realization that imagery can play a similar, generalizing role as, for instance, sententiae seems to me crucial; so too his awareness that the function of such devices is identical, irrespective of the particular form which they assume, whether, that is, they appear as an explicit statement (as for example with the utterances of the chorus in Schiller's *Braut von Messina*) or as an artistically more subtle (because integrated) gesture:

Schiller hat sich dazu in der *Braut von Messina* entschlossen, ermutigt durch das antike Beispiel, wo öfter der Chor in der Exodus das erlittene Schicksal den ewigen Gesetzen des Daseins einfügt. Im allgemeinen wird der Dichter jedoch *nicht so ausdrücklich verfahren* und sich lieber mit einer möglichst umfassenden Gebärde begnügen, von der das Lebendige nicht, wie von einer Sentenz, erdrosselt zu werden Gefahr läuft (in his *Braut von Messina* Schiller was encouraged by the example of Classical Antiquity where in its *exodus*—closing song—the chorus frequently ascribed the Fate suffered by the hero to the eternal laws of existence. But in general the poet *will not proceed so explicitly*; he will rather content himself with a sweeping gesture. When confronted by this the life force will not run the risk of strangulation as it does when confronted by a sententia) (my italics).[31]

---

[30] Emil Staiger, *Grundbegriffe der Poetik* (6th edn., Zurich, 1963), 166.
[31] Ibid. 168–9.

Imagery would also, clearly, come under this more sophisticated category of generalized utterance in drama. Staiger does not draw the full inference from his own theory of 'das Dramatische' as an architecturally complex structure in which the composite parts do not have independent, free-standing significance but fulfil a strategic role within the overall design of a work which is primarily constituted to generate 'Spannung' (tension). However, I believe that it does follow that a similar incompleteness may characterize generalizing image-patterns themselves. I believe too that Klotz's term 'metaphorische Verklammerung' indicates as much and that consequently we find works in the German dramatic repertoire in which a high degree of organization prevails in the deployment of imagery to such an end. Among German and Austrian dramatists of the nineteenth century Kleist's[32] and Grillparzer's[33] dramas have already been mentioned as outstanding examples, rich in image-patterns which act as implicit commenting devices. From the Classical tradition, Goethe's dramas also display a plentiful variety, especially *Iphigenie* (e.g. the imagery of healing and rejuvenation which is so closely woven into the main action); *Tasso* (wreath imagery) and *Egmont* (charioteer imagery) exhibit very similar features, their author being equally subtle in his disinclination, to paraphrase Staiger's words, to allow crass statement to crowd out and strangle all the vitality and delicacy of poetic utterance. It is most revealing to find, however, that, among German Classical dramatists, Schiller, as Staiger himself astutely notes, often prefers the explicit mode of utterance (is this because rhetorical statement comes so naturally to him?). It will be important in the chapters which follow to bear in mind this strategic function of image-patterns within the dramatic framework. It may also be interesting to bear in mind the view of one commentator (Harald Reger) on the role of imagery in the dramas of Grillparzer, a major practitioner among the 'Classicists'. Reger confines such strategic and interpretationally vital functions as are performed by Grillparzer's imagery exclusively to non-Naturalistic usage, saying:

[32] On Kleist's imagery see D. G. Dyer, 'The Imagery in Kleist's *Penthesilea*' *Publications of the English Goethe Society*', (1961), 1–23; also the present author's *Kleist and the Tragic Ideal* (Berne, 1977), esp. 98 ff.

[33] On Grillparzer's, see Harald Reger, 'Metapher und sprachliches Symbol im Drama', *Muttersprache*, 82 (1972), 324–33.

der poetische Leistungswert der sprachlichen Symbole besteht darin, daß sie für den Aufweis der tragischen Antinomien in Schauspielen mit nichtnaturalistischem Sprachgebrauch und für die Erschließung des Grundgehalts eine sprachimmanente und damit formale Interpretationskategorie erstellen (the poetic value and function of linguistic symbols derives from their ability to construct a category of interpretation which is built-in linguistically—and thereby formal—which can be applied to the display of tragic antinomies in dramas utilizing non-naturalistic language and can help to elucidate their basic meaning).[34]

Reger seemingly takes the opposite position to Klotz, who had restricted such 'sprachliche Symbole' (linguistic symbols), as we have seen, to 'open' form, which, if we consider his examples, is frequently 'realistic' and non-tragic. But this view may eventually prove to be too narrowly determined by genre to be convincing either: the case of Gerhart Hauptmann, who makes extensive use of the device, even in his Naturalist dramas, would certainly have to be explained.

A Theory of Leitmotiv: Richard Wagner

As my examples above indicate, it would indeed be possible to demonstrate the thesis I have outlined by referring to dramas of an earlier period than the twentieth century. Equally, of course, there are no reasons except practical ones why discussion should be restricted to works from the German tradition. There could be certain advantages in restricting the enquiry, in its practical aspects at least, to, say, the period of approximately fifty years extending from the works of Hauptmann to Brecht; for as well as being full of high quality drama, this period is extremely innovative; moreover, it encompasses sharply contrasting literary movements such as Naturalism and Expressionism, all of which exhibit an abundance of perspectival commentary of the kind I have been describing. However, on reflection, and in view of the need to concentrate my study and keep the lines of enquiry as clear as possible, I propose instead to adopt the somewhat surprising expedient of focusing on Brecht's drama alone (and of that only a sample which will be treated as 'exemplarisch') and analysing it not only from the angle of his own theories (which has often been done before), but also

[34] On Grillparzer's, see Harald Reger, 'Metapher und sprachliches Symbol im Drama', *Muttersprache*, 82 (1972), 333.

from the angle of a leading nineteenth-century theorist, Richard Wagner, whose ideas, though derived from a close study of the drama form, have not—presumably because he is perceived primarily as a composer and scarcely at all as a dramatist or theorist of drama—been thought to have much bearing on the drama form. There are a number of reasons for bringing these strange bedfellows together.

First, it is my intention to demonstrate the special areas in which Brecht's own theories fail to cover important aspects of his dramatic practice. In the critical secondary literature devoted to Brecht two schools seem to dominate: first, those who often state the principle of contradiction whereby the two domains, theory and drama, are seen to be going in *different* directions (e.g. Esslin); secondly, the new theory-based critics who are trying to connect Brecht's own theoretical aims with modernist abstract theory (Structuralism, Post-Modernism, etc.). Members of this second group take a diametrically opposed stance to the first: that is, they see little contradiction between Brechtian theory and practice and take Brecht's theoretical statements at face value. A second aim of my study which still relates specifically to Brecht is to demonstrate how truly diverse his dramatic practice really is—and that applies both to drama which he consciously intended to work within the known parameters of 'epic' theatre and drama written without such considerations in mind. The extensive amount of imagery and image-networks which Brecht employs and the different forms which this imagery assumes—descriptive or analytical, operating in primary or secondary roles within a hierarchical structure or configuration—is a feature of Brecht's writing which I believe to have been almost totally neglected.

Wagner and Brecht

One particular purpose of the study is, therefore, to demonstrate Brecht's reliance in certain works on forms of expression which he never acknowledges openly and of which he is perhaps not even consciously aware. An additional question is the extent to which, despite all appearances, his reliance on these forms may be rooted in more traditional features of the drama form. And on the aesthetic level it will be pertinent to enquire how fruitful the tension may be which is created between such subtly concealed perspectives and the more overt forms assumed under the banner of 'Trennung' or of Brecht's much vaunted 'Gestus' (which will be discussed in Chapter 3). The endeavour here is not, it must be made clear, to offer a *complete* interpretation of the particular dramas of Brecht's which I have selected. Certain elements which might belong to such an interpretation, such as the operation of the 'Fabel', the 'Spruchbänder', or the 'split' characterizations, are only considered if they shed light on the image-networks themselves.

However, in thus illuminating a neglected aspect of Brecht's practical technique, I would hope that a general purpose might also be served. I return to my sense that so many twentieth-century genre-related theories have not served the dramas themselves to best advantage. In particular, the failure to consider except peripherally (that is as 'Metatext') any reflective or evaluatory, commenting device flies in the face of the evidence of a dramatic repertoire extending from Hauptmann to Brecht which possesses an abundance of examples. Specifically—and here the role of Wagner's theory will become clearer—the proliferation of image-networks or leitmotivs and their deployment within the hierarchical dramatic structure can be shown to provide a major source of perspectival commentary. The establishment of such a transcending principle must render the continued application of polarizations like 'epic'–'dramatic' (together with subsidiary antitheses like 'closed' and 'open' form) highly dubious. Indeed the usefulness of the two terms may be open to question.

Finally, another area of general interest on which I would hope to shed light is the relationship of music and text in both Wagner and Brecht. This is an issue which will be examined as part of the investigation into, and the attempt to establish, a unifying principle of commentary.

2

Leitmotiv and Commentary in Richard Wagner's Theory of Drama

The Status of Wagner's Theory

Wagner's theories of drama, opera, and music drama—despite, or perhaps mainly because of, their great bulk and daunting aspect—have been ignored by students of drama and only peripherally discussed by students of music and opera. By their very nature they set us considerable problems: to which side of the fence do they belong—music or literature? On closer examination we realize that the interdisciplinary challenge which they present is one which the late twentieth century with its compartmentalized, technically orientated specializations is poorly equipped to deal with. Music-ologists in Germany, for example, seem to be deeply immersed in the important business of fundamental scholarship, especially editions of the great German Masters: Bach, Mozart, Beethoven, Schubert, Schumann, etc.[1] In America and England, on the other hand, formal analysis has been gaining ground. However, the influence of Structuralism upon this discipline and in particular upon the so-called Schenkerian School, which is characterized by an austere rigour, has not so far succeeded in serving inter-disciplinary studies too well. A form like opera, and more particularly music drama, with its 'mixed' heritage and its strong literary and dramatic connections, is bound to present special difficulties and to resist an exclusively abstract approach. A new specialist technical language would need to be developed to deal with this awkward hybrid, for how can the techniques applied to the 'pure', unprogrammatic forms of, say, Brahms and Schoenberg be adequate to deal with others which so untidily straddle several

---

[1] In addition, critical editions of 'modern' Classics, e.g. Arnold Schoenberg and Paul Hindemith are continuing.

disciplines?[2] Joseph Kerman has done important pioneering work with his popular study of opera as drama,[3] but among leading musicologists the name that stands out is that of the late Carl Dahlhaus,[4] who in a comprehensive series of publications, several of which are devoted to Wagner, has more than any other sought to bridge the great divide between the disciplines. Dahlhaus's approach remains, however, predominantly that of the musicologist, albeit one who commands an enviably wide range in the sphere of aesthetics, and I believe that a number of key areas remain where literary and dramatic aspects are not given due weight—or even where major misunderstanding may arise. I shall be discussing these below.

Until recently, the situation 'on the other side' was far more dismal. When examining the theoretical principles on which their subject rests, students of German drama from the eighteenth century onwards—leaving aside altogether drama in the wider context of European or world literature—have managed to get along quite nicely, or so they would appear to believe, by scrutinizing the extensive corpus of texts offered by such venerated figures as Lessing and Schiller (in the case of German Classical drama) and Brecht (for twentieth-century drama). As all students of German literature are aware, particularly if they themselves originate from a different (e.g. Anglo-Saxon) tradition, one of the most striking ways in which their subject differs from those other traditions is in the existence of an extensive body of theoretical writings which German writers, but most especially dramatists, seem to have found it necessary to articulate, either to support or to complement their own creative activity. Self-analysis and reflective-ness have for long been identified as hallmarks of the German psyche: nobody exemplifies this better than Schiller (cf. *Über naive und sentimentalische Dichtung*), but they are manifest throughout the literature. And since, for reasons which cannot be discussed

---

[2] Schenker's own theories of 'Urlinie' and 'Ursatz' and 'hierarchical differentia-tion' of musical components work from musical principles (e.g. the triad) alone. The later application of mathematical Group Theory to musical analysis similarly takes no account of dramatic or textual considerations. See article on 'Analysis' in *The New Grove Dictionary of Music and Musicians*.

[3] Joseph Kerman, *Opera as Drama* (New York, 1956).

[4] See esp. Carl Dahlhaus, 'Zur Geschichte der Leitmotivtechnik bei Wagner', in *Das Drama Richard Wagners als Kusntwerk*, ed. Dahlhaus (Regensburg, 1970), 17–40, and *Richard Wagners Musikdramen* (Velber, 1971; repr. Munich, 1988); the latter also in English trans. by Mary Whittall (Cambridge, 1979).

here, drama has since the eighteenth century been regarded as the foremost genre in German literature, much attention has been paid to analysing and dissecting these theories and trying to establish their precise relationship to the creative works. It could well be that Lessing set this particular ball rolling when he made his celebrated self-deprecatory remarks about having to 'prop up' his creative works with theoretical 'crutches', and to find inspiration from distance sources ('fremdes Feuer', borrowed flames). Since, as I hope to show, there are important links between both Lessing's and Schiller's theories, on the one hand, and Wagner's, on the other, it will be necessary to find some explanation for the persistent refusal of German scholars to accord the latter a place of honour in the theoretical canon which has now consolidated around the triad: Lessing, Schiller, Brecht.

Some awareness of Wagner reception in the late nineteenth and early twentieth century seems to me to hold the key to this 'missing link' in German dramatic theory, and in particular I am struck by the crucial role played here by a celebrated non-dramatist, Thomas Mann. As an ardent, but not uncritical Wagnerite, whose essays and utterances on the Master span a lifetime's experience of his works,[5] Mann seemed to feel it incumbent upon him to use Wagner almost as a marker, or yardstick of measurement for his own literary aims. More relevant to our purposes, though, than the question of Wagner's influence on Thomas Mann's own creative work is the latter's unique role as a standard-bearer of German culture whose pontifications were rhetorically persuasive and highly influential among countless educated Germans between the Wars. Taken out of this historical context, however, the rhetoric may often appear thin, the judgements a shade dogmatic, and their basis at times questionable. So far as Wagner's theoretical works are concerned, I believe this may have done untold damage, as can best be illustrated by quoting a passage from an essay of 1911, in which Mann's indictment of Wagner the theorist is breath-taking in its derogatory outspokenness:

Wäre sie [die Theorie] nicht so durchaus etwas Sekundäres, nicht so ganz nur eine nachträgliche und überflüssige Verherrlichung seines Talentes, so wäre sein Werk ohne Zweifel so unhaltbar geworden, wie sie, und nie hätte

---

[5] 'Versuch über das Theater' (1908), 'Uber die Kunst Richard Wagners' (1911), and 'Leiden und Größe Richard Wagners' (1933) seem to me to represent the most important of Mann's various attempts to come to terms with Wagner.

jemand sie auch nur einen Augenblick ernst genommen ohne das Werk, das sie, solange man im Theater sitzt, zu beweisen scheint, und das doch eben nichts weiter beweist als sich selber. Ja, hat überhaupt je jemand ernstlich an diese Theorie geglaubt? An die Addition von Malerei, Musik, Wort und Gebärde, die Wagner für die Erfüllung aller künstlerischen Sehnsucht auszugeben die Unbefangenheit hatte? An eine Rangordnung der Gattungen, in welcher der 'Tasso' dem 'Siegfried' nachstünde? Werden denn Wagners Kunstschriften auch nur gelesen? Woher eigentlich dieser Mangel an Interesse für den Schriftsteller Wagner? Daher, daß seine Schriften Parteischriften und nicht Bekenntnisse sind? Daß sie sein Werk, worin er wahrhaftig in seiner leidenden Größe lebt, sehr mangelhaft, sehr mißverständlich gelten lassen. Es ist wahr, man kann aus Wagners Schriften nicht viel über Wagner lesen (if theory were not of such secondary importance, nor so much a mere retrospective, superfluous celebration of his talent, then his work would undoubtedly have become as untenable as the theory has. Nobody would ever have taken the theory seriously even for a minute if it were not for the work which seems to be giving evidence of it for as long as one sits in the theatre—a work which, in the end, though, gives evidence only of itself. Has anyone, at any time, ever seriously believed in this theory? Believed in the aggregation of painting, music, words, and gestures which Wagner was naïve enough to proclaim as the fulfilment of all artistic longing? Believed in a hierarchical arrangement of genres, according to which *Tasso* would occupy second place to *Siegfried*? And does anyone even read Wagner's writings on art? What is the reason for this lack of interest in Wagner the author? Is it because the writings are polemical pieces and not confessions? Is it because they give such an inadequate and misleading account of the work—where he truly exists in all his suffering, all his greatness? Truly, one cannot glean much about Wagner himself from his writings).[6]

These remarks, written around the time of *Der Tod in Venedig*, when Mann was himself cultivating a strict Classicistic—and parodying—style, repay some analysis. First, they are factually inaccurate with respect to Wagner's estimation of the 'art-work of the future' (one of his many alternative terms for 'Gesamtkunstwerk'). Wagner did not see his new form as superior to Goethe's *Tasso*, a work which he venerated, just as he did other masterpieces by Shakespeare and Beethoven.[7]

[6] 'Über die Kunst Richard Wagners', *Gesammelte Werke*, (2nd edn. Frankfurt-on-Main and Hamburg, 1974), 841–2.
[7] See D. Borchmeyer, *Das Theater Richard Wagners* (Stuttgart, 1982), 12 and 'Tristan, Tasso und die Kunst des "unendlichen Details" ', *Jahrbuch der Bayerischen Staatsoper*, 3 (1979–80), 23–32.

Secondly, the charge of inconsistency between the operatic practice and the theory ('mangelhaft', 'mißverständlich', inadequate, misleading) is one which could be levelled against every theorist of note who has ever written dramatic works. Consistency among the theoretical works would be no more to be expected, given the long span during which Wagner occupied himself with theorizing—it was at least thirty years—any more than such consistency is evident in the theoretical works of Lessing or Schiller. Thomas Mann himself shows a scant disregard for consistency in his various essays and statements on the subject of Wagner which spread over many years.[8] Thirdly, he makes some demonstrably inaccurate comments about the theory. The most important and substantial of all Wagner's theoretical works, *Oper und Drama*, was certainly not written 'nachträglich', that is *after* the work to which it most applies, namely the *Ring* tetralogy. Rather, it arose out of a mood of intense self-scrutiny in the wake of *Lohengrin*, in a period which was uniquely fallow from the creative point of view and when Wagner was taking stock of his position and of the direction in which he planned to take opera before addressing himself to the task of composing the music for his vast work, having started to plan a scenario for the *Ring* and completed the 'Textbuch' for *Siegfrieds Tod*. It is often the case when eminent writers or artists assess each other's work that their statements tell us more about their instigators than about those works themselves. Mann is no exception, and one would be well advised to look elsewhere for objective assessments of Wagner's theories. I have already hinted at another difficulty, which is the fact that, as a major exponent of a genre, the novel, which had had its nose pushed out of joint by the much exalted drama during the course of the nineteenth and early twentieth centuries, Mann seemed almost to labour under a kind of literary inferiority complex. At any rate, his essays bear witness again and again to his need to assert the importance of the novel against the hegemony of the drama. One way in which he tended to do this was by attacking the drama form itself. It might be argued that his fascination with Wagner was more adequately expressed in his literary or fictional response to the content of the music dramas—one thinks here of *Wälsungenblut* and *Tristan*—and that

---

[8] Take, for example, his inconsistent attitude towards Wagner's theoretical writings and the apparent volte-face expressed in 'Leiden und Größe Richard Wagners'.

when he considered the more technical aspects of the music drama he was on less secure ground. We shall return at a later stage to the question of Mann's attitude towards the leitmotiv technique.

It is little wonder, given this emphatic directive to ignore Wagner's theoretical works, that many students of German drama have not felt much need to explore them. When one also considers the damaging effects of a rebarbative, over-complex prose-style and the rather quaint attempts to reinstate 'Stabreim' (alliterative verse) in the text of the *Ring*, we have a situation in which the stage is set for general scorn and derision, certainly at the more popular end of the scale. In this connection it is perhaps symptomatic to record that not even the anniversary year of 1983 was cause enough to persuade a German publisher to bring out a complete edition, let alone a critical one, of the theoretical writings.[9] Lesser figures than Richard Wagner have fared a lot better.

Notwithstanding this, there have been signs over the past ten years or so that a new attitude is slowly starting to develop. First, Marianne Kesting's illuminating essay (1977) on Wagner, Meyerhold, and Brecht[10] has brought into the arena the link figure of Meyerhold, enabling us to register the influence which this inspired theatre director exercised on Brecht. Meyerhold's productions were notable for their utilization of all the theatrical means at his disposal—music, pantomine, acrobatics—and could thus in their own way be regarded as a kind of 'Gesamtkunstwerk'. For those who have been disposed to regard Meyerhold as a forerunner of 'epic' theatre, it may come as a surprise to see his work within this broader spectrum. But even more surprising, perhaps, is Meyerhold's unconditional enthusiasm for Wagner's theoretical works: 'aber er hat auch zehn Bände außerordentlich interessanter Essays geschrieben, ich habe sie alle gelesen' (but he has also written ten volumes of extraordinarily interesting essays—I've read them all).[11] An unfashionable view, no doubt, for 1937, but surely significant,

---

[9] Although an attractive selection of the writings appeared in that year (in Insel-Verlag), the standard edition to date remains the late 19th-cent. one: *Gesammelte Schriften und Dichtungen* (12 vols., Leipzig, 1871 ff. (5 editions) (to which mention is made throughout (as *GSD*) unless otherwise stated. The 1887 edition forms the basis for a facsimile edition produced in 1976. Additionally, an extended version of the edition (with index) in 16 vols. (no date) exists.

[10] Marianne Kesting, 'Wagner/Meyerhold/Brecht oder die Erfindung des "epischen" Theaters', *Brecht-Jahrbuch* (1977), 111–30.

[11] Quoted by Kesting, 121.

coming as it does from a dedicated and practical man of the theatre, one who, although he must have been able to read and understand German, did not belong to that tradition whose spokesman was Thomas Mann: 'Wenn ihr diese zehn Bände zuzieht mit den Zetteln, auf die ich meine Anmerkungen geschrieben habe, werdet ihr verstehen, was mich interessiert hat' (if you take a look at these ten volumes along with the notes on which I've written my observations, you will understand what it is that interests me).

Even more significant than Meyerhold's testimony, however, has been the recent large-scale reinstatement of Wagner, the theorist of drama, instigated by Dieter Borchmeyer.[12] One hopes this book will serve not only students of German drama (and drama in general) but also musicologists, who may need more convincing that a book written 'aus literaturgeschichtlicher Sicht' (from a literary-historical perspective) can also have validity and make a major contribution to the more broadly based, interdisciplinary dialogue which would seem especially important for opera. The placing of Wagner's music drama, together with its appropriate theoretical underpinning, within an entire literary tradition stretching from Lessing to Schiller and the nineteenth century is one of the most striking and significant achievements of Borchmeyer's book. Particularly salutary is the following statement of the importance of Wagner's theories: 'wir dürfen seinen Autor [des Welttheaters] als den bedeutendsten schöpferischen *Vermittler der deutschen Literatur* [*my italics*] ans europäische Publikum zwischen Heine und Thomas Mann bezeichnen' (we may describe its author as the most significant creative *exponent of German literature* to the European public from Heine to Thomas Mann).[13] How many students of German literature would at this time be prepared to go along with this claim? Very few, I suppose. Yet I hope to demonstrate that by analysing Wagner's major commenting device, the leitmotiv, it is possible to give further substance to the claim. I also endorse (with one reservation) Borchmeyer's other powerful statement on the matter: 'Wagners ästhetische und dramaturgische Schriften [gehören] zu den faszinierendsten kunsttheoretischen Dokumenten des bürgerlichen Zeitalters' (Wagner's aesthetic and dramaturgical writings are among the most fascinating theoretical documents in the history of bourgeois art).[14] Only, why restrict the

---

[12] Borchmeyer, *Das Theater Richard Wagners.*
[13] Ibid. 16.   [14] Ibid. 14.

influence to 'des bürgerlichen Zeitalters'? Marianne Kesting has already pointed a way forward from Wagner to Brecht. I would hope to be able to shed further light on the concept of 'epic' theatre by analysing Wagner's theoretical writings. Lessing and Schiller have both been called in to shed light on Brecht's theories, so why not Wagner too?

Antecedents for Wagner's Theories: 1. Lessing

In order to give further substance to the claim that Wagner's theory of music drama has a wide-ranging relevance, it is necessary to linger for a moment on those points of substance in Lessing's and Schiller's theories on which Wagner was able to draw for the purpose of formulating his own views about how drama and music could be brought together for mutual benefit. Although musicologists are probably well aware of the fact, students of drama need to recognize that Wagner's first premiss was that no progress could be made with the opera as it was developing in Germany and elsewhere in the nineteenth century—that is, as a 'number' form in which the aria had assumed ever greater independence. To Wagner's mind the worst example of this development was Rossini,[15] who had made melody virtually an end in itself, concentrating on vulgar and showy feats of vocal virtuosity which could only impede the flow of any dramatic action that was developing on stage. Wagner did have some appreciative comments to make on the daring reforms of Gluck (as summarized in the famous Preface to *Alceste*)[16] and in general approved of the French operatic composers like Spontini, Méhul, and Cherubini who followed in his wake at the Paris Opéra at the turn of the eighteenth and nineteenth centuries.[17] He was also, as is well known, impressed by certain aspects of Weber's *Der Freischütz*, notably the

---

[15] 'Oper und Drama', *GSD* iii (Leipzig, 1897), esp. 251–5. Note Wagner's contemptuous reference to Rossini's 'narkotisch-bearauschende Melodie' (intoxicating and narcotic melody), a particularly interesting choice of words in view of Brecht's later comments about Wagner! See Ch. 3 below, p. 93–4.

[16] Although he qualifies his praise on the grounds that, while Gluck did much to restore the dignity of the composer (who had been losing out badly to demanding virtuoso singers) and thereby struck a blow for the integrity of composition itself, his reforms did little or nothing to alter the rigid structure of the 'Nummeroper' (number opera) with its relentless alternation of recitative, aria, and dance. 'Oper und Drama', *GSD* iii. 237–8.   [17] Ibid. 239 f.

famous wolf's glen scene which is presented in the form of a 'Melodram', a heightened form of speech which is complemented by suitably dramatic and atmospheric music. But Wagner was doubtful about the usefulness of Beethoven's *Fidelio* as a contribution to the genre of opera and regarded it as a prime example of how a great composer—and Beethoven's symphonies were for Wagner indubitably the greatest thing in all music—had been impeded and stifled by a hopelessly primitive and out-of-date structure. Beethoven, he argued, unable to exploit the dramatic possibilities of the genre, concentrated all his pent-up energies into the Overture. It is, possibly, a point in favour of this argument that Beethoven composed no fewer than four versions of the Overture: *Fidelio* and *Leonore* Nos. 1, 2, and 3, and that the magnificent *Leonore* No. 3 was conceived on such a grandiose scale that, despite its having been intended to accompany a new performance of the opera in March 1806, it completely broke asunder the normal proportions and functions of the overture form.[18] Again it is clear that the source of Wagner's dissatisfaction is to be located in what he sees as the one-sided development of the opera form: the elaboration of purely musical effects and the under-exploitation of the rich vein of dramatic potential which, to his mind, the hybrid form cries out to express.

As Borchmeyer has reminded us,[19] Wagner found support for his ideas on the relationship between drama and music not from the ranks of the composers but from those of the dramatists, Lessing and Schiller. Lessing's never completed continuation of and companion piece to the Laocoon essay 'Über die Grenzen der Malerei und Poesie' which was to have taken the form of a comparison between literature and music would have held some surprises for anyone inclined to regard him as a severe Classicist who believed that the different art forms should be kept strictly within their boundaries. Lessing was strongly of the opinion that 'Poesie' and 'Musik' had much to contribute to one another and

[18] See 'Über die Ouvertüre', *GSD* i. 197. Of *Leonore* No. 3: 'Dies Werk ist nicht mehr eine Ouvertüre, sondern das gewaltige Drama selbst' (this work is no longer an overture, but a powerful drama in its own right).

[19] And he has done a service in recalling earlier, long-forgotten, but no less valuable pioneering contributions to the theme by Konrad Burdach in 'Schillers Chordrama und die Geburt des tragischen Stils aus der Musik', *Vorspiel: Gesammelte Schriften zur Geschichte des deutschen Geistes*, ii, (Halle, 1925), 116–237.

that they should be brought more closely together. Surprisingly—like Wagner[20]—he seems to have conceived of the complete unity of the two forms in earlier times: the 'Trennung', he believes, only came about much later (unlike Wagner, who had views about this, Lessing does not suggest how). As things then (i.e. around 1770) stood, Lessing thought the only way in which they could be brought together again was via the opera: 'Hernach ist noch auch dieses zu erinnern, daß man nur eine Verbindung ausübet, in welcher die Dichtkunst die helfende Kunst ist, nämlich in der Oper, die Verbindung aber, wo die Musik die helfende Kunst wäre, noch unbearbeitet gelassen ist' (accordingly, note must also be taken of the fact that there is only one example of a practical alliance in which literature is the 'helping' art-form—namely opera. An alliance, however, in which music were to assume that role remains as yet untried).[21] As Borchmeyer rightly observes, the reference to the undeveloped potential of the literary element in the opera of Lessing's day (it is so far only a 'helfende Kunst', that is, subordinate to the music) is a remarkable anticipation of Wagner's theories in *Oper und Drama*.

This is not the only example of such a train of thought in Lessing's writings; the question of the role which music could play in the development of the drama is also ventilated in the *Hamburgische Dramaturgie* (26th and 27th sections), where Burdach[22] had already suggested that Lessing was pointing forward to the concept of music drama as developed by Wagner, even down to the actual technical means that should be brought into play in order to enhance the dramatic effect. First, Lessing had focused attention on the role of the orchestra, which he saw as a possible substitute for the Greek chorus in its commenting function. He was aware of and appreciative of the developments taking place in the music of his day. We should perhaps recall that the foundations for the Classical symphony were at this very moment being laid by Haydn, who would soon be followed by Mozart. The new expressive possibilities of the art-form should, so Lessing thought, be exploited for the drama too. Secondly, he was even more explicit about the techniques that might be dramatically fruitful, pointing

---

[20] See *GSD* iv. 91 ff. For an interesting recent analysis of Wagner's theories of language see Mary Cicora, 'From Metonymy to Metaphor: Wagner and Nietzsche on Language', *German Life and Letters*, 42 (1988), 16–31.

[21] Lessing, *Werke*, ed. Georg Wittkowski (Leipzig and Vienna, n.d.) iv. 309 f. (Paralipomena to 'Laocoon').   [22] Burdach, *Vorspiel*, 176–7.

to devices which, I believe rightly, can be said to anticipate the letimotiv: the repetition, that is, of thematic material with dramatic associations which has the effect of taking the listener 'hinter das Geheimnis des Ausdrucks' (behind the mysteries being expressed). And in another area too Lessing—as Burdach again observes— shows much originality and perspicacity. In the context of his investigation of the role of incidental music, he is able to observe great practical advantages for the drama, particularly at points where there is a wide range of expression and sudden transitions of mood, when the spectator will be forced to realign his responses fairly drastically in response to developments in the action: 'die Motivierung der plötzlichen Übergänge ist einer der größten Vorteile, den die Musik aus der Vereinigung mit der Poesie zieht, ja vielleicht der allergrößte' (the capacity to motivate sudden transitions is one of the greatest advantages that music derives from its union with literature, indeed possibly the greatest advantage of all).[23] How interesting to observe that within thirty years of this remark being made we find a remarkable example of music performing this function and controlling dramatic transitions quite brilliantly. I am thinking of the incidental music which Beethoven wrote for Goethe's drama *Egmont*, where at the point in Act V at which many would say that Goethe fails to convince us with his sudden transitions (Egmont's apotheosis and the transfiguration of his beloved, Klärchen, into an embodiment of freedom), Beethoven's music possesses just the right quality of nobility to raise us from prosaic reality into the realm of the ideal.

One must always, of course, bear in mind the considerable differences in the respective attitudes of Lessing and Wagner to the role of music in drama as a means of effecting transition. For Wagner such incidental music as Lessing envisages is only one of the many possible relationships between the two art forms. But none the less Lessing's observations are remarkable for their time. His statements represent the first tangible evidence of a *rapprochement* between music and drama, instigated from the literary-dramatic end. Before we turn to Schiller's contribution to the process, it will be opportune to cast a brief glance at Wagner's own method of approach, since *his* starting-point is the complete reverse of Lessing's. Working from his profound dissatisfaction with

[23] Lessing, *Werke*, ed. cit. v. 14.

operatic music of the early nineteenth century, Wagner demands an alliance between music and drama on the evidence of new and exciting possibilities which had been taking place in the field of music, particularly Beethoven's symphonies. If Lessing (not known in any case as a musical connoisseur) was able to observe the beginnings of this new movement in the music of C. P. E. Bach, Haydn, and possibly Gluck, it is clear that by the time Wagner appeared music had developed to unprecedented heights and German music now reigned supreme.[24]

But there is another development of which Lessing could not have been aware, although he himself had made a major contribution to its evolution. This was the fact that not only had German orchestral music reached a pinnacle by the mid-nineteenth century, but German drama—and German literature in general—thanks to his pioneering attempts—had itself developed to almost similar heights (the dramas of Goethe, Schiller, and Kleist rank among the finest achievements in post-Shakespearian European drama). But by 1850, having rapidly scaled such peaks of excellence, the drama had virtually exhausted itself and stood ready to receive a transfusion. In a position as he was to look back now on these twin achievements of music and drama, painfully aware too of the inadequacy of the operatic form, the movement of Wagner's mind towards a synthesis of the best elements from each seems both logical and timely. Equally understandable is his opposition to what he would have regarded as the polarization of music and drama implicit in the great debates that raged among the representatives of 'absolute' music (e.g. Hanslick, Brahms) and the adherents (like Berlioz and Liszt) of 'mixed' forms, such as 'programme music' and opera. The sheer thoroughness of Wagner's theoretical exegesis in *Oper und Drama* and his other contemporaneous theoretical writings and the sense of urgency which he conveys through them have to be understood against this background. But it is worth noting that, despite the vigour and almost messianic fervour with which he engages with his theme, Wagner disdains a narrowly polemic stance and eschews all personal

---

[24] If any confirmation of German supremacy in the field of music in the 19th cent. is needed, it can be found in P. Scholes, *The Oxford Companion to Music* (9th edn. 1955), 400: 'for a time she dominated the whole of the musical world, provoking outside her borders in the mid-nineteenth century the revolt to which the name of Nationalism is attached'.

attacks or vindictive outbursts.[25] As it turned out, German drama had already, though unbeknown to all, received its transfusion through the works of the precocious genius Georg Büchner, but would not be able to rise until those works were 'rediscovered' at the end of the nineteenth century, unleashing a new spate of original dramas by first the Naturalists, then the Expressionists. This new direction in drama, however, showed a scant regard for the 'sister-art' of music until the arrival on the scene of Bertolt Brecht. By rediscovering music's role Brecht neatly turned the wheel full circle. While Wagner's dreams of the integration of the two art forms are inconceivable without the complex, historically conditioning factors which he inherited from the *Zeitgeist*, it is less clear that his own particular dramatic-operatic 'solutions' left much of an opening for future composers, despite the daring innovatory musical language in which they were presented. Rather, they appear as a culmination of previous trends and a highly original fusion of the two forms which no other operatic composer has achieved so completely ever since.

At the centre of Wagner's concerns not only in *Oper und Drama*, which is the most systematic and far-reaching of the theoretical writings, but in other essays as well (e.g. 'Das Kunstwerk der Zukunft'), lies the concept of the 'Gesamtkunstwerk' to which we must now attend before proceeding to a consideration of its chief instrument, the leitmotiv. 'Gesamtkunstwerk' is a term for which Wagner did not care too much, often preferring terms like 'Kunstwerk der Zukunft' (art-work of the future), 'musikalisches Drama', etc., and indeed it is ambiguous since, as Dieter Borchmeyer points out,[26] it denotes a Utopian construct in which all the arts, poetry (that is, literature), music, and the visual arts, lose their own identity and are amalgamated in something else. Such a construct looks suspiciously like nineteenth-century man's long-awaited answer to the ever-present challenge presented by the visible perfection of Greek culture. But there is a second, less high-falutin

---

[25] See Wagner's letter to Uhlig (10 Mar. 1851): 'Es wäre doch entsetzlich, wenn das Buch für einen bloßen Angriff auf Meyerbeer angesehen werden könnte' (it would be a terrible thing if the book were to be regarded as a mere attack on Meyerbeer), Richard Wagner, *Sämtliche Briefe*, ed. G. Strobel and W. Wolf, iii (Leipzig, 1975), 522. Klaus Kropfinger presents helpful information relating to Wagner's revisions of the manuscript of 'Oper und Drama', see *Oper und Drama*, ed. Kropfinger (Stuttgart, 1984), 465.

[26] Borchmeyer, *Das Theater Richard Wagners*, 70–1.

aspect of the concept, as Borchmeyer is equally well aware, a concrete dramaturgical principle which, more modestly, sets out to bring about the *rapprochement* of music and drama (the visual aspect is very much in the background), which had hitherto been distinct forms, following the principles laid down in *Oper und Drama*. Wagner makes it clear that the dramatic element, so long neglected in opera and treated merely as a means to an end, will become a primary determinant of the form, structure, and even the musical language that is adopted (later, it is true, he had other views). In the light of Brecht's strictures, it is important to notice that the process of integration envisaged by Wagner between gesture, poetic-dramatic content, and musical expression in no way implies an obliteration of the primal characteristics of each individual component. In short, Wagner is far from envisaging music drama as a featureless amalgam. It is not—*pace* Brecht—a question of integration implying unification at the level of 'lowest common denominator'. Far from it. Wagner would see the process of merger, rather, as enabling each respective art form to reach new, hitherto unexplored levels of expressiveness. Despite the seeming bias towards the dramatic element in theory—which is really a corrective to the given position of imbalance that prevailed—posterity would surely not complain that in Wagner's music drama the music has lost out!

Antecedents for Wagner's Theories: 2. Schiller

If Lessing's inspired gleam of a proto-'Gesamtkunstwerk' could only take a theoretical form (and a sketchy one at that), Schiller felt sufficiently emboldened to venture along the road by putting theory to the test. It is well known that around 1800 both he and Goethe were much preoccupied with the problems of drama at the Weimar Court and particularly interested in allying drama and music through such popular forms as the 'Singspiel' (cf. Goethe's *Claudine von Villa Bella*) and the 'Melodram' (cf. Goethe's *Proserpina*). Schiller's main contribution to these experiments is, of course, his chorus drama *Die Braut von Messina*, together with its pendant, the essay 'Über den Gebrauch des Chors',[27] in which he

---

[27] Wagner knew Schiller's *Braut* from early days (his sister played the part of Beatrice in a performance in the Königliches-Sächsiches Hoftheater, Leipzig, on 26

set out his reasons for taking what must have appeared the drastic step of reintroducing the long-abandoned, though still much lamented chorus. By such means Schiller hoped to introduce a perspectival role via the chorus, which would combine lyrical and musical reflective functions. Schiller's rather spectacular failure with the new form in many ways highlights the problems that Wagner too had to face in his ambitious enterprise. Schiller, though, was ill-advisedly persuaded by his friend Körner to drop the musical-orchestral accompaniment which he had originally intended for his choric interludes; instead of this, the verses of the chorus were chanted by large groups in parrot-fashion, a kind of 'Geplapper' which bore an unfortunate resemblance to schoolboy recitation. Then the chorus was divided into two partisan groups— a practical compromise which Schiller attempts rather unconvincingly to defend in his essay. This destroyed the possibility of its achieving a perspective of detachment or universality which, as we also learn from that essay, was to have been its prime function. The flop was highly embarrassing for all concerned in Weimar: Herder was openly scornful; Goethe, who had aided and abetted the venture, maintained a dignified silence about the reception of the work, which spoke volumes.

For Wagner there must have been important lessons to be learned. First, this botched attempt on the part of the two greatest exponents of the drama form in late eighteenth- and early nineteenth-century Germany to bring musical-choric elements together with drama made a successful attempt at further amalgamation with the drama as starting-point look increasingly unviable. Secondly, problems were bound to arise if a composer was called in to compose music for a drama that was already complete; examples such as Beethoven's incidental music to *Egmont* must, to Wagner's mind, have lacked that dimension of immediacy which renders total dramatic cross-fertilization possible.

May and 18 June 1830). He himself wrote an Overture to the drama (now lost), see J. Deathridge, M. Geck, and E. Voss, *Verzeichnis der musikalischen Werke Richard Wagners und ihre Quellen* (Mainz, 1984), 70–1. He would also appear to have been familiar with Schiller's essay 'Über den Gebrauch des Chors' as can be seen from the (recently discovered) review he wrote of Bellini's *Norma* on the occasion of its first performance in Königsberg (8 Mar. 1837). Here he finds in Bellini's opera a realization of the spirit of Classical Antiquity along the lines urged by Schiller in the latter's essay. See F. Lippmann, 'Ein neuentdecktes Autograph Richard Wagners: Rezension der Königsberger "Norma" Aufführung von 1837', *Festschrift Karl Gustav Fellerer*, ed. H. Hüschen (Cologne, 1973), 373–9.

When we look back on the successful musical-literary collaboration between Richard Strauss and Hugo von Hofmannsthal, while bearing in mind the point that it is doubtful whether the fruits of that collaboration would have met Wagner's criteria for music drama, we are struck by the painstaking efforts made on both sides—admittedly not without their acrimonious interludes—to give equal weight to words and music. Wagner was able to solve the problem of balance by the simple expedient of writing his own 'Textbücher' (he disliked the more commonplace word 'libretto'); by taking over both roles he could better organize the process of integration. Thus the Textbuch of the *Ring* tetralogy was more or less completed before Wagner addressed himself seriously to writing the music, as if to underline the primacy of the textual and dramatic aspects of the enterprise.

Burdach suggests that Schiller can be regarded as a 'Vorkämpfer des Gesamtkunstwerks' (pioneer of the *Gesamtkunstwerk*), but he may be exaggerating, and certainly Lessing's insights come rather closer to Wagner's model. Taken together, Lessing's and Schiller's contributions to the debate represent different approaches towards a common goal, namely the abiding need for a dimension of perspective and commentary upon a dramatic action as it unfolds. For Schiller a major consideration here was the disturbing effect that tragedy could produce on the psyche of the spectator, if allowed to take its course on stage; choric intervention at highly charged moments would serve a moderating function and the aesthetic balance which had been disturbed by the display of violent emotion would be restored. One can see from this how far Schiller's aims are from Wagner's. Musical-reflective perspective is clearly for him a device which has to be used sparingly, only, that is, at critical points in the action. Lessing had seen the usefulness of the commenting, evaluating aspects as well, but had considered their operation specifically in the restricted context of disjoined musical interludes before and between the acts ('Zwischenspiele'); these could be provided by instrumental music, he thought. I have already emphasized that that particular insight into the potential usefulness of the orchestra is a strong link between Lessing and Wagner. While Schiller was still thinking in terms of prose dialogue alternating with 'vocalized' sections—not so very different in effect, one supposes, from 'number' opera—and saw no independent role for an orchestra, Lessing had already opened the way for a

'Durchkomponierung' of music and text. Another leap and an extension of his ideas into the terrain of the 'Melodram' (cf. Weber's *Der Freischütz*) would enable the orchestra to function both within and without the dramatic action. From that point to complete 'Durchkomponierung' is not such a large step.

The Role of the Orchestra as Commentator

Wagner's realization that the orchestra could play a vitally important role in the coming together of music and drama in the 'Gesamtkunstwerk' is a momentous breakthrough in what, during the first half of the nineteenth century, had virtually become a dead-end issue. It is this—together with its corollary, the leitmotiv—that makes both his theory and practice (especially as exemplified in the *Ring* tetralogy) so revolutionary. His deep knowledge of the drama—not only German Classical drama but also Ancient Greek drama (in particular the works of Aeschylus and Sophocles)—had imbued in him a sense of the overriding need for drama to return to an 'interdisciplinary' model after the seeming abandonment of this ideal at the hands of Shakespeare (of whose achievements, however, as we shall see below, Wagner was no less appreciative). Again and again in *Oper und Drama* Wagner insists on the need for the composer-dramatist to make his intentions clear to his public. Such a 'dichterische Abischt' (poetic design) could not be read from between the lines, as it were; it had to be rendered clear and intelligible by means of a commanding presence.[28] For Wagner the great advantage which the orchestra in its new commenting role can offer is that it is omnipresent and its main function is coincidental to the dramatic action on stage. Its role between sections is not by any means diminished, however; the 'Zwischen-spiele' in the *Ring* and elsewhere (like Siegfried's Funeral Music, for example) can perform an important structural function, enabling the spectator and listener to register recapitulatory and anticipatory material in a reflective frame of mind. This variation in the

---

[28] It would be interesting to know how convincingly certain modern theories, e.g. Structuralism and Post-Structuralism, can accommodate such a spectacular example of *intentionality* on the part of the creative artist as Richard Wagner's. The post-Jungians like Robert Donington have already exhaustively investigated the other, i.e. subconscious, angles. See *Wagner's 'Ring' and its Symbols: The Music and the Myth* (2nd edn., London, 1969).

commenting techniques and the temporary absence of the demanding extra dimension of direct action and visual immediacy provides
him with a much needed respite and gathering of forces before the
resumption of the stage action.

In Wagner's new conception, then, the synchronization of
commentary and dramatic action is complete: Siegfried's naïve and
nonchalant melodic statements and themes can be allied to
ominous motivs and harmonic ramifications presented by the
orchestra, these can both hark back to his doom-laden origins as
the product of the incestuous union of Sieglinde and Siegmund and
point forward to his tragic end. In the case of a character possessing
so little self-awareness this is of inestimable importance for the
audience's understanding of the whole. Wagner makes this commenting role even more precise; it is explicitly compared to that of a
human commentator and virtually acquires the human function of
speech ('Sprachvermögen'). He is clear that such a degree of
expressiveness is only possible because of the technical and musical
developments associated with the early nineteenth century (the
example of Beethoven's Ninth Symphony is ever before him): 'Das
Orchester besizt unleugbar ein Sprachvermögen und die Schöpf-
ungen unserer modernen Instrumentalmusik haben uns dies
aufgedeckt' (indubitably, the orchestra possesses the power of
speech and the creations of our modern instrumental music have
revealed this to us).[29] This means that it is therefore in a position to
achieve all that the Greek chorus—which was chiefly a vocal
device—was able to do for Greek tragedy, namely provide a
simultaneous evaluation and commentary upon events: 'Dieser war
stets gegenwärtig, vor seinen Augen legten sich die Motive der
vorgehenden Handlung dar, er suchte diese Motive zu ergründen
und aus ihnen sich ein Urteil über die Handlung zu bilden' (this was
ever present, the motives behind the action as it proceeded were
expounded; it sought to fathom these and thence to form a
judgement about the action).[30]

But Wagner sees his orchestra doing even more than the Greek
chorus was able to, since the latter necessarily played a non-
participant and comparatively inactive role in the action and
reflected upon it from a distance, whereas the modern orchestra, by
dint of its intimate musical relationship to the whole—as the

---

[29] 'Oper und Drama', *GSD* iv. 173.
[30] 'Zukunftsmusik', *GSD* vii. 130.

supplier of the harmonies which reinforce and complete the vocal melodic line ('die harmonische Trägerin der Versmelodie', the harmonic bearer of the verse-melody)[31]—is at one and the same time integrated into the whole and yet able to oversee it and preside over it with sovereign detachment. Wagner would seem to be walking a tightrope as far as the question of audience response is concerned: on the one hand, aiming to create an intellectually detached perspective, on the other, a total emotional involvement on the part of the audience. Such a manifold appeal to our faculties, emotional and intellectual, is a highly complex matter. We are constantly being invited—and the orchestra's new commenting role is central here—to compare, contrast, and adjudicate upon human (and divine) actions; we are forced into a highly attentive state, directed towards the intricacies of motivation for events, towards an understanding of their shape and pattern. Wagner seems to have been well aware of the demands he was making; one of his most endearing traits is that he does not underestimate the audience's capacity to rise to the challenge. Indeed he suggests in *Oper und Drama* that the dynamic processes instigated by the orchestra place the spectator in the same intellectually active position as the composer himself, who makes us 'zu organisch mitwirkenden Zeugen dieses Werdens' (participant witnesses of this organic process).[32] We can only acquire this status as 'participant witnesses' if we are being made consciously aware of the nature of the events enacted. I shall return at a later stage to this important point, which has often not been fully taken by commentators.

Mode of Commentary: Epic or Dramatic?

Wagner sees the orchestra's role as an alternative to the wholly inadquate vocal choruses so beloved of nineteenth-century Italian and French operatic composers. Where such choruses appear as useless, unmotivated excrescences, his orchestra will in its omni-presence function in a purposeful and aesthetically pleasing fashion: 'in stets gegenwärtiger, nie aber störender Weise' (in ever-present but never-intruding fashion).[33] This remark—and others in

---

[31] 'Oper und Drama', *GSD* iv. 160.
[32] Ibid. 186–7 (in italics in original).
[33] 'Zukunftsmusik', *GSD* vii. 131.

a similar vein—has not gone unnoticed by many commentators who have a stake in the business of identifying 'epic' features in Wagner's music dramas and theories. For surely, as they see it, this all-encompassing perspectival stance upon the dramatic action is closely akin to the stance of an omniscient narrator in the novel? Marianne Kesting, certainly, is struck by the resemblance to Flaubert's self-styled stance as novelist-narrator who is 'überall anwesend und nirgends sichtbar' (omnipresent, but nowhere visible).[34] Even more influential, perhaps, has been Thomas Mann's attempt in the essay 'Versuch über das Theater' to argue for the superiority of the novel form over the drama specifically in terms of the latter's failure as a genre to provide this all-important distancing perspective upon the action. The drama, according to Mann—or perhaps the theatre, since the focus of his argument switches curiously between the two—is viewed in terms of a totally illusionist, direct replication ('Mimik') and he has misgivings about what he sees as the consequent direct appeal which it makes to the senses (there is not a little ambivalence in his stance and we have the impression that he rather fears its seductive appeal). Mann casts around in vain for signs of a detached perspective in drama: 'Wo ist die Stimmung, der Ernst, die berühmte "interesselose Anschauung" so beständig bedroht und in Frage gestellt wie dort . . . ?' (Where are the atmosphere, the gravity, the celebrated 'disinterested intuition' so threatened or challenged as they are here?).[35] But largely, I believe, he has an axe to grind—and with Thomas Mann one can never ignore the element of personal prejudice which detracts from the purported objective status of his remarks, while one can still admire the stylish and arresting way in which these remarks are presented. I have already suggested a reason for this: it is Mann's need to 'reinstate' the novel at the expense of the drama.

When he turns for a moment to concede the high quality of German drama of the Classical period—that of Goethe, Schiller, Grillparzer, and Kleist—and has even a kind word for later practitioners like Hauptmann, Wedekind, and Hofmannsthal, Mann produces a startling rationalization to explain their success, suggesting that these works do not depend on the theatre and are, in fact, better suited to reading than to theatrical staging. Wagner's theatricality, on the other hand, makes him more dependent on the

---

[34] Kesting, 'Wagner/Meyerfield/Brecht', 118.
[35] Thomas Mann, 'Versuch über das Theater', *Gesammelte Werke*, ed. cit., 39.

stage, giving his works, in Mann's view, an ambiguous quality.[36] It is amazing to note how far Mann is prepared to go in defence of his own position! The superb quality of these 'Lesedramen' like Schiller's, he continues, is to be attributed to their Classical and Hellenic inspiration, a feature which makes them 'epic' rather than 'dramatic' (we note the hopeless confusion which reigns about the definition of 'epic'). In what seems to me a convoluted manœuvre, Mann sums up his position: 'Man sieht, wie hier eine Behand-lungsweise, die dem antiken Dichter als dramatisch gegolten hätte und den antikisierenden Dichter als dramatisch galt, von einem modernen Standpunkt aus geradezu als "episch" bezeichnet wird' (we can see how a technique which would have been considered as dramatic by a Classical author, and was considered as such by the classicizing one, is described here, from the modern perspective, as 'epic').[37] Mann's point that the terminology 'epic'/'dramatic' has undergone a drastic realignment since Classical Antiquity is certainly interesting, but is rather sketchily indicated. There is something rather reductive about his categories: all 'good' art, it seems, must be 'epic'; this being so, Wagner, whose music drama is obviously 'good', has also to be claimed as an exponent: 'Was er schuf, war ein szenisches Epos—etwas Wundervolles aber kein Drama, im modernen [*i.e. Ibsen's analytical technique*] nicht und gewiß nicht im Sinn der Tragödie' (what he created was an epic in scenes—something marvellous, but in no way a drama, not in the modern sense, let alone in the sense of tragedy).[38]

To my mind Mann gives a false emphasis to the direct role which he regards the orchestra as playing in a Wagnerian music drama, suggesting that instead of enhancing it this detracts from or rather invalidates any immediacy and directness of the stage action ('die Gegenwärtigkeit des Dramas'). But in doing so he notes correctly its role as commentator upon the work: 'dies Werk, das dort oben in kindlich hohen Gesichten erscheint, während die Musik ihre singende, sagende Flut zu den Füßen der Ereignisse dahinwälzt (the work which appears up there in childlike, lofty faces, while the music surges at the feet of the events on a tide of song and narrative).[39] One would not wish to quibble with Mann's view that the perspectival role assumed by the orchestra—one which he finds

---

[36] Ibid. 37. Note Mann's further polarizations of 'drama' and 'theatre', 'epic drama' and 'theatrical drama' on p. 46.   [37] Ibid. 47.
[38] Ibid. 48.   [39] Ibid. 31.

missing on the contemporary stage with its seductive appeal to the senses and its cult of the actor—has existed within the drama form since time immemorial (one need only think of the role of the Greek chorus). So far, so good, but that is to say no more, surely, than that this commenting function is an essential part of the genre of drama, not that the 'epic' (however defined) is itself primary or superior to drama. Although there is strong evidence to show that, despite all his dismissive statements about them, Mann was well acquainted with Wagner's theoretical works,[40] it is a pity that he was not able to analyse them objectively or in the depth that they require.

We shall be returning presently to the central issue of terminology and the continuing tendencies in the critical literature to treat 'epic' and 'dramatic' as polarized forms. For the moment I should like to draw attention, however, to Dieter Borchmeyer's disappointingly uncritical acceptance of the idea of such polarity and—this despite his own awareness of Mann's unreliability to which I have just drawn attention—his apparent agreement with the views of Thomas Mann. The chapter entitled 'Die Erlösung des Romans im musikalischen Drama' (The redemption of the novel in musical drama) seems to me to contain the weakest arguments in an otherwise valuable book and it would appear that Borchmeyer has been caught up in the universal tide of 'epic' thinking about drama. Briefly, his thesis is that Wagner's theory of music drama is simply another version, this time achieved through music, of the nineteenth-century novel: it is, in fact, an 'umgestülpte ('upturned') Roman-theorie'.[41] Not surprisingly Borchmeyer seeks to illustrate this bold hypothesis by drawing 'novelistic' parallels between Wagner's works and the novel form. Many of these are disappointingly superficial. For example, he develops the theory that Wagner's music is analogous to prose (the fact that the 'endless melody' is never end-stopped, or only very rarely, is seldom rhymed, and that Wagner introduced 'Stabreim' is presented as evidence of this.[42]

[40] As Borchmeyer rightly observes (see p. 150), there is evidence that Mann was acquainted with Wagner's theoretical writings well enough to quote from them without acknowledgement: 'Selbst da, wo er gegen Wagner polemisiert, bedient er sich seiner Argumente' (even when he is polemicizing against Wagner, he uses the latter's arguments).

[41] Borchmeyer, *Das Theater Richard Wagners*, 151.

[42] Borchmeyer also identifies prologues and narrative sections as 'epic' character-istics in Wagner's music dramas. His examples follow those of Thomas Mann quite closely. See p. 150.

The fact that drama can equally well be presented in prose as in verse does not appear to trouble Borchmeyer.

Now it is indubitably true that Wagner enthused about the novels of Balzac and Scott (who did not in the nineteenth century?). But it is also true, as Borchmeyer is well aware, that he regarded the genre of the novel as symptomatic of a 'fallen' era, one characterized by rationalism and historicism.[43] That meant that for the 'art-work of the future' new forms had to be developed. To describe Wagner's music dramas as 'secret novels', as Borchmeyer is disposed to do, is a distortion of Wagner's aims. Again, confusion reigns regarding the definition of 'epic' at this point. Borchmeyer equates the term with the novel, then with the medium of prose (as opposed to end-stopped verse). At other times he identifies it as a principle of commentary and perspective comparable to the role of the narrator, as when, for instance, he analyses the interaction of the orchestra with the action on stage and sees this as directly analogous to authorial stance. It would appear that in claiming Thomas Mann as his major authority on the matter of definition of the term 'epic', Borchmeyer has perpetuated the state of general confusion.

Simply in order to attempt to bring some clarity into these muddied waters, let me anticipate a little and explain the point of view from which I am working. It is that the terms in which Wagner himself presents his ideas in *Oper und Drama*—which are those of drama not epic—seem to me to provide a useful basis on which to proceed. Since the composer is at pains to emphasize this point and since the very feature which he had found lacking in nineteenth-century opera was the drama, it seems unreasonable to assume on such flimsy evidence that he got things badly wrong, particularly when one considers his elaborate efforts to relate his contribution to what had gone before. I am not suggesting that it is indefensible to query the basis of a creative artist's assumptions when he attempts to build a theoretical edifice to 'explain' his endeavours. Indeed I shall later try to examine Brecht's theory of drama from just such a critical standpoint and 'against the grain'. I will only state here that it seems to me that Wagner's premisses and the painstaking way in which he sought to substantiate his theory by

---

[43] 'Oper und Drama', *GSD* iv. 34. Borchmeyer (*Das Theater Richard Wagners*, 136) notes this point but still holds to his notion that for Wagner the 'art-work of the future' represents an ideal solution in *epic* form.

showing its relationship to past tradition has in its favour a coherence and a sense of historical continuity which other theoretical systems of the twentieth century may lack. Wagner's technique of the leitmotiv was one of the most potent weapons in his quiver towards the achievement of his radical goals and it must now receive our close attention. I shall try to bring out its dramatic significance and intended function within the overall structure of the music drama form.

The Wagnerian Leitmotiv

First, it is interesting to observe that the new orthodoxy concerning the 'epic' quality of Wagner's music drama has caught on equally strongly in discussion and analysis of the technique of leitmotiv itself, not only in the ranks of the literary scholars but also those of the musicologists.[44] It is unclear whether the outspoken views of Thomas Mann or the post-Brechtian theorists have been the more decisive, but one thing is certain and it is that when we return to Wagner's own theoretical writings, particularly *Oper und Drama*, it is plain that the composer himself took the opposite view. Whenever he is expounding the theory of leitmotiv, or *Grundmotiv* (primary motiv), for the former term, which has proved irresistible, was invented by Hans von Wolzogen, Wagner emphasizes its functionality—the way, that is, that it is both prompted by dramatic events and fully integrated into the dramatic action. It is just this lack of a purposeful dramatic coherence which had caused him to reject Beethoven's *Fidelio*. 'Das Zusammenhanglose war so recht eigentlich der Charakter der Opernmusik' (opera music was really characterized by its lack of structural connections).[45] The alternative to such baggy shapelessness was the development of a network ('Gewebe')[46] of musical 'themes' or motivs which are

---

[44] Carl Dahlhaus takes it over without discussion and, perhaps rather unwisely, adopts the over-simplified categorization of Volker Klotz, describing the structure of the *Ring* as 'open', see Dahlhaus, *Richard Wagners Musikdramen*, 107; on the 'epic' character of the Norns scene see Dahlhaus, 'Zur Geschichte der Leitmotivtechnik', 34 f. Following Dahlhaus, Mann, Kesting, and Borchmeyer, Annette Ingenhoff has been tempted into even crasser categorizations in *Drama oder Epos? Richard Wagners Gattungstheorie des musikalischen Dramas* (Tübingen, 1987), 10, 13, *et passim*.   [45] 'Oper und Drama', *GSD* iv. 201.

[46] 'Über die Anwendung der Musik auf das Drama', *GSD* x. 185:'Dennoch muß die neue Form der dramatischen Musik, um wiederum als Musik ein Kunstwerk zu

intimately associated with key elements in the action—often, in turn concentrated into concrete objects (e.g. 'gold', 'sword', 'apples') or characters (e.g. Siegfried, the Wanderer, the Valkyries, etc.)—or with more insubstantial notions (e.g. Valhalla, which is in one sense concrete, in that in *Das Rheingold* it appears visibly before us, but later becomes more abstract when its falseness—the fact that it has been built by Wotan by means of the Giants' forced labour—is exposed). These motivs are subjected to all kinds of complex contextual associations, their transformation being a good example of the interaction of the dramatic and the musical. Thus, for example, the Valhalla motiv, despite its outward nobility which is so wonderfully conveyed by the leitmotiv, becomes tinged with associations of illusion and false idealism. What is at work here, as Dieter Borchmeyer has well expressed it,[47] is a 'semanticization' (Semantisierung) of a musical theme so that it becomes saturated with ideas and associations and can be brought out again and again—for repetition is a basic characteristic of leitmotiv—to convey such meanings and become subject to even more transformations.

To explain further: in its semantic multi-valency the Valhalla leitmotiv operates in much the same way as a literary motiv. A comparison with Goethe's *Faust* illustrates the point, for one could compare the 'noble' Burg with Faust's equally noble-seeming, half-altruistic attempt to colonize the land he has wrested from the sea.

bilden, die Einheit des Symphoniesatzes aufweisen, und dies erreicht sie, wenn sie im innigsten Zusammenhang mit demselben, über das ganze Drama sich erstreckt, nicht nur über einzelne kleinere, *willkürlich herausgehobene* Teile desselben. Diese Einheit gibt sich dann in einem das ganze Kunstwerk durchziehende Gewebe von Grundthemen, welche sich, ähnlich wie im Symphoniesatz, gegenüberstehen, ergänzen, neu gestalten, trennen und verbinden . . . (my italics) (nevertheless, for it to be in turn an art-work in the form of music, the new dramatic music must display the unity of the symphonic movement. It does so by extending over the whole drama in the closest possible relationship with this, not merely over individual, smaller, and arbitrarily selected parts. This unity is then manifest in a network of basic themes spread out over the entire drama, which, as with the symphonic movement, contrast, supplement, refashion, separate, and combine with one another). Note that Schiller uses the term 'lyrisches Prachtgewebe' (finely-spun lyric web) to express the structural role of the chorus. See 'Über den Gebrauch des Chors', *Sämtliche Werke*, i, ed. H. Koopmann (Munich, 1968), 820: 'Der tragische Dichter (umgibt) seine streng abgemessene Handlung und die festen Umrisse seiner handelnden Figuren mit einem lyrischen Prachgewebe' (the tragic poet surrounds his strictly controlled action and the firm outlines of his participant characters with a finely-spun lyric web).

[47] Borchmeyer, *Das Theater Richard Wagners*, 13.

In both instances ambiguous and suspect means are employed to achieve grandiose ends and the degree to which the schemes are shot through with the hubristic arrogance of their initiators, both of whom are prepared to stoop to extortion and violence, casts a dubious light over the entire venture. It is difficult to envisage many examples from opera where such a density of meaning and reference is achieved that meaningful comparisons can be made with literary drama, but such is Wagner's success with leitmotiv technique that he achieves a similar semantic density. Of course, it goes without saying, that in achieving such density Wagner is developing and extending the range of musical language to an extraordinary degree as well. In particular he can draw fully upon resources such as tonality, rhythm, harmony, and counterpoint, to create multi-textured variations and, above all, simultaneity to a degree unparalleled in word drama. The virtuosity with which he manages to control such patterns and associations has been the subject of much critical attention[48] and scarcely needs to be amplified here: motivs can be combined as well as developed (the sword leitmotiv, to take a very obvious example, magically reappears along with the Valhalla motiv, bringing two sets of associations into direct juxtaposition). It goes without saying that such a degree of concentration, involving the listener in comparison and planting suggestions in his mind, presupposes a highly attentive state on the latter's part. It was not Wagner's fault—*pace* Thomas Mann—that his listeners were not always equal to the task;[49] he certainly gave them ample scope to use their faculties.

Wagner expounds in some detail how his *Grundmotive* (primary motivs) can perform the intricate task of developing and transforming motivic-thematic elements in response to the necessities of the dramatic action (cf. Borchmeyer's 'Semantisierung'). He uses

[48] See esp. Carl Dahlhaus, 'Zur Geschichte der Leitmotivtechnik', and Anthony Newcomb, 'The Birth of Music out of the Spirit of Drama: An Essay in Wagnerian Formal Analysis', *Nineteenth Century Music*, 5/1 (1981–2), 38–66. Also, by the same author, '*Siegfried:* The Music', *Siegfried*, ed. N. John (ENO and Royal Opera Guides; London, 1984), 21–41.

[49] See G. B. Shaw's riposte to Ernest Newman: 'nobody can "spontaneously correlate" either musical motives or anything else until he has found for them a refuge in the memory from the category of time, as Parsifal did in the Grail Temple ... If Mr. Newman cannot spontaneously correlate every thematic reference in *Tristan* or *The Mastersingers* on the first night, the moral is, not to call Wagner a blunderer, but simply to go again', *The Complete Music Criticism*, ed. Dan H. Lawrence (3 vols; London, 1981), iii, 563.

terms like 'Ahnung' (anticipation) and 'Erinnerung' (recollection) to define these functions structurally, and hints—without giving specific examples, for he did not wish to encourage the pedants too much—that such key motivs will occur precisely at those points in the action which are the most laden with meaning for both the past and the future. He felt it was important for the listener that there should not be a bewilderingly large number of primary, or *Grundmotive*. When we compare the near-equivalents of these motivs in a word drama, namely image-patterns (a somewhat imprecise term), we can see that like these—and possibly less like other more explicit or sententious utterances in drama (cf. Klotz's 'Integration Points')[50]—Wagner's *Grundmotive* are not intended to provide an explicit commentary nor do they necessarily present a clear-cut overview. Rather they bring to light all the complex associations which have been building up within the intricate structure and draw the threads of the action together. A key passage from *Oper und Drama* will serve to clarify this point (others both from this work and from other essays, e.g. 'Zukunfts-musik', could be cited to reinforce it). In the nearest thing we have to a definition of leitmotiv/*Grundmotiv* Wagner starts with the term 'melodische Moment'—again he wishes to underline the dramatic impetus which produces these musical realizations—then links this with the more familiar term *Grundmotiv*:

Diese melodischen Momente, in denen wir uns der Ahnung erinnern, während sie uns die Erinnerung zur Ahnung machen, werden notwendig nur *den wichtigsten Motiven* des Dramas entblüht sein, und die wichtigsten von *ihnen* werden wiederum an Zahl denjenigen Motiven entsprechen, die der Dichter als zusammengedrängte, verstärkte Handlung zu den Säulen seines dramatischen Gebäudes bestimmte, die er grundsätzlich nicht in verwirrender Vielheit, sondern in plastisch zu ordnender, für leichte Übersicht notwendig bedingter geringerer Zahl verwendet. In diesen Grundmotiven, die eben nicht Sentenzen, sondern plastische Gefühls-momente sind, wird die Absicht des Dichters, als eine durch das Gefühlsempfängnis verwirklichte, am verständlichsten; und der Musiker, als Verwirklicher der Absicht des Dichters, hat diese zu melodischen Momenten verdichteten Motive, im vollsten Einverständnis mit der dichterischen Absicht, daher leicht so zu ordnen, daß in ihrer wohlbedingten wechsel-seitigen Wiederholung ihm ganz von selbst auch die höchste einheitliche

---

[50] Klotz, *Geschlossene und offene Form*, 111 ff. See my Introduction, Ch. 1, p. 19.

musikalische Form entsteht—eine Form, wie sie der Musiker bisher willkürlich sich zusammenstellte, die aus der dichterischen Absicht aber erst zu einer notwendigen, wirklich einheitlichen, das ist: *verständlichen*, sich gestalten kann (these melodic impulses, when we recall the feelings of anticipation even as they are turning recollection into anticipation, will necessarily have issued from the most significant motivs in the drama alone, and the most significant of these will in turn correspond in number to those motivs which were destined by the poet to be compressed into action and thus to form the very pillars of his dramatic edifice. These latter he is careful to deploy not in such vast numbers as to confuse, but restricts them to a more modest number in order to enable the whole scene to be more readily surveyed. In these primary motivs—which must be distinguished from sententious utterances, being tangible impulses based on the emotions—the poet's design becomes more intelligible and is realized through sense perceptions. And it is the task of the performing artist—the agent, that is, who carries out the poet's design—to arrange these motivs, condensed as they are into melodic impulses, so elegantly and in such complete harmony with the poet's design that there comes into being, quite spontaneously according to a process of judicious repetition on both sides [i.e. impulses/motivs], a truly unified musical form. Such a form the musician had hitherto had to cobble together arbitrarily by himself; now in its truly unified structure it can appropriately and intelligibly reflect the poet's design).[51]

Certain key words and images stand out in this wordy 'definition': 'Drama' and 'dramatisch', for instance, the image of the leitmotiv as a pillar supporting an architectural structure ('Gebäude'); the related motiv conveying the idea of the concretization of physical energy and force: 'verstärkt', 'zusammengedrängt'; the idea of the economical distribution of these motivs within the whole structure: 'in plastisch zu ordnender, für leichte Übersicht notwendig bedingter, geringerer Zahl'; finally, the omnipresent starting-point for the whole structure: 'des Dichters Absicht'.

None of these endeavours to describe the nature of the leitmotiv seems to me to correspond to any of the meanings which the term 'epic' has acquired, whether in its 'Homeric' association with the rambling narrative or in its 'reincarnation' in the modern novel of Balzac. The loose, paratactic structure identified by Emil Staiger as 'epic'—in which a relaxed view is taken of digressions—seems to accord more with Wagner's own reaction to the nineteenth-century opera: 'jedes einzelne Gesangstück war eine ausgefüllte Form für

---

[51] 'Oper und Drama', *GSD* iv. 201.

sich' (each individual vocal number was a completely rounded form in itself).[52] This indeed corresponds closely to Staiger's idea of 'Selbständigkeit der Teile' (independence of the parts) as a distinguishing characteristic for 'epic'. Even if nowadays Staiger's purist insistence on the Homeric model for his definition of 'epic' may seem unhelpful, his identification of the dramatic principle— which he is careful to distinguish from 'drama' or 'theatre'—falls in very well with Wagner's own conception, which we have just glimpsed from the latter's 'definition' of the leitmotiv. Purposeful organization of the parts within the total structure (like Wagner, Staiger uses the architectural analogy),[53] the sense of incompleteness, of forward movement, and the creation thereby of 'Spannung'—all these aspects feature unmistakably in Wagner's own statements, both here and throughout *Oper und Drama*. Wagner is fond, too, of referring to the 'Handlung' as a central focus—here he follows closely Aristotle's strictures concerning the basic distinguishing features between 'epic' and 'dramatic'.

Of course this does not mean that one will not find certain sections of the *Ring* which appear to be more loosely integrated into the whole structure than others. If one chooses to become side-tracked, as Thomas Mann and others have been, into byways, or if one singles out one particular scene—the Norns in *Götterdämmerung* (Vorspiel) seem to be everybody's favourite in this respect—one might be able to make a case (I do not believe it would be a good one) for treating this as a self-contained episode or as a kind of potted history of the action to date, relayed for the benefit of those members of the public who have joined late. However, it is important not to be hoodwinked into the assumption that a scene like this—just because it seems reflective in style, detached from the action, and thereby in contrast with the forward-driving impulse of the 'Handlung'—must therefore be dubbed 'epic'. On closer inspection it can be seen that this wonderful scene (on which Wagner lavished much attention) does serve a number of crucial dramatic functions. As well as providing recapitulation of the material from the three preceding sections of the tetralogy, as is not uncommon in such a literary form, it also introduces as delayed

---

[52] Ibid.

[53] Staiger, *Grundbegriffe der Poetik*, 162: 'ein Ganzes . . . [wird] in Teile zerlegt und die Ordnung der Teile genau bedacht' (an entity is divided up into parts and the disposition of parts carefully considered).

exposition important new material relating to Wotan's desecration of the World Ash Tree. Moreover, the scene has the even more potently dramatic function of foreshadowing the catastrophe that lies ahead. It is in more ways than one a drawing-together of the threads, a concentration and intensification of the action and a means, above all, of underlining its fateful propensities. Motivs occur in abundance and intertwine here, but none are more multivalent than the close musical resemblance established between the World Ash Tree and the Valhalla motivs.[54]

Clearly the Norns—like Erda—serve the purpose of an oracle, just as in Ancient tragedy. Commentators need to be reminded of the fact that the precise shape of the action in the *Ring* is that of a tragedy—or rather several tragedies, since Wotan's problematical situation represents one action, and the Siegmund and Sieglinde and Siegfried and Brünnhilde 'stories' represent other, interlocking actions with tragic implications. The tetralogy form itself is designed to create a portentous, doom-laden atmosphere: prefigurations and the creation of a mood of inevitability are at the very heart of such a tradition. This is why 'Ahnung'—one of the crucial features of leitmotiv—about which some commentators make heavy weather[55] is so well served by this particular scene.

In his otherwise quite excellent and stimulating discussion, Carl Dahlhaus seems to me to be in danger of forgetting this fairly basic feature of the *Ring* tetralogy. Arguing along his familiar genetic lines and mindful of Wagner's earlier difficulties with the Siegfried material and, in particular, with this very scene, at which he had come to a full stop, Dahlhaus is disposed to regard the impressive array of leitmotivs simply as a retrospective attempt by Wagner to impose order on an otherwise loosely related episode to which Dahlhaus gives the portmanteau description of 'epic'.[56] This is

[54] For a discussion of the structural and semantic implications see Christopher Wintle, 'The Questionable Lightness of Being: Brünnhilde's Peroration to *The Ring*', *Götterdämmerung*, ed. N. John (ENO and Royal Opera Guides; London, 1985), 46.

[55] See esp. Jack Stein, *Richard Wagner: The Synthesis of the Arts* (Detroit, 1960), 77: 'Thus the presentiment is conceived as the reflection of a feeling which is real enough, but which has not yet been placed in connection with a specific object.' The 'vagueness' of which Stein complains is surely a function of the *futurity* of the 'Ahnungsmotive', which, however, on their ultimate realization, may be just as 'concrete' as their counterparts, the motivs of reminiscence.

[56] Dahlhaus, *Richard Wagners Musikdramen*, 107: 'Die Motivtechnik . . . ist charakteristisch für die offene oder epische Form des Dramas' (the motiv technique . . . is characteristic of the open or epic variety of drama).

despite the fact that they are embedded in what has now become a coherently anchored 'Erinnerung' (reminiscence) of episodes, all of which, according to the principles outlined in *Oper und Drama*, have been given visible expression ('vergegenwärtigt') at earlier points. I shall discuss Dahlhaus's view of 'epic' and 'dramatic' in greater detail below, but for the present we should note this demotion of Wagner's idea that the structural function of the leitmotiv principle is to contribute to the dramatic organization of the work and to its tragic shape and patterning. If we accept Dahlhaus's view, we are soon back with Thomas Mann again, who had said: 'Und . . . ich begreife nicht, wie man im "Leitmotiv" ein wesentlich dramatisches Mittel erblicken kann. Er ist im Innersten episch' (and I cannot comprehend how anyone can regard the leitmotiv as an essentially dramatic tool. It is inherently epic).[57] Later, in the Introduction to *Der Zauberberg* Mann will describe his own adaptation of the leitmotiv technique in the novel (comparing it with *Tonio Kröger* in this respect) as virtually identical to that of Wagner. He aims, as Wagner had certainly done, to use the device as a structural principle which spreads over the entire work (did he have in mind Wagner's own terms 'Verknüpfungen' and 'Gewebe'?), 'auf die komplizierteste und alles durchdringende Art' (in the most complex, all-pervading manner).[58] I shall later examine such phenomena as examples of a 'horizontal' principle of leitmotiv technique. It should be noted in any case that, whatever Mann might say, the complete identification of his technique of leitmotiv with that of Wagner's theoretical statements is rendered invalid by the absence in the novel genre of any exact equivalent to the principles of immediacy and concretization ('Vergegenwärtigung'). For Wagner this was, theoretically, a prerequisite for all leitmotivs.

It is significant that in the essay I have referred to above Carl Dahlhaus never actually defines the term 'epic'. Sometimes he uses it in the sense of 'episch-kontemplativ', i.e. 'reflective'; at others in the sense of 'pertaining to narrative material'. Delving deeply into the genesis of the *Ring* from its first form, *Siegfrieds Tod*, to the completed tetralogy, Dahlhaus identifies 'epic' elements which were

[57] Thomas Mann, 'Versuch über das Theater', *Gesammelte Werke*, x. 27.
[58] Thomas Mann, Einführung in den Zauberberg', *Gesammelte Werke*, xi. 611.

never, despite all Wagner's herculean efforts, he believes, converted into a finished dramatic shape. Although Wagner certainly believed he had overcome the structural problem by developing the 'antecedents' of the Siegfried action backwards and building an elaborate leitmotivic structure to underpin the dramatic action, Dahlhaus will not concede his success, largely because of his insistence on the work's 'epic' character. In affirming Wagner's own view that the music drama (and its principal technical tool, the leitmotiv) are essentially dramatic in origin and in function ('dramatic' in the sense of Emil Staiger's definition),[59] one is not thereby suggesting that the pitch of dramatic intensity which is envisaged in the theory can (far less should) be maintained at all times over the length and breadth of the large work. Contrastive and retarding elements have always been at the heart of the very greatest literary dramas; if nothing else, it makes good practical sense to allow the listener/spectator moments of respite, of apparent relaxation of the tension, of reflection, of contrasting pace, so that he may return to the intensity of the visibly unfolding stage action with refreshed interest and renewed concentration. The complaint sometimes registered about Siegfried's Funeral Music (*Götterdämmerung*, Act III, scene 2) that, like the Norn's scene, it fails to 'vergegenwärtigen', is entirely irrelevant. Once more a consideration of the tragic context will make this clear. The Funeral Music is a threnody, an epilogue, which provides a commenting perspective of the most intense kind. Contextuality plays a vital part in creating the overwhelmingly tragic and noble effect (an effect which is, conversely, lacking when the entr'acte is detached, as is frequently the case, and performed separately as an orchestral piece). The fact that Dahlhaus is able to identify a series of purposeful leitmotiv networks in both these scenes does nothing to disprove their dramatic functionality within the tetralogy structure or their tragic relevance. Rather the reverse.

Why does it matter what the origins of the leitmotiv technique really are? Francis Bulhoff, for one, cannot see any point in such an enquiry and criticizes scholars like Ronald Peacock for even having raised the issue.[60] It is not 'verfehlt' and 'unergiebig' (Bulhoff's

---

[59] Staiger, 'Das Dramatische', in *Grundbegriffe der Poetik*.

[60] Francis Bulhoff, *Transpersonalismus und Synchronizität: Wiederholung als Strukturelement in Thomas Mann's 'Zauberberg'* (Groningen, 1966), 15. R. Peacock, *Das Leitmotiv bei Thomas Mann* (Bern, 1934), 45–6, maintains an

words) to resuscitate this once so hotly debated—but unresolved—
issue? But surely some explanation is required for the fact that the
now widely accepted consensus view of the 'epic' nature of
Wagner's *Ring* and of the leitmotiv technique conflicts totally with
Wagner's own theoretical statements (and I do not believe that on
such a fundamental issue one can take refuge in that hoary old
chestnut of theory and practice never coinciding, since even in
instances where this is true, the lack of coincidence is a matter of
degree). The issue involved is quite basic: it is the question to what
extent the twentieth-century view of 'epic' drama is not itself based
on false polarities and premisses, a situation which has been further
sharpened by the now almost universal reinstatement and mis-
application of the term 'epic' in the wake of Brechtian dramaturgical
theory. And at the centre of the new orthodoxy, as I have tried to
demonstrate, there lies the fundamental issue of perspectival
technique—appraisal, evaluation, interpretation, pointing of the
way, and all the numerous other devices, without which the genre
of drama, despite all appearances to the contrary, simply cannot
exist, least of all when it has applied itself to a form like tragedy,
which is constantly seeking meanings and explanations that lie
beyond and behind the 'action' itself.

Steeped as he was in European drama—Ancient as well as
Modern—Wagner noted perceptively the effect of the banishment
of the chorus from Greek tragedy upon more recent forms,
especially Shakespeare's dramas. It was not the case that all need
for such a function was removed from the drama, although
Shakespeare's 'solution' was original indeed: 'Shakespeares
Tragödie steht insofern unbedingt über der griechischen, als sie für
die künstlerische Technik die Notwendigkeit des Chores vollkommen überwunden hat' (Shakespeare's tragedies are clearly
superior to the Greek form in this respect: they have entirely
outgrown the need for a chorus for technical or artistic purposes).[61]
The fact of the matter is that, as Wagner notes, Shakespeare found

---

entirely neutral position on the question of the 'epic' and 'dramatic' origins of the
leitmotiv. Peacock's still useful study does not aim at a thorough analysis of
Wagner's theory of leitmotiv, but concentrates instead on analysing the function of
the device within Thomas Mann's literary works. It is therefore more a contribution
to practical criticism than to the debate about the theoretical issues underlying the
technique.

[61] 'Oper und Drama', *GSD* iii. 268.

ways of *dispersing* the commentary function, moving it into the sphere of characterization and character-interaction. He notes in this connection the greatly increased number of dramatis personae which follows on the removal of the chorus and the much enhanced role of character within the whole structure. The practical upshot of this is, of course, that the element of perspectival commentary becomes implicit, i.e. integrated, rather than explicit, i.e. disjoined, as it had been with the chorus; further, more scope is thus given to the spectator to make sense of the work by reading between the lines and, where characterization is concerned, learning to analyse so-called 'direct characterization'.[62]

As Shakespeare scholars have made clear, however, where perspectival direction of the reader or spectator is concerned, the situation is not so anarchic as might be supposed. The use of songs as perspectival devices has often been noted; it is a device of which the German dramatists, e.g. Goethe and Büchner, with their tremendous enthusiasm for Shakespeare, were to avail themselves to the full.[63] Furthermore, and probably with even greater subtlety, the networks of symbolic imagery which Shakespeare spins and which have been so expertly unravelled by Wolfgang Clemen,[64] provide one of the most powerful alternative means of evaluation and commentary which the modern dramatist has at his disposal. The fact that neither Wagner nor, to my knowledge, any theorist since Wagner has linked this phenomenon with the Ancient chorus (or with the leitmotiv) is not perhaps surprising, since these intricate symbolic constellations often work by stealth and upon our imagination and subconscious (in this respect closely corresponding to Wagner's 'Verknüpfungen' and 'Gewebe'). The fact remains, however, that they are a persistent element in virtually all modern drama since Shakespeare and that they reach a very high point of development among German dramatists belonging to what we loosely term the 'Classical' period: Goethe and Kleist, for example (Schiller to only a very limited extent)—and also Grillparzer. That they may also be identified among the more modern

[62] For a thorough analysis of the concept of 'direct characterization' see Matthias Sträßner, *Analytisches Drama* (Munich, 1980).

[63] G.-L. Fink, 'Volkslied und Verseinlage', in *Georg Büchner*, ed. W. Martens (Darmstadt, 1965), 443–87.

[64] Wolfgang Clemen, *Shakespeares Bilder: Ihre Entwicklung und ihre Funktion im dramatische Werk* (Bonn, 1936); English version: *The Development of Shakespeare's Imagery* (London, 1977).

dramatists (e.g. Wedekind),[65] many of whom have been claimed as forerunners of the Brechtian 'disjunctive' mode of perspective, may come as a greater surprise.

As we attempt to bear in mind such parallels between the Wagnerian leitmotiv and the modern drama, it is helpful to abandon completely the 'epic' terminology which has caused such confusion over recent decades and to concentrate our attention on the ways in which various techniques in drama, such as leitmotiv, actually function. It is certainly not helpful either to join forces with those who regard the leitmotiv as a ridiculous excrescence (cf. Neitzsche's 'Polyp') without examining the complex ways in which it operates; here the musicologists are able to present abundant proof, if proof were needed, of its complexity as a technique.[66] It is well known, and indeed regrettable, that so many pedants, especially in the early days of Bayreuth, which coincided with the heyday of Positivism, went on a hunt for leitmotivs and drew up their absurd lists for identifying these (the procedure has not been entirely abandoned even today as one can see from certain paperback publications of the 'Textbücher', and indeed one has to concede that it has a certain limited usefulness). The effect of such presentations, however, was to establish in the popular mind the notion that the leitmotiv is a mannerist tic, superimposed upon the music dramas in an arbitrary fashion. The commonest example of reductionism in Anglo-Saxon criticism of the leitmotiv is the term 'visiting-card';[67] it serves no useful critical purpose.

But the leitmotiv technique has attracted some powerful criticism from the ranks of those one might expect to know better. For Theodor Adorno, for instance, it is an allegorical, not a symbolic device which atomizes and fragments the works. Further, he stresses the rigidity and stasis which he believes it produces: the music 'kennt keine Bewegung, indem sie ihren eigenen Zeitverlauf widerruft' (avows no movement, thereby revoking its own chronological sequence).[68] This flies in the face of all that has been

---

[65] See Gerd Witzke, *Das epische Theater Wedekinds und Brechts*, diss. Tübingen, 1972), esp. pp. 108 ff.

[66] Anthony Newcomb's contribution could be regarded as among the most luminating examples of musical analysis in this area: 'The Birth of Music out of the spirit of Drama: An Essay in Wagnerian Formal Analysis'.

[67] Debussy, not the Anglo-Saxons, appears to be the author of this tag, however; see *Debussy on Music*, ed. F. Lesure and R. L. Smith (London, 1977), 80.

[68] Theodor Adorno, *Versuch über Wagner* (Frankfurt-on-Main, 1974), 41–2.

achieved in Wagner criticism over the past fifty years or so, for which the versatility and complexity of Wagner's technique has provided much stimulus and challenge. Particularly unjust, it seems to me, is Adorno's technique of hoisting Wagner on the petard created by his critics. Because critical interpretation has lavished so much attention on the leitmotiv itself, this is seen as proof of the 'bankruptcy of Wagner's own "aesthetics of immediate unity" ' (die Bankrottierung von Wagners eigener Ästhetik des unmittelbaren Einen). The argument then develops along speculative lines when Adorno blames Wagner for producing the decadence ('Verfall') to which the leitmotiv technique was subjected when it got into the hands of Richard Strauss, Wagner's 'disciple'. In the hands of this composer he thinks it was reduced to 'geschmeidige Illustrationstechnik' (glib illustrative technique), and, worse still, it was taken over thereafter by writers of film music: 'wo das Leitmotiv einzig noch Helden oder Situationen anmeldet, damit sich der Zuschauer rascher zurechtfindet' (where the sole function of the leitmotiv is to herald heroes or situations so as to help the spectator more swiftly to find his bearings). This looks suspiciously like a variation on the 'visiting-card' theory, dressed up in more pompous language but bearing the same dismissive implications and thus lending a rather spurious intellectual respectability to an otherwise threadbare popular critique.

It would seem probable, therefore, that Wagner's development of the leitmotiv 'web' derives mainly from a largely subconsciously determined method of presenting perspectival commentary which has been a notable, though scarcely noted, feature of the literary form since Shakespeare. While Wagner was fully conscious that the orchestra would now take over the chief function that had been performed by the Greek chorus, he would seem to have been unaware of the fact that his elaborate leitmotiv technique neatly assumes the mantle of, and creates a new, modern substitute for the chorus in its commenting role. There is a coherence and consistency about this development, and it comes about, I believe because of Wagner's very searching scrutiny of the fundamental principles on which all drama is based. While one would wish to draw the links between the opera-based leitmotiv 'Gewebe' and drama-based symbolic configurations very tightly indeed—and not simply regard the relationship in terms of a loose-knit analogy— one is also forced to admit that under Wagner's transforming musical genius the principle acquires a unique and distinctive status: it is at one and the same time clearly a blood-relation of the literary structure, indeed it could be described as its offspring, but it differs from it substantially too, as offspring are wont to do from their parents. Firstly, of course, the new integration of music and drama in the 'Gesamtkunstwerk' marks the culmination of many piecemeal attempts to explore the possibility of a synthesis. Secondly, this very synthesis makes possible a complete synchronization of the modes of action and reflection, which had traditionally proved difficult to integrate. Then, too, Wagner had, by developing the leitmotiv technique within this framework, succeeded in imparting to music—which on its own, as he saw it, possessed no 'meaning'—a literary and dramatic dimension by the process which Borchmeyer calls 'Semantisierung'. In the course of doing so, however, he had fully deployed and developed the many resources at his disposal which were unique to the art of music—tonality, harmony, polyphony, rhythm, etc. The fundamental similarities between music drama and literary drama, therefore, which Wagner had carefully established in *Oper und Drama* mask some pretty obvious secondary differences between his fully developed techniques and their point of departure (it is for the musicologists to decide in what way symphonic structure, which they tend to see as a crucial ingredient of Wagner's musical language, relates to the literary-dramatic determinants of Wagner's leitmotiv technique with which we are concerned here). Approaches towards a synthesis via the other route—drama—and the development of other alternative forms of perspectival expression such as had been mooted by Lessing and attempted by Schiller had in the end failed (though the unobtrusive, non-explicit symbolic patterns spun by Grillparzer may have been sufficiently well developed for dramatists not to feel the need—at least for the time being—to invade the territory of music in pursuit of an extension of their expressive range). It remains to be seen what further progress towards amalgamation and *rapprochement* between drama and music would be achieved by Brecht and his composers, who later were to approach the problem once again from the literary end of the spectrum.

Integrated and Disjoined Perspectival Structure

There is an important and rather complex point to be considered here, namely the double-sided aspect assumed by Wagner's perspectival structure of which leitmotiv is the main ingredient. On the one hand, the orchestral 'choric' function of which he is aware seems, physically at least, to operate from without the action and to be disjoined from it. On the other, via the leitmotiv network it interacts fully with the stage action, complementing and supporting it in a myriad of ways, and in this sense is wholly integrated into the structure. Thus perspectival commentary can be achieved by both integrated and by disjoined techniques, an achievement to which no commentator, so far as I can discover, has drawn attention, and an example of the ambiguity of means and ends which has been the source of much misunderstanding, as first one function has been identified, then the other. Wagner himself attempted to express this complexity by means of a number of images pertaining to water, drawing at one moment on the contrasting principles of horizontality and verticality, while in another extension of the image he compares the orchestra first to a ship which sails serenely over the waves in total control of its destiny: 'als Bewältiger der Fluten der Harmonie' (as controller of the floods of harmony), then alters the imagery slightly so that the ocean becomes a mountain lake: in these less turbulent surroundings the idea of reflection is then introduced. The barque is identified with the melodic line created by the singer; the orchestral harmony is now associated with the water itself: 'Der Nachen ist ein durchaus anderes als der Spiegel des Sees, und doch einzig nur gezimmert und gefügt mit Rücksicht auf das Wasser und in genauer Erwägung seiner Eigenschaften' (the barque is quite different from the reflected surface of the lake, and yet is uniquely constructed and fitted together with respect to the water and after a detailed consideration of its qualities).[69] It is easy to smile at the earnestness (and long-windedness) with which Wagner attempts to make clear the complex relationship. He himself is quite self-deprecating about such analogies ('Ich habe nicht nötig, dies Gleichnis näher zu deuten', there is no need for me to spell out this analogy more clearly), pointing out that, when

[69] 'Oper und Drama', *GSD* iv. 172.

following them through, one should only pay attention to those features which the two parts have in common, not the differences between them. What this particular image does bring out clearly, to my mind, however, is just this ambiguous relationship between orchestra, leitmotiv, harmony, and melodic line, and the mutual interdependence of all these elements, which at the same time retain their distinctness and independence. This ambiguity is further emphasized when the orchestra's role is described as 'ein selbständiges, an sich von jener Versmelodie unterscheidendes Element' (an independent element which in itself must be distinguished from that verse-melody) which has yet the important function of 'carrying' the melody along on its (horizontal) course and, musically speaking, being harmonically determined by the very form that this melody assumes. It is important not to jump off at this point, as some commentators do, to make another raid on the 'epic' larder, under the misguided impression that the image is exclusively about the disjoined type of commentary which we associate with Brecht[70] and that Wagner is therefore to be seen as a forerunner of 'epic' theatre!

Before concluding this analysis of Wagner's theories of music drama and leitmotiv, it might be useful to draw attention to the manifold and complex nature of the reception process to which they have given rise. Despite the popular view—much ventilated by Brecht—that the effect of a Wagner music drama is a wholesale bombardment of the listener's emotions (mostly the baser ones), we are confronted by a complex and ambiguous situation. Certainly Wagner is intent in involving his audience, there can be no doubt about that; this aim lies behind all the emphasis on dramatically compelling structures which we have just examined. But the involvement appears to operate by means of a variety of stimuli, some emotional, some purely aesthetic, some intellectual. Little wonder, when we are being asked to retain so many impressions simultaneously and to keep a sense of the whole structure in mind at virtually every moment, that this complex process operates upon us at two major and different levels: the conscious level, when, for

[70] I believe Marianne Kesting may be guilty of this ('Wagner/Meyerhold/Brecht'): 'Was Wagner mit Hilfe seiner Leitmotiven Technik suggerierte, wollte Brecht durch die Schauspielerkunst und ihre Verfremdungstechnik bewirken, ferner durch den Kommentar auf der Szene' (what Wagner was suggesting via his leitmotiv technique, Brecht sought to achieve via acting skills and alienation technique, and also via commentary on stage) (p. 119).

example, we are fully aware of this functionality and are made to realize the deeper purposes and implications of a specific 'Moment'—say, when Siegmund wrests the sword Nothung from the tree in which Wotan had embedded it (*Die Walküre*, Act I, scene 2); or conversely, at climactic moments, when the sheer expressive power of the music may appear to predominate over its structural organization, or, again, when leitmotivs are 'planted' in our minds for future reference and clarification. At such points the appeal would seem to be to subconscious processes, which are also in operation, it would seem, at the big 'closure' points, e.g. Wotan's sentence on Brünnhilde at the end of *Die Walküre* which concludes with Loge casting a girdle of fire round the mountain top on which the sleeping Valkyrie is placed. Even at such climatic points, however, we are never allowed to 'wallow' in emotion; the continual momentum which the music sustains is an effective deterrent, so too are the leitmotivs, which are never far away, and indeed, at such immense 'closures' (of which *Götterdämmerung* too has its fair share) bring forward seemingly endless chains of retrospective allusions, some of which—depending on our state of alertness—we are able to register consciously, while others will perhaps escape most of us at the conscious level, but may yet be impressed upon our subconscious minds. There are so many levels on which Wagner's music drama operates that we must beware of noticing only the most obvious and blatant of the leitmotivs, the most 'expressive' or emotionally laden.

It should be clear from the above that the theory and practice of the Wagnerian 'Gesamtkunstwerk', music drama and leitmotiv, are a paradox: drawing us in through the most expressive and beguiling means, while at the same time, through the orchestra's special function of perspectival commentary, requiring us to use all our critical faculties and apply ourselves to the business of uncovering the hidden meanings below the surface level. This combination of self-consciousness and analytical awareness, on the one hand, and intuitive sureness and persuasiveness, on the other, is present in Wagner to an extent surely unparalleled among creative artists. The double aspect is reflected even in the rather strange circumstances in which he wrote *Oper und Drama* around 1850, and to which I have already alluded. It was a fallow period as far as his creative work was concerned: after the completion of *Lohengrin* in 1848, there were to be no further operatic works until *Das*

Rheingold was finished in 1854 (the completion of the entire *Ring* cycle would have to wait until 1874, after *Tristan* and *Die Meistersinger von Nürnberg* had first forced their attentions upon the composer). For Wagner to forego musical composition even for a few years in mid-career in order to concentrate exclusively on theoretical matters reflects the importance he attached to the reform of the opera, as well as his own acute need for self-knowledge before taking what Carl Dahlhaus has described as the 'quantum leap' from *Lohengrin* to the *Ring*. A parallel might be drawn with Schiller, whose long break in mid-career (at roughly the same age as Wagner) brought forth a similarly rigorous and searching exploration of aesthetic principles which were enshrined in a number of theoretical essays and subsequently in a series of dramatic masterpieces. Possibly Schiller's analyses were more general in scope than Wagner's (particularly *Oper und Drama*, which concerns itself closely with matters related to the genre of music drama and the theory of leitmotiv), but they were no less important for his own development as a dramatist.

The complex interaction of intuition and reflection both in the creative process and in audience reception puts one in mind of a short, but very succinct essay written by Heinrich von Kleist for the *Berliner Abendblätter* entitled 'Von der Überlegung: Eine Paradoxe' (On Reflection: A Paradox), which, I believe, to a greater extent than the much more celebrated 'Über das Marionettentheater' (the ending of which is extremely ambiguous)[71] provides sharp insights into the paradox at the roots of spontaneous action. In Kleist's essay the need for reflection *and* intuition is stressed in the successful achievement of an undertaking which is both complex and hazardous (although the terms of reference here are not aesthetic but practical, they are not at all dissimilar to those of a dramatic action). Kleist argues that everything hinges on appropriateness and timing: thus, reflection *during* the action is harmful to its successful execution, whereas after the event (which is the same thing as *before* the next one, though at not too close a proximity) reflection and analysis can bring great gains which can be exploited during subsequent engagements: 'dagegen sich nachher, wenn die Handlung abgetan ist, der Gebrauch von ihr machen läßt, zu welchem sie dem Menschen eigentlich gegeben ist, nämlich

---

[71] See H. M. Brown, 'Kleist and Diderot', *Heinrich von Kleist Studies*, ed. A. Ugrinsky (Berlin and New York, 1980), 142–4.

dessen, was in dem Verfahren fehlerhaft und gebrechlich war, bewußt zu werden, und das Gefühl für andere künftige Fälle zu regulieren' (afterwards, on the other hand, once the action is complete, it is put to the use for which it has actually been bestowed upon Man: so that he becomes aware, that is to say, of what was deficient and vulnerable in the process and can regulate his faculty of feeling in preparation for other future cases).[72] The 'paradox' here, then, is that reflection can and should operate in complex circumstances which seem to call for purely intuitive responses, but according to what seems to be a continuous and ongoing process of flux, so that reflection carries over into intuition. I believe it is perhaps this kind of paradox which Carl Dahlhaus has in mind when he refers to 'zweite Unmittelbarkeit' (second immediacy)[73] as both a creative principle to which Wagner subscribed and as an aesthetic principle which he was encouraging his listeners and spectators to adopt in their reception of the music drama. In this respect, it is perhaps relevant to recall Wagner's constant exhortation in *Oper und Drama* that the listener/spectator should participate as fully as possible in the processes in which the composer himself is engaged.[74] Carl Dahlhaus well summarizes this complex response:

Daß die Reflexion in Gefühl und Anschauung aufgehen soll, schließt ein, daß sie zunächst als Reflexion wirksam ist, um dann vergessen zu werden. Die erste Unmittelbarkeit ist nichts als ein blindes Gefühl, dem die Musik der *Ring*-Tetralogie in ein Gewoge verschwimmt. Man muß die musikal-ischen Motive, die Gefühlswegweiser durch das Drama, wie Wagner sie nannte, unterscheiden, wiedererkennen und in ihren wechselnden Zusammenhängen und Funktionen verfolgen können, wenn die Musik nicht zu dem 'Schwall' verfließen soll, als die sie von den Klassizisten unter ihren Verächtern verpönt worden ist. Erst aus aufgehobener Reflexion erwächst ein Gefühl und eine musikalische Anschauung, die mehr ist als ein akustisches Anstarren (for reflection to be transposed into feeling and intuition implies that it can be forgotten after having first worked effectively. The first direct response is nothing but a blind emotional reaction which sweeps up the music of the *Ring* tetralogy in a tidal wave. It is necessary to recognize the musical motivs a second time, those emotional

---

[72] Heinrich von Kleist, *Sämtliche Werke und Briefe*, ed. H. Sembdner (2nd edn., Munich, 1961), ii. 357.

[73] Dahlhaus, *Richard Wagners Musikdramen*, 83.

[74] Wagner's avowed aim is to make the listener 'an essential co-creator in the work of art' ('zum notwendigen Mitschöpfer des Kunstwerks'), *GSD* iv. 186.

signposts through the drama, as Wagner called them, and to be able to keep them in mind in the course of their changing contexts and functions. This is necessary if the music is not to be dissipated in the 'riot of sound' which is the term of abuse coined for it by the classicists among its detractors. Only on the basis of the dialectic of reflection and non-reflection can emotional responses and musical intuitions develop which are more than mere acoustical gawping).[75]

I would suggest that this principle—by means of which our reflective and intuitive responses to Wagner's music are constantly being required to alternate, adjust, and interact during the actual performance itself (and not just, as Dahlhaus seems to be suggesting, at the first or second hearing, i.e. from one performance to the next), represents an important clue towards the understanding of what are often seen as contradictory techniques (e.g. reflective commentary which makes us stand back from the action, and expressive musical statements which seem to draw us in). Given the many popular misconceptions about the effect of Wagner's music, I believe it is important to try to understand its complexities. But in all this—and particularly in view of the élitist image which Wagner has acquired for many—it is salutary to recall once again that the composer neither looks down on his public from the cliché pinnacle of popular imagination, nor sets himself apart in any other way. In view of the cults that have been formed in Wagner's name and which still persist, his lofty ideal may seem excessively Utopian. The challenge, however, is one that students of drama ignore at their peril, so thoroughly charted are the foundations on which it rests. The following pages will attempt to demonstrate this in greater detail.

[75] Dahlhaus, *Richard Wagners Musikdramen*, 83.

3

Brecht: Modes of Perspective in 'Epic' Theatre

Introduction: The Nature of the Problem

Brecht's own views—to say nothing of the critics' interpretations of them—are bedevilled by overstatement, concealment (not always deliberate), and a special fondness (especially on the part of his interpreters) for attaching labels to sometimes complex concepts, which has the effect of reducing their significance. We are not dealing with the kind of earnest, even rather scholarly endeavour with which Wagner approached his theme of the relationship between music and drama. A body of theory that belongs so clearly to that kind of tradition will not present readers with anything like the difficulties that Brecht's does; it will yield more readily to the conventional tools of scholarship and yardsticks of measurement. Brecht's theory is neither systematic nor always coherent; and yet to hear the critics talk, these are precisely the qualities which you would expect of it. If Wagner can sometimes be faulted for overdeveloping his points and becoming long-winded in the process (though I believe that some of the criticism along these lines is not fully justified), then Brecht can be equally faulted for being over-laconic, for leaving an argument so undeveloped that it is hardly any wonder that there is scope for misinterpretation. As we shall observe, one of the most flagrant, but also most fateful examples of what we may term the 'Brecht factor' is the celebrated presentation of the essential features of 'epic' theatre in tabular, polarized form which is slotted into the 'Anmerkungen' to the *Mahagonny* opera. It is hard to think of another example anywhere, by any author, which has had an equally potent or misleading effect. Brecht's own later retreat from this position (in the 'Nachträge zum kleinen Organon für das Theater' of 1954) has had little impact on the critical debate, which has been obscured by polemics. There he conceded that the term 'episches Theater' had been too vaguely defined: 'es ist der Begriff nur zu ärmlich und vage für das gemeine Theater' (the concept is too vague and inadequate for the ordinary theatre) and furthermore that the opposition of the terms 'epic' and 'dramatic' (from which dramatic theory has drawn sustenance for the past fifty years) was too naïvely formulated: 'Außerdem stand es [i.e. 'episches Theater'] zu unbewegt gegen den Begriff des Dramatischen, setzte ihn oft allzu naiv einfach voraus . . .' (moreover, the term 'epic theatre' was set too rigidly in contrast to the concept of the dramatic; the presuppositions were often excessively naïve).[1] A better example of the perils of uncritical acceptance of ready-made slogans and the danger of taking Brecht's statements at face value could scarcely be imagined.

The problem, then, is not only how to read and evaluate Brecht's theoretical works, but how to deal with the confusions that these have created in the ranks of his interpreters, given that not only his works, but those of dramatists preceding him—Wedekind, for example, springs to mind—have been approached again and again via Brecht's—ultimately, on his own admission—inadequate terms of reference. Brecht's persuasive tongue, to say nothing of his bullying manner of presenting his ideas, may be held partly to blame, and we must now learn to stand back from these foreground distractions and use more reliable tools if we are to penetrate Brecht's many masks and his chameleon-like capacity for altering his position. Brecht himself cannot be blamed in all this: the *Zeitgeist* was working powerfully through him, even if he may not have realized it. As it happened, the *Zeitgeist* of the 1920s and 1930s decreed that ahistoricism should reign supreme in the creative arts. It also decreed that ahistoricism should continue in the guise of Existentialism, then Structuralism and Post-Structuralism, enjoying a long reign in twentieth-century literary criticism. The upshot is that very little attention has been paid to relating Brecht to the context of his own times or to viewing his clearly articulated statements about his aims and achievements within those traditions and contexts which now, at the beginning of the 1990s, have been growing clearer to us. There are a few exceptions, of course (notably Hans Mayer),[2] and more are appearing bit by

[1] *Gesammelte Werke* (*GW*) Werkausgabe edition suhrkamp (all subsequent references are to this edition, unless otherwise stated), xvi. *Schriften zum Theater 2*, 701.

[2] Hans Mayer, *Bertolt Brecht und die Tradition* (Pfullingen, 1961); also Reinhold Grimm, *Bertolt Brecht und die Weltliteratur* (Nuremberg, 1961).

bit. The case of Brecht's response to Wagner is especially relevant in this respect for it has now been demonstrated that Brecht was participating in a European-wide reaction during the 1920s which commenced in France among composers and writers, then swept through Germany, where it became identified with such things as Neo-Classicism in music or with the movement known as 'Neue Sachlichkeit' (Brecht shares certain concerns with this supposedly sober movement, but was never very closely identified with it).[3] We shall do well to bear in mind the wilful interpretations of history which often underly Brecht's statements about theatre and apply to them such perspectives as are now accessible to us. There is no doubt that self-exemption from the chore of placing his aims within a tradition had a liberating effect on Brecht—just think of Wagner's laborious and detailed attempts to do precisely that—allowing him to concentrate on his new ideas without let or hindrance. But it also means that from our point of view his theoretical works have an 'unfinished' and provisional appearance and have to be regarded more as raw material on which we ourselves are required to do more work than as complete statements of dramaturgical principles.

Until the new historical–critical edition of Brecht's works[4] is further advanced, we have to make do with some very messy editions and anthologies of the theoretical writings, to say nothing of some dubius chronology. But for the theme of music (which will be of some importance for my discussion) we are fortunate to have access to the useful new compendium of Lucchesi and Shull,[5] which not only contains all the relevant documents but also a commentary and a much more accurate chronology of the various writings than has hitherto been available. Brecht's views on the role of music and 'epic' perspective are to be found scattered through his writings, but are most coherently gathered together in three groups of essays spanning a period of over twenty years: the 'Anmerkungen' to the opera *Mahagonny* of 1930,[6] a collection of assorted pieces grouped

---

[3] See A. Subiotto, 'Neue Sachlichkeit: A Re-assessment' in *Deutung und Bedeutung*, ed. B. Schludermann *et al.* (The Hague and Paris, 1973), 248–74. Also Ulrich Weisstein, 'Brecht und das Musiktheater: Die epische Oper als Ausdruck des europäischen Avantgardismus', *Kontroversen, alte und neue*, Akten des VII. Internat. Germanisten-Kongresses (Göttingen, 1985), ix. 72–85.

[4] Bertolt Brecht, *Große kommentierte Berliner und Frankfurter Ausgabe GKA* (30 vols.; Berlin and Frankfurt-on-Main, 1988 ff.)

[5] Joachim Lucchesi and Ronald Shull, *Musik bei Brecht* (Frankfurt-on-Main, 1988).

[6] *GW* xvii. *Schriften zum Theater 3*, 1004–16.

together under the title 'Über Bühnenbau und Musik des epischen Theaters' (1935–52),[7] and the most systematic of all (as well as the most bland), the 'Kleines Organon für das Theater' (1948).[8] Other substantial contributions to dramatic theory (e.g. *Der Messingkauf*) exist, of course, but the three above-mentioned are the most relevant to my thesis. Neither the views put forward in these three works nor the style and presentation are consistent. I shall nevertheless point out various important changes of emphasis in the course of my examination of certain key concepts.

'*Trennung der Elemente*'

Brecht's renunciation of 'pure' drama is an amazingly consistent feature of his dramatic theory and practice. His earlier dramas, such as *Baal, Trommeln in der Nacht, Im Dickicht der Städte*, although far from being 'operas' in the sense that *Die Dreigroschenoper* or *Aufstieg und Fall der Stadt Mahagonny* can be so described, nevertheless make use of the interpolated songs (lyric verse in the case of the first) and ballads. Looking back at these songs from the later standpoint of the 1930s Brecht saw them as being relatively casual interpolations 'in ziemlich landläufiger Form' (in fairly customary form) and with an element of 'naturalistische Motivierung' (naturalistic motivation), by which I understand him to mean that they were fully integrated into the dramatic action.[9] All the same, he thought they introduced a 'lighter, more elegant' touch to the drama, which had recently suffered from the claustrophobic inwardness of the Impressionists and the 'manic one-sidedness' of the Expressionists. From about 1926–7, the period when he began to consider the Marxist theory of society and started to formulate the principles of 'epic' theatre, his interest in hybrid forms of drama—forms, that is, in which music plays an increasingly important role—becomes ever more clearly articulated.

Theoretically, Brecht identifies only three 'Elemente' in his first full-scale attempt to formulate a theory in the 'Anmerkungen':

---

[7] GW xv. *Schriften zum Theater 1*, 439–97. These are rather misleadingly lumped together in this collection; they have been detached from one another and, where appropriate, arranged in new chronologies by Lucchesi and Shull, *Musik bei Brecht*.

[8] GW xvi *Schriften zum Theater 2*, 661–700.   [9] GW xv. 472.

namely 'Wort', 'Musik', and 'Darstellung' (word, music, and presentation). As if taking up Wagner's point in *Oper und Drama* about the rival claims of music and drama to be *the* primary elements, Brecht declares that a relationship of democratic equality shall reign between them and that this will actually be promoted by the 'radical' separation between them which he envisages. There should be no argument, therefore, as to whether 'die Musik der Anlaß des Bühnenvorgangs, oder der Bühnenvorgang der Anlaß der Musik [ist]' (music motivates the stage action or the stage action motivates the music).[10] All the same, one cannot help thinking that in works like the *Dreigroschenoper* and *Mahagonny*, at least, music occupies a dominant role within the total structure. As Brecht puts it after presenting one of his notorious 'tables': 'Die Musik ist der wichtigste Beitrag zum Thema' (music makes the most significant contribution to the theme).[11] We shall examine this point in greater detail below. Furthermore, one notices that 'Darstellung' (presentation; also known as 'Bild') occupies rather less of the argument at this stage. A brief reference to Caspar Neher's use of the technology of film projection registers one significant principle of separation, however: 'Die Projektionen Nehers sind ebenso ein selbständiger Bestandteil der Oper wie Weills Musik und der Text' (Neher's projections are just as much an independent component of the opera as are Weill's music and the text).[12]

However, so far as the traditional 'Bühnenbild' (stage-set) is concerned, Brecht does not seem to regard this as very significant. He even makes a statement to the effect that the written text is as important as the spoken: 'Beim Lesen gewinnt das Publikum wohl am ehesten die bequemste Haltung dem Werk gegenüber' (the audience achieves its most convenient perspective on the text from reading it).[13] This seemingly less than full-blooded support for the primacy of the theatrical enactment could perhaps be compared to Wagner's references to the desirability of listening to music with one's eyes shut, and his comparative indifference to overwhelming visual effects such as were associated with the stage-sets for Romantic opera.[14]

[10] *GW* xvii. 1010.   [11] Ibid. 1011.
[12] Ibid. 1012.   [13] Ibid. 1012.
[14] Apropos Wagner's statements about stage-scenery in *Oper und Drama*, Ernst Schumacher observes: 'Wagner wetterte . . . gegen die romantische Prunkoper . . . zu deren Verkörperung er in den Augen der fortschrittlichen Musiker und Dramatiker

Brecht's theory of 'Trennung der Elemente' (separation of the elements) has sometimes been seen as a purely negative counterpart to Wagner's idea of the 'Gesamtkunstwerk'. If this is indeed the case, one would not expect to find evidence of any debate with the complex ideas which Wagner put forward in *Oper und Drama* and elsewhere. Indeed there is absolutely no evidence to suggest that Brecht had ever read Wagner's essays and it would seem more likely that his notions of the 'Gesamtkunstwerk' were culled entirely from secondary sources. This may explain that reductionism and scaling down of complex issues to almost slogan-like status which is an unfortunate characteristic of Brecht's utterances on this and other matters—though his highly developed political and polemical instincts also explain the aggressive form in which he clothed his theoretical ideas. Manfred Voigts is disposed to regard the 'Gesamtkunstwerk' as a fundamental starting-point for Brecht's theorizing throughout his life: 'das Gesamtkunstwerk [ist] negativer Fixpunkt des Brecthischen Denkens' (the 'Gesamtkunstwerk' is a negative focal point in Brecht's thinking).[15] This raises an interesting question: did Brecht's ideas about 'Trennung' stem from a positive source, a belief, that is, in a particular form of theatre based on first principles, or is it not rather the case that he was led to formulate his theories (including the theory of 'Verfremdungseffekt'—alienation effect—and indeed the entire theory of 'epic' theatre) purely by a spirit of contradiction, and an opposition to all that seemed conventional and outmoded?

Brecht himself would certainly not have regarded the lack of originality implicit in such an approach as a slur on his status; indeed he would probably have exulted in his apparent liberation from all traditional shackles. But that is not to say that elements from such sources, even the 'Gesamtkunstwerk' itself, do not linger on, transformed and not immediately recognizable, in some of his own works. It will be a major objective in the analysis section of this book to demonstrate how a system of leitmotivic imagery operates in the case of certain Brechtian dramatic masterpieces in a fashion not dissimilar to Wagner's leitmotiv, which, as we saw in

der zwanziger Jahre werden sollte' (Wagner fumed against the plush Romantic opera, whose embodiment he himself was destined to become in the eyes of avant-garde musicians and dramatists of the 1920s), *Bertolt Brecht: Die dramatischen Versuche 1918–1933* (Berlin, 1955), 217.

[15] Manfred Voigts, *Brechts Theaterkonzeptionen* (Munich, 1977), 101.

the previous chapter, was a central plank of the 'Gesamtkunstwerk'. However, such is the distance between this practical level and that of Brecht's theorizing that we have constantly to take into account the fact that Brecht has drawn the terms of reference for the latter in an extremely tight circle, so that the stark simplicity of his categorizations beg, or ignore, many of the central questions which had hitherto concerned theorists of drama. One only needs, however, to pause for a minute to be struck by the paradox that such a richly creative, even chaotic talent as Brecht displayed up to 1926, the year of his awakening to a theoretical interest in Marxism, could within a few short years proceed to something as drastic as the theory of 'Trennung der Elemente'. It does not require much imagination to see that such a process could only be effected by imposing an iron discipline upon his natural inclinations. In other words, a juxtaposition of *Baal* and Brecht's first 'systematic' formulation of his ideas in the 'Anmerkungen zu *Mahagonny*' may tempt the attentive reader to ask what price had to be paid for the suppression of all manifestations of the subconscious in Brecht's theory of drama and to wonder to what extent such a position could be maintained during the creative process itself. And if it could not, one is not unmindful of the inner tension that would be set up, nor of the likelihood that an over-dependence on external stimuli for theoretical purposes—like, for instance, the repeated attacks on the 'Gesamtkunstwerk'—would leave a great many questions unanswered and lead to defensive postures, frequently masked by aggressive statement. Brecht's theories on 'Trennung' are probably unique in the extent to which they mislead, though they exert a fascination by virtue of their apparent rationality and clarity.[16]

Let us examine more closely, then, the notion of 'Trennung der Elemente', specifically against Brecht's view, however imperfectly understood, of the 'Gesamtkunstwerk'. The radicality of the separation of the component elements of 'Work', 'Musik', and 'Darstellung' is most aggressively promoted in the 'Anmerkungen',

---

[16] Several commentators have pointed to Brecht's curious lack of insight into the subconscious aspects of his own theories and to the extent to which he was 'unbewußt', among these being Marianne Kesting, 'Wagner/Meyerhold Brecht, 121: 'Meyerhold . . . war sich—anders als Brecht—des Ursprunges der umfunktionierten Äethetik bewußt' (unlike Brecht, Meyerhold was conscious of the origins of the restructured Aesthetic).

where it is set against the opposing principle (as Brecht sees it) of intermingling, 'Verschmelzung der Elemente', which is regarded by Brecht as the distinguishing feature of the 'Gesamtkunstwerk' (one notes that Brecht uses quotation marks which may, or may not, suggest that he is taking issue with interpreters of Wagner's theories rather than with the composer's own writings). To this adverse notion of 'Verschmelzung'—a term, incidentally, which I do not believe Wagner himself employed—is added an idea taken from the natural sciences, namely the principle of degradation.[17] This is a well-known technique in chemistry whereby substances are broken down and lose their individual properties, but Brecht imbues it with an unscientific disdain, suggesting a process of reprehensible deterioration.

Although the form of the argument is not entirely convincing—Brecht quickly mounts a pulpit rather than engaging in a close analysis of the phenomena he alludes to metaphorically—his point seems to be that amalgamation of the component parts necessarily entails loss of their distinctive or distinguishing features—the term 'Aufwaschen', meaning 'washing everything in the same liquid' underlines this—and that this loss is not compensated for by any counterbalancing enhancement of the end-product. By an extraordinary shifting of the terms of reference (which may be a defensive measure to conceal some deeply rooted bias, though it is difficult to prove such things), Brecht moves from this largely technical matter of the relationship of the 'elements' to the emotive issue of a spectator reaction and uses the term 'Verschmelzung' loosely as a bridge between the two: 'Der Schmelzprozeß erfaßt den Zuschauer, der ebenfalls eingeschmolzen wird und einen passiven (leidenden) Teil des Gesamtkunstwerks darstellt' (the melting process extends to the spectator, who likewise gets melted down and becomes a passive (suffering) part of the 'Gesamtkunstwerk').[18]

I shall be examining Brecht's use of the term 'Verschmelzung' in further detail at a later stage. Here it is sufficient to notice the vehemence of the invective against the principle of intermingling of different art-forms and the point that Brecht is concerned to wage his war on grounds which smack much more of moral superiority than they do of aesthetic or even logical principles of evaluation. 'Trennung' does not in itself make for aesthetically superior drama,

---

[17] *GW* xvii. 1010.   [18] Ibid.

nor does Brecht manage to demonstrate that the antipodal 'Gesamtkunstwerk' necessarily implies inferior art. The underlying premisses are rather different.

In his later discussions of 'Trennung' Brecht is much more guarded about the negative aspects implied by an assimilation of individual parts and he concentrates instead on what he sees as the more positive features of separation itself: independence, for instance (the parts remain 'completely independent'), since each is slotted into its position as in an assemblage of mechanical parts ('kennbar einmontiert', conspicuously assembled). The question of how these parts relate to one another is expressed in somewhat paradoxical terms: they are acting together—and yet at the same time do not sacrifice anything of their individual identity: 'Die drei Elemente Aktion, Musik und Bild traten vereint und doch getrennt auf' (the three elements of action, music, and set were presented all together and yet separately).[19] Again more attention seems to be paid to the first two elements, 'Aktion' and 'Musik', although at another point Brecht makes the interesting observation that the 'Bühnenbild' (in the form of film projections) can at certain times work *together with* the music and *independently of* the action. He cites an example from *Aufstieg und Fall der Stadt Mahagonny* which serves to demonstrate the principle of simultaneous independence and interaction: the same event ('Vorgang') is described separately by a chorus which provides musical commentary, by an actor who is impersonating a glutton but who does not identify with that role, and by a film projection of the action. One might comment here on the prolixity of such a presentation and question the need to use more than one method for making such an obvious point. Brecht himself rather weakens his case by admitting that the examples he cites are extreme: 'Diese Beispiele sind verhältnismäßig extrem . . . sie sind hauptsächlich angeführt, um zu zeigen, was unter *Trennung der Elemente* zu verstehen ist' (the examples are relatively extreme: they are cited mainly to show what is to be understood by 'separation of the elements').[20]

At another point in the same series of essays, 'Über Bühnenbau und Musik des epischen Theaters', we find a rather surprising reference to the enhancing effect which music can have on the

---

[19] *GW* xv. 495. As is often the case with Brecht, there may be political overtones here: the autonomy of parts within an aesthetic whole could suggest opposition to the Stalinist model of the monolithic state.   [20] Ibid.

whole work: the phrase 'zur Erhöhung der Gesamtwirkung' (to heighten the total effect) surely suggests an interaction of some kind between the various elements to produce a heightened effect, and one which, after all, is not dissimilar to the role which Wagner allocated to music within the construct of the 'Gesamtkunstwerk' where it served the function of intensification ('Verstärkung der Handlung'). Brecht, of course, would doubtless distinguish between Wagner's notion of intensification via interaction of one 'element' upon another and his own notion of intensification in totality, which is achieved by an oppositional relationship of these same elements towards one another. And he would certainly have us believe that the totality of the 'Gesamtkunstwerk' represents less (i.e. is a degradation) than the totality of the component parts. But the absence of precise details to support his arguments leaves us unconvinced, particularly if we compare his dogmatic presentation to the complexity of Wagner's analysis of the process of interaction.

More specifically Brecht defines the relationship between the 'elements' in terms of contrast and contradiction (this matter will be examined later when we consider the special role assigned to music). Thus the actors (who are unceremoniously lumped together along with the 'Bühnenbau') are invited to maintain an oppositional position: 'Das Zusammenspiel der Künste wird so ein lebendiges; der Widerspruch der Elemente ist nicht ausgelöscht (the interplay of the different art-forms thus comes to life; the contradiction of the elements is not extinguished).[21] The later essay 'Das kleine Organon für das Theater' tackles the question of interaction of the parts in an even more general way: there is much stress on the idea of participation of individual elements not just for their own sake (this was always a rather puzzling feature of the early formulation, since individual liberty was not exactly a principle which Brecht held dear during his first, most zealous period of enthusiasm for the Communist revolution, as we can see when we consider, for instance, the 'Lehrstücke). Rather it is for the general good and in the interests of 'die gemeinsame Aufgabe' (the common task). These 'elements' still enter into a contrastive relationship, indeed the word 'verfremden' is used here for the first time to express their relationship to one another, thus linking them clearly to Brecht's most celebrated theatrical device, the 'Verfremdungseffekt' (aliena-

---

[21] Ibid. 441.

tion effect): 'ihr Verkehr miteinander besteht darin, daß sie sich gegenseitig verfremden' (their relationship to one another consists in their producing a mutual alienation),[22] but that does not seem to affect the closeness, even intimacy which is expressed by the term 'Schwesterkünste' (sister-arts), not even at times the (incongruous) sense of a crusade for the liberation of the various art-forms: music recovers its 'Freiheit', likewise the choreographer and the 'Bühnen-bildner' (stage-designers) are emancipated. Given the notorious difficulties which Brecht experienced with his composer collabor-ators (e.g. Weill and Paul Hindemith), this glib statement masks a whole series of problems which arise in the setting of a dramatic text to music which Brecht pretends do not exist.

We note, finally, that the number of participants—together with their appropriate art-forms—has risen considerably. We are no longer dealing with three 'elements' alone (remember that 'Bühnen-bild' had incorporated both acting, stage-sets, and such things as film projections). Brecht now itemizes a whole panoply of 'Schwesterkünste', stating that the whole work is produced by 'den Schauspielern, Bühnenbilnern, Maskenmachern, Kostüm-schneidern, Musikern and Choreographen' (the actors, stage-designers, mask-makers, costume-tailors, musicians, and choreo-graphers). The relatively subsidiary position which he allocates here to music is especially interesting in the light of its central importance in the earlier essays and we shall return to this point later. The new emphasis on what are generally regarded as technical matters (e.g. costume-making) may also be a significant reflection of Brecht's own very intensive participation in the practicalities of theatrical production which accompanied his work as director at the Theater am Schiffbauerdamm after his return to East Germany.

It is important to observe the differences in style and presentation when one compares Brecht's theoretical statements over the period in question. The exaggerated language of the 'Anmerkungen': 'radikale Trennung', 'Schmelzprozeß', 'Degradierung', 'Auf-waschen', is anything but sober and matter-of-fact. By 1936 a certain amount of venom is still retained for the 'Gesamtkunstwerk': while the earlier 'radical' separation of the 'elements' has been reduced to being merely 'strict' (streng), the relationship of the

[22] *GW* xvi. 698–9.

'elements' within the 'negativer Fixpunkt' (Voigts)—otherwise 'Gesamtkunstwerk'—still suggests an arbitrary violence ('einer rastlosen Verschmelzung aller Kunstelemente', a radical melting together of all artistic elements). Furthermore, we must not forget that it is in the section entitled 'Über Bühnenmusik' (On music for the stage), which has now been redated to 1943, that we encounter Brecht's statement: 'Bismarck hatte das Reich, Wagner das Gesamtkunstwerk gegründet, die beiden Schmiede hatten geschmiedet und verschmolzen, und Paris war von beiden erobert worden' (Bismarck had established the Reich, Wagner the 'Gesamtkunstwerk'; the two smiths had forged their metals and put them in the melting-pot and Paris had been conquered by them both).[23] This assertion is notable for its colourful extravagance rather than its historical accuracy for one thing, Wagner's reception at the hands of the French was almost uniformly hostile during his lifetime).

In the 'Kleines Organon', however, the language is much more neutral and, for Brecht, perhaps even a shade academic and colourless: instead of 'Degradierung' and 'Verschmelzung', the component 'elements' that make up the 'Gesamtkunstwerk' are said to 'surrender' and 'lose themselves', while in Brecht's own counterpart to the 'Gesamtkunstwerk' the elements 'have a common task': 'So seien all die Schwesterkünste der Schauspielkunst hier geladen, nicht um ein "Gesamtkunstwerk" herzustellen, in dem sie sich alle aufgehen und verlieren, sondern sie sollen, zusammen mit der Schauspielkunst, die gemeinsame Aufgabe in ihrer verschiedenen Weise fördern . . .' (so let us invite all the sister-arts of drama, not in order to create a 'Gesamtkunstwerk' in which they give in and are destroyed, but so that, along with the drama, they promote the common task in their various ways).[24] One explanation for this new, more sober tone could be Brecht's recently developed admiration for Francis Bacon: at any rate he appears for once to adopt the tone of academic discourse rather than the harsh invective which had been his wont.

Such changes may be more than skin deep and perhaps the clear

---

[23] For redating (to 1943) see Lucchesi and Shull, *Musik bei Brecht*, 208. The quotation itself can also be found in *GW* xv. 486.

[24] *GW* xvi. 698–9. The political overtones (to which attention was drawn in . 19 above) are possibly present here too, as Brecht's opposition to Stalinism finds expression in a more humanized system of Communism.

emphasis on the principle of enjoyment in art ('Vergnügung'), a principle which, while not entirely absent before from the Brechtian canon, was now seen as an important adjunct to the learning process itself, has brought with it a softening of the style. Certainly, too, there is a broadening of the vistas in this essay: the prominence of the concept of the 'scientific age' (here Brecht can link hands with Bacon) replaces the narrower Marxist, anti-Capitalist focus which had earlier prevailed. Especially interesting for our study, however, as I mentioned earlier, is the different emphasis now accorded to music in Brecht's theory of 'Trennung'. For while in the 'Anmerkungen' it was the prime instrument of Brecht's reforming zeal (despite the allegedly 'democratic' relationship of the 'elements' to one another), now it appears to be merely one among a whole battery of theatrical devices to which the later Brecht lays claim. Secondly, the less strident emphasis on the principle of 'Trennung' itself (with its strong disjunctive and anti-empathetic implications and its practical application in the 'Verfremdungseffekt') may well be connected with the restoration of 'Vergnügung' as an admissible principle. I shall be examining this point in greater detail in my analysis of the late masterpiece, *Leben des Galilei*.

The Role of Music in Brecht's Theory of 'Trennung der Elemente'

(1) Social Critique

In the summarizing remarks[25] which he appended to the notorious schematized tables used to demonstrate the polarized relationship between 'die dramatische Form des Theaters' (the dramatic form of theatre) and 'die epische Form des Theaters' (the epic form of theatre) ('Anmerkungen' to *Aufstieg und Fall der Stadt Mahagonny*), Brecht accorded a special role to music, as we have already observed. Furthermore, the general tables are followed by another set which presents the two forms of opera in similarly polarized terms: 'dramatische Oper' and 'epische Oper'. In a footnote Brecht even specifies the number of instruments which he regards as the outside limit (30 in all, which may seem larger than we might

[25] *GW* xvii. 1011.

expect, but is still only a small proportion of the vastly swollen forces that compose the Wagnerian orchestra with its special reinforcements of harps and brass instruments, including 'Wagner tubas').

The five functions which Brecht allocates to the music of 'epic opera' all share one important feature and that is the role of perspectival commentary upon the text through the medium of music: 'die Musik vermittelt' (the music mediates); 'den Text auslegend' (expounding the meaning of the text); 'den Text voraussetzend' (providing the basic assumptions behind the text); 'Stellung nehmend' (taking up a position); 'das Verhalten gebend' (prescribing rules of behaviour). Commentary, of course, pre-supposes something on which to comment, and Brecht is soon involved in specifying what kinds of content ('Inhalt') are per-missible and what are not: the permissible are mainly social and political. Such philosophical ('weltanschaulich') ingredients as, for example, had been presented in opera by Wagner and his followers is quickly dismissed: 'Jedoch war das Weltanschauliche, etwa das Wagners, stets so kulinarisch bedingt, das der *Sinn* dieser Opern sozusagen ein absterbender war und dann in den Genuß einging' (and yet the philosophical dimension—such as Wagner's—was always so restricted by the 'culinary' effects of these operas that the meaning was virtually in abeyance and degenerated into sensual enjoyment).[26]

This is a curious argument: Brecht cannot gainsay a strong philosophical element in Wagner's works (he may be mindful of the influence of Feuerbach, which pervaded the earlier operas, or Schopenhauer, who left his mark on the later ones), but he disclaims their lasting appeal in those terms, suggesting that contemporary opera-goers can no longer respond in the same way as Wagner's own contemporaries did—a historical relativism which would equally apply to other composers of opera as well, e.g. Mozart and Beethoven, whom, however, Brecht still finds 'relevant' for his own day. Thus he dismisses the formidable element of content in Wagner's operas: 'Der Inhalt war in der Oper abgelegt' (the content in opera was discarded). Not so Mozart or Beethoven, whose 'Inhalt' finds approval because their 'Weltanschauungen', as expressed in works like *Die Zauberflöte*, *Le Nozze di Figaro*, and

---

[26] Ibid. 1013.

Fidelio, have the required political or social relevance: 'weltan-schauliche, aktivistische Elemente' (philosophical and activistic elements). Not only do these works provide material of lasting appeal (mythology, it seems, does not!), but they are able to present an attitude, a position towards that material which is 'critical' (this is synonymous in Brecht's parlance with 'progressive').

There is no doubt that behind the invective there lurks here an interesting fundamental point: by what means can music—itself, as Wagner was well aware, 'inhaltlos' (without content)—become the vehicle for expressing political attitudes or social critique? Are we dealing with an extension of instrumental 'Sprachvermögen' (power of language) (I think this is doubtful), or are we perhaps back to Borchmeyer's notion of 'Semantisierung', the process, that is, whereby through its association with words and particular meanings, this content-less-art-form can itself become a bearer of 'meaning'? However, that might presuppose some bridging device such as leitmotiv, which, as has been demonstrated in the previous chapter, is regarded by Wagner as ideally suited to fulfilling such a role but which, as subsequent chapters of this study will try to demonstrate, is not without its counterparts in Brecht's own dramatic practice although it is a device about which he is totally silent in his theoretical works. Brecht's theoretical alternative, however, is something new and altogether different. His essay entitled 'Über gestische Musik' (On gestic music) of 1937 shows how such a political and social meaning can be conveyed in musical terms and without (theoretically at least) the benefit of such a link device as leitmotiv. This becomes clearer when one examines the key concept of 'Gestus', which, is, in effect, Brecht's bridging counterpart to the Wagnerian leitmotiv. It is a notion which Brecht expounds in some detail but one about which for the most part quite a lot of heavy weather has been made in the secondary literature.

In his 'definition' of 'Gestus' Brecht is at pains to distinguish it from 'Gestikulieren', that is expressive hand-movements which convey particular attitudes, e.g. rage, joy, etc. 'Gestus' could, it seems, take that form; indeed these represent one of the important elements that go to make up a complex range of responses: ('ein Komplex von Gesten'). But it would only fulfil Brecht's require-ments if it related to a general rather than a specific response ('es handelt sich um Gesamthaltungen', it's a matter of overall attitudes),[27] and, in particular, to socially directed rather than private or individual human behavioural patterns. As such, as Hans Martin Ritter has noted in his valuable study, it is ideally suited to the medium of theatre: 'das Theater als Kunstform [ist] nicht nur der Ort, von dem aus der Begriff bei Brecht entwickelt worden ist, sondern auch der Ort, auf den er in seinem eigentlichsten Sinn ausgerichtet ist' (as an art-form the theatre is not only the starting-point for Brecht's development of the concept, but also the place towards which it is directed in its most basic sense).[28] We shall find that others may claim its primary presence in other art-forms, but I believe it is difficult to sustain such a hypothesis when it is tested out specifically against Brecht's own definition.

Brecht's theory of 'Gestus' revolves very much around the process of giving effective verbal expression to such socially directed 'perspectives' (see especially the essay 'Über reimlose Lyrik mit unregelmäßigen Rhythmen' and *Me-ti/Buch der Wendungen*, where the origins of Brecht's ideas can be located in his Chinese source, for whom language is regarded as 'ein Werkzeug des Handelns', a tool of action). Brecht himself cites a celebrated sentence from Luther's Bible as an illustration of the 'gestic' principle: 'Wenn dich dein Auge ärgert, reiß es aus' (if thy eye offend thee, pluck it out), a forceful, well-balanced piece of syntax, built on the two connected notions: the reasons for a particular action followed by the action itself. The syntactical structure itself, therefore, is mimetic of the precise form of action to be taken. This is a principle which is very much at the heart of Brechtian dialogue, as has been demonstrated by various commentators. It is, of course, not unique to Brecht, but may be found in the dialogue of many excellent dramatists.

However, verbal means in themselves do not satisfy Brecht in his search for methods of conveying 'attitudes', 'critical responses', or 'perspectives'. He has recourse to other, non-verbal forms of expression to supplement linguistic and syntactical devices which he himself could supply in considerable abundance. And music was one of the expressive modes on which his eye lighted with special interest. Brecht attempts to define musical 'Gestus' thus:

Es ist ein vorzügliches Kriterium gegenüber einem Musikstück mit Text, vorzuführen, in welcher Haltung, mit welchem Gestus der Vortragende die

---

[27] GW xv. 482.
[28] Hans Martin Ritter, *Das gestische Prinzip bei Bertolt Brecht* (Cologne, 1986), 7.

einzelnen Partien bringen muß, höflich oder zornig, demütig oder verächtlich, zustimmend oder ablehnend, listig oder ohne Berechnung' (an excellent method of judging a piece of music with text is to assess the kind of attitude, of 'Gestus', with which the performer has to render the individual sections, whether politely or disapprovingly, craftily or without calculation). ('Über gestische Musik')[29]

He admits to a predilection for the commonplace, banal, and vulgar in order better to focus attention on political issues: 'Dabei sind die allergewöhnlichsten, vulgärsten, banalsten Gesten zu bevorzugen. So kann der politische Wert des Musikstücks abgeschätzt werden' (for this purpose the forms of 'Gestus' to be preferred are the most commonplace, the most vulgar, the most banal. In this way one can gauge the political value of the musical piece).[30] But what becomes apparent when one compares the musical 'Gestus' with the purely linguistic variety is the adversative relationship that prevails between music and text in specific examples of 'Gestus'. When we consider the examples of *Die Dreigroschenoper* and *Aufstieg und Fall der Stadt Mahagonny*, operas which were both written in collaboration with Kurt Weill at the height of his and Brecht's joint theoretical interest in 'gestische Musik', we cannot fail to observe the extensive use of parody, which becomes the major vehicle for 'Gestus'. The virtuoso use by Weill of standard operatic devices, e.g. duets, trios, finales, and his well-placed deployment of strict academic forms like fugue (e.g. the instrumental music accompanying 'Der reitende Bote' in the former opera, or the typhoon in the latter) are obvious instances. Such devices, when placed disjunctively, i.e. in conspicuous opposition to the seedy and sordid tenor of the action and the theme of the falseness and hypocrisy of bourgeois society, are an effective way in which Brecht and his composer are able to express political and social critique. This would appear to be a clear example, then, of one way in which music can participate in a 'gestic' perspective. What remains unclear, however—and this is a matter of some theoretical importance, as we shall see when we examine Brecht's and Weill's contrasting views on the relationship between text and music—is whether the 'content-less' form of music is independently capable of conveying such semantic information and whether such 'gestic' perspectives as are so effectively achieved in the two above-

[29] *GW* xv. 485.   [30] Ibid.

mentioned operas (though perhaps not always quite in the sense that Brecht would have liked) could have been equally well expressed by non-contrastive, non-contradictory means.

(2) Kurt Weill and Musical 'Gestus'

That Kurt Weill played a major role in the practical and theoretical explorations being conducted by the two men is clear from an examination of the composer's own essay, entitled 'Über den gestischen Charakter der Musik' (On the gestic charcter of music), ideas for which may well have been formulated before Brecht's and many of which are restated in Brecht's 'Anmerkungen' to *Mahagonny*. Weill insists repeatedly on the primacy of music within the 'gestic' alliance between his art and verbal forms of expression; as we have already seen, Brecht, perhaps rather surprisingly, allows him to get away with this, to the extent even that he himself spells out the primary importance of music in his 'counterpart' to the 'Gesamtkunstwerk' based on 'Trennung der Elemente'. Weill argues the toss for music taking a 'vorherrschende Stellung' (predominant position) and refuses to yield ground to the two other 'elements', here termed 'Wort' and 'Bild'. Like Brecht, he sees no role for music in the area of psychological characterization (Brecht, of course, true to his Behaviourist leanings,[31] is theoretically opposed to all such nuanced characterization, regarding man purely as a social being). Again like Brecht, Weill views music as a major means of conveying 'Gestus': 'Dafür hat die Musik eine Fähigkeit, die für die Darstellung des Menschen auf dem Theater von entscheidender Bedeutung ist: sie kann sogar eine Art von Grundgestus schaffen' (instead music has a capacity which can be of decisive significance for the theatrical representation of Man: it can even produce a kind of basic 'Gestus').[32] This is a particularly interesting insight into the structural relationships produced by Gestus' and I am tempted to draw a parallel here with Wagner's *Grundmotiv* (primary motiv) which, however difficult it may be to exemplify or pin down precisely in each individual music drama, at least theoretically, suggests a hierarchical arrangement of these

---

[31] On Brecht's relationship to Behaviourism see the valuable essay by J. J. White, 'A Note on Brecht and Behaviourism', *Forum for Modern Language Studies*, 7 (1971), 249–58.

[32] Kurt Weill, 'Über den gestischen Charakter der Musik', *Ausgewählte Schriften*, ed. David Drew (Frankfurt-on-Main, 1975), 42.

devices according to which individual leitmotivs may be subordinated to overarching ones which assume a major perspectival
role within the whole structure, becoming primary bearers of
meaning. Similarly here, then, Weill sees the musically conveyed
'Grundgestus' (or 'Grundton' which is another term he uses to
convey the hierarchical notion) as a great advantage to both the
composer and librettist who aim to present clear, unequivocal
statements and perspectives.

At the same time, however, Weill insists that 'gestic' music is able
to make its impact independently and unaided by any textual or
verbal 'contamination': 'Natürlich ist gestische Musik keineswegs
an den Text gebunden' (gestic music is, of course, in no way limited
to the text),[33] which seems to me a point that he does not succeed in
proving. The 'splendid isolation' of music is an odd idea for a
composer to embrace who has deliberately cast loose from
'absolute' music and who is seeking an alliance between his art-
form and another on which it must necessarily be dependent to
some extent. Weill quotes a number of musical (mainly operatic)
examples—Bach Passions, Bizet, Offenbach, Mozart (where he
finds the device 'überall'), and Beethoven's *Fidelio* (these last two
examples of musical 'Gestus' he shares with Brecht), but I do not
find his arguments convincing. For example, he cites what he sees
as the built-in 'dramatic' 'Gestus' in Mozart's operas and other
music as well: 'wenn wir Mozarts Musik überall, auch außerhalb
der Oper als "dramatisch" empfinden, so kommt das eben daher,
daß sie nie ihren gestischen Charakter aufgibt' (if we perceive
Mozart's music everywhere—even outside the opera itself—to be
'dramatic', then that is because it never sacrifices its gestic
character).[34] But he is frequently to be found using a circular
argument, for the very 'dramatic' quality which Weill frequently
identifies in Mozart's operas owes much to the situation and
characters for whom the composer is 'indebted' to his librettist,
even although he may have transformed the bare bones of the
libretto and contributed what amounts to his own inspired
interpretation of these essentially 'literary/dramatic' elements.

Weill's analysis of his examples seem to me to betray a confusion
of ends and means. His example from Mozart's *Die Zauberflöte*

[33] Kurt Weill, 'Über den gestischen Charakter der Musik', *Ausgewählte Schriften*,
ed. David Drew (Frankfurt-on-Main, 1975). 42.
[34] Ibid. See discussion by Ritter, *Das gestische Prinzip*, 76–7.

(Tamino's aria: 'Dies Bildnis ist bezaubernd schön') is a prime example of musical illustration, the meaning of the key words 'Götter' and 'Herz' providing the inspiration for the composer to place the climax of the melody (on an Ab) by making the tenor scale the daring interval of a seventh on 'Götter', while the richly associative 'Herz' elicits a twofold embellishment through lingering, melismatic extensions on the respective leading notes (an Eb and a G respectively. It is surely erroneous to suggest, as Weill does, that these rich musical embellishments are not prompted by the words and their contextual associations, for these are their very starting-points.

Another example by means of which Weill attempts to argue for the primacy of musical 'Gestus' yields further interesting points. Both Brecht and Weill apparently shared a strong interest in the recitatives used by Bach in his great Passions, and as we can see from Weill's analysis of one particular example from the St John Passion they were both particularly fascinated by the way in which entirely contrasting 'Gesten' could be contained within the scope of a single piece of recitative. In the particular example selected for discussion[35] this contrastive principle is seen to be reflected in the juxtaposition of a musically expressive (and, note, once more descriptive) 'Gestus' of lamentation consisting of a coloratura extension on the word 'gekreuziget' which contrasts strikingly with the sparse and, melodically, relatively colourless intonation of the purely narrative *recitativo* section. Granted that the contrast of 'Gesten' is indeed striking, one might argue nevertheless that such a contrast represents in microcosmic form a principle in which the entire work—which is structured around alternating *recitativo*, arias, and choruses—rests and to which the listener becomes well accustomed. This in itself must weaken the case for the particular example being perceived as disjunctive or deliberately obtrusive. Moreover, the fact that the lamentation expressed at the word 'gekreuziget' is thus extended is a prime example of musical underlining of associative verbal significances.

Hans Martin Ritter is disposed to believe that Weill's view of the independence of musical 'Gestus' has something to commend it and that 'man tatsächlich die Haltung eines Menschen und ihre Nuancen schon in der musikalischen Formulierung festlegen kann'

---

[35] See discussion of Brecht's reaction to the recitative 'Jesus ging mit seinen Jüngern über den Bach Kidron' in Albrecht Dümling, *Laßt euch nicht verführen: Brecht und die Musik* (Munich, 1985), 293; also Ritter, *Das gestische Prinzip*, 75.

(one can actually specify a man's attitude, its nuances, too, from the way the music is presented).[36] This is a point which might possibly relate better to examples such as have been examined above, where the musical 'Gestus' repeats, embellishes, and underlines, than to those suggesting contradiction or contrast. The Bach example, according to Weill's theory, should, strictly speaking, reveal how such an individual example of musical 'underlining' of text must be seen in the context of the hierarchical arrangement of 'Gesten' and the dominance of a 'Grundgestus' within the principle of 'Trennung der Elemente'—which would subvert that particularly successful fusion of music and words which is achieved within the smaller unit. And yet that cannot be the true effect of the sharp contrast of 'Gesten' so admired by both Brecht and Weill, nor does Weill suggest it is. The truth would seem to be, then, that he had not given sufficient thought to the ways in which a 'Grundgestus' interacts with what could be termed a partial or 'Teilgestus', and seemed unaware of the fact that if a disjunctive effect was not achieved (as the example from the Bach Passion might have warned him it might not be) then a traditional—though not necessarily artistically inferior—effect of underlining and illustration of verbal meaning through musical means would predominate for the listener. This is a point of some substance when one reflects on Weill's own musical practice in the two collaborative operas, *Dreigroschenoper* and *Mahagonny*.

The example of the 'Alabama Song' from the latter opera which Weill discusses shows him making one important concession to the primacy of verbal stimuli in the process of setting a text to music. Weill points out that in his own setting ('Oh moon of Alabama . . .' he had taken over the basic 'Grundgestus' from Brecht's own original version which was based on the inherent rhythmic cadences of the text: 'diese rhythmische Fixierung, die vom Text her erreicht wird, bildet aber nur die Grundlage einer gestischer Musik' (this process of securely fixing the rhythm which is achieved by the text forms merely the basic level of a gestic music).[37] As Ritter points out, he does not care to specify what precisely this primary or 'Grundgestus' might be, and if he did would probably have got into further difficulties *vis-à-vis* his stated belief that a 'Grundgestus' is dictated by music and not by semantic transference *from* the text *to* the music.

---

[36] *Das gestische Prinzip*, 77.　　　　[37] Weill, *Ausgewählte Schriften*, 43.

The 'Alabama Song' is, in fact, a very good example of the basically reactive relationship between music and text in Brecht and Weill's conception of disjunctive and contrastive 'Grundgestus' which is central to their joint policy of 'Trennung'. The exaggeratedly meretricious, schmaltzy melody and Hollywood harmonies supplied by Weill have to be placed in the context of an overarching 'Grundgestus' of ironic parody. This is further served by what—*pace* Weill—is a purely textual/dramatic context, since the popular and, to some tastes, even attractive qualities of this song are subverted by the distancing achieved by its first being sung by the prostitute Jenny at the time when the grotesquely capitalistic and materialistic city of Mahagonny is founded (scene 2); later it is repeated (scene 9) at a point when the same city is about to be destroyed by a hurricane. The ironical, even satirical 'Gestus' is demonstrably clear within the context of the action. Divorced from this context, however, the song is liable to produce enthusiastic identification on the part of the listener or spectator, who may respond exclusively to its immediate 'Inhalt'—i.e. as a highly successful blend of music and words—precisely the opposite to the effect intended. This ambiguity which lies at the heart of Weill's musical practice—and in itself seems to have created major problems in his partnership with Brecht, as we shall discover—has been frequently commented on.[38] The ambiguity is not resolved by Brecht's insistence on fragmentation in his presentation of songs and action and his (theoretical) abandonment of contextual continuity.

As a footnote to Weill's interpretation of the concept of 'Gestus' (his essay is dated March 1929, i.e. just after the *succès fou* of the *Dreigroschenoper*) we should bear in mind Brecht's somewhat guarded remarks concerning the degree of success with which he believed Weill had dealt with 'gestic' music: 'Ich möchte nicht unerwähnt lassen, daß meiner Meinung nach die Weillsche Musik zu dieser Oper nicht rein gestisch ist . . . (I must mention that in my opinion Weill's music for this opera is not purely gestic).[39] That sounds grudging; so too does the continuation, which takes the line 'half a loaf is better than no bread', as if to suggest that Weill's music had made some dent on the Establishment, but had not gone

---

[38] See, for example, Peter Branscombe: 'Brecht, Weill and Mahagonny', *Musical Times* (Aug. 1981), 486: 'Weill's success . . . is such that the audience is tempted to wallow rather than study critically—a point that Brecht made in his essay on the use of music in the epic theatre'. Also Ritter, *Das gestische Prinzip, passim.*

[39] GW, xv. 476.

as far as Brecht would have liked. At this point one enters the difficult terrain of operatic collaboration which, despite all the high-falutin statements in Brecht's theoretical works about 'equality' which the new principle of 'Trennung' is supposed to have inaugurated, was to prove just as troublesome in practice as in other partnerships (cf. Strauss–Hofmannsthal). I believe that in the case of the collaboration between Brecht and Weill the cause of their undoing was built in from the outset and emanated from two inherently contradictory sources: first, Weill's misconception about the absolute primacy of music in any collaborative enterprise; secondly, his adoption of a principle of 'Gestus' which differed markedly from Brecht's aggressively contrastive approach with its heavy emphasis on musical parody and ironic distancing. Weill was certainly a master of musical parody—he was, after all, a fully fledged composer and a former pupil of Busoni—and in complete command of both the popular and Classical ends of the musical spectrum. But the 'culinary' aspects to such parodistic imitations were by no means eliminated; listeners and spectators could not always be expected to make comparisons or see underlying contradictions between the musical forms and the textual substance; in short, to identify a 'Grundgestus' of which the composer himself was only vaguely aware.

It is particularly interesting to find that, theoretically, Weill attached little importance to the principle of irony and refused to admit that the 'Gestus' which Brecht approved for music in his collaboration relied heavily on ironic effects: 'Es ist dringend abzuraten, die Darstellung des Werkes nach der Seite des Ironischen oder Grotesken zu verschieben' (any bias in the presentation of a work towards the ironical or the grotesque is emphatically to be discouraged).[40] But how else could Brecht's intentions be implemented, other than by sardonic and ironical methods when one considers his position in the hard-hitting world of 1920s Germany, a world in which, nurtured by an explosive political atmosphere, art achieved new heights of expressive savagery and even hatred (consider the visual arts and the works of Otto Dix, Max Beckmann, and George Grosz)? That is not to say, however, that Brecht's ideas on musical 'Gestus' which, as we have seen, are heavily reliant on the principle of parody, may not themselves

[40] 'Preface' to the 'Regiebuch der Oper *Mahagonny*', Weill, *Ausgewählte Schriften*, 59.

contain the seeds of ambiguity. This is a point which I shall develop further when I turn to his dramatic masterpiece of this period, *Die Heilige Johanna der Schlachthöfe*.

Brecht's own statements about musical 'Gestus' and his interest in extending parody into the field of music are not informative. They reach a peak around 1930, the time of the collaboration with Weill (whose brain he seems to have picked quite effectively) and are most apparent in the 'Anmerkungen' to *Mahagonny*. In the much later 'Kleines Organon für das Theater' Brecht reiterates the need for music to avoid the menial role of mere accompaniment and for it to assume a 'gestic' character and a commenting role: 'Die Musik muß sich ihrerseits durchaus der Gleichschaltung widersetzen, die ihr gemeinhin zugemutet wird, und die sie zur gedankenlosen Dienerin herabwürdigt. Sie "begleite" nicht, es sei denn mit Komment' (for its part music must strongly resist being brought into line, as is commonly expected of it, or being turned into a mindless handmaiden. Unless it provides commentary, music must not accompany at all).[41] As if to demonstrate that musical 'Gestus' is still alive and well, Brecht appreciatively cites the example of Hanns Eisler's music for *Galilei* (it is noteworthy that by this time Brecht had moved away from any traditional idea of operatic collaboration—an enterprise in which composer and dramatist are jointly involved in creating an entire work—to a relationship in which a composer could be 'called in' to supply music for certain 'numbers' (e.g. songs) and where the dramatist is in overall command of the situation). Brecht may have been trying to convince himself when he made exaggerated claims for the brilliance of Eisler's contributions: citing, for instance, the deft way in which he manages conspicuously to juxtapose contrasting styles in the mass and the 'academic' scenes of *Galilei* respectively. Earlier, Brecht had cited Eisler's music to *Die Mutter* as perfectly fulfilling the requirements of musical 'Gestus' despite the reluctance of American audiences to appreciate its qualities. Brecht's lack of concern for audience reaction is a worrying feature in all this, although perhaps understandable in view of the tremendous response to the two 1920s operas for what Brecht regarded as the wrong reasons. It is an indubitable fact that of all the collaborations in which he engaged it is Weill's music—with which he expressed

[41] Brecht, *GW* xvi. 697.

dissatisfaction—which has prevailed, while Eisler's, which met his intentions almost perfectly, has certainly not achieved comparable popular acceptance. Does this possibly suggest the limitations of Brecht's theory of 'Gestus' itself, at least in its application to music?

(3) The Attack on 'Verschmelzung'

If music assumes a distinctly double-edged character in Brecht's theorizing in the extent to which it can present socio-critical commentary upon an 'action' (Brecht, as is well known, disdains the Aristotelian term 'Handlung', preferring 'Fabel', but cannot really get by in his drama without this central prop), then the underlying causes may well reside in his own deeply ambivalent attitude towards this particular art-form.[42] It is instructive to recall that he had an almost unnatural distaste—bordering on horror— towards any kind of 'pure' or 'absolute' music. Nowhere does this ambivalence become clearer than in the various sections of his dramatic theory in which he deals with the question of audience response, especially the principle of pleasure ('Vergnügung') and the tendency of listeners and audiences towards emotional passivity and indulgence in general, and what he termed 'Hörfaulheit' (aural laziness) in particular. It is clear to any student of Brecht's early Marxist phase (i.e. *c.*1929–31) that he had a puritanical disgust when confronted by any art-form which might be suspected of affording entertainment or innocent amusement to an audience and that music was, in his eyes, a major offender in this sphere. A sharp dichotomy is opened up between the 'Vergnügungtheater' (often even more pejoratively described as 'kulinarisch') and the 'Lehr-theater'. Although one can still find traces of this severity lingering on in the 'Kleines Organon', the position is considerably more relaxed towards 'Vergnügung'—indeed the principle is now officially admitted into the canon of appropriate responses to

[42] Surprisingly, Bach's '48' (along with the Passions) remained a source of lifelong fascination. There are a number of revealing remarks, for instance in the *Arbeitsjournal*, which reflect Brecht's obsession with the physical effects (e.g. increased pulse rate) which certain music produced in him (he appears to have had hypochondriacal tendencies, possibly because of the diagnosis in childhood of a weak heart). See Lucchesi and Shull, *Musik bei Brecht*, 212. Note, too, Brecht's concern, expressed in 1936 (and later expunged from the published account), that there was 'little knowledge about the precise effects of music upon the human organism' (Uber die präzisen Wirkungen von Musik auf den Organismus ist wenig bekannt'), *ibid.* 166.

theatre. However, the polemic against Aristotle—or more precisely the Aristotelian view of catharsis seen through Brecht's eyes—is an issue which he refuses to let go of—at least at the conscious level of theorizing, while simultaneously, as many have noticed, his own works permitted more and more 'culinary' intrusions, which set up a fascinating tension within them. It is tempting to see this development in terms of a repressive tendency within the dramatist which finally yielded to a greater spontaneity and expressiveness and such a view would chime in with the popularly accepted three-stage scheme of development in Brecht's work.[43] But the salient point, which is to be examined here, is the nature and form of Brecht's repressive tendencies. In order to highlight these I propose to compare Brecht's position *vis-à-vis* music with those of Schiller, a dramatist with whom he shares some remarkable common ground. The similarities in thought and attitudes are nowhere more evident than in matters like audience response to a work of art and specifically to music.

In all three of the theoretical works of Brecht's which we have been examining what is perceived as passivity in the audience's response becomes codified (which is as much as to say 'reduced') into the term 'Verschmelzung', together with its cognates (e.g. 'Schmelzprozeß', 'einschmelzen', etc.). Frequently, the term occurs in the context of attacks on the notion of the 'Gesamtkunstwerk' and with reference to the relationship to one another of the component parts that constitute a mixed form like opera or music drama. But, as I indicated earlier, the term is also applied, by an illogical jump in thought, to the supposed reaction of a listener to such an interdependently structured work as well. 'Der Schmelz-prozeß erfaßt den Zuschauer, der ebenfalls eingeschmolzen wird und einen passiven (leidenden) Teil des Gesamtkunstwerks darstellt' (the melting process extends to the spectator, who likewise gets melted down and becomes a passive (suffering) part of the 'Gesamtkunstwerk').[44] (This last point is surely a conceit: how can the listener-spectator himself be regarded as a constituent part of the work to which he is responding, unless Brecht is anticipating 'reception-theory', which I think is unlikely.) At other points the smear-word 'kulinarisch' is trotted out to suggest brutish responses,

---

[43] On the continuing prevalence of this view, which was first eloquently advanced by Martin Esslin (*Brecht: A Choice of Evils* (London, 1959)), see E. Wright, *Postmodern Brecht* (London, 1988), 6.

while the term 'Hörfaulheit' exaggeratedly suggests a completely uncritical response to art-works. Both terms carry unmistakable overtones of censure and moral superiority towards what is regarded as a state of physical dependence. Words like 'narkotisch' and 'Rausch' (intoxication) make this point over and over again. Once more, the 'Anmerkungen' of 1930 represents a high point of Brecht's superior rationalism. The bad taste and paucity of expression which accompany this always comes as surprise in a writer who was such a master of language, but the degree of stridency and vehemence may be in proportion to Brecht's defensive position, and as much a personal aid as anything else.

Turning to Schiller, we shall find better manners superficially, perhaps, on the subject of listener response, but that may be more a reflection of the different styles that characterize the eighteenth and twentieth centuries and certainly a strong element of overstatement can be found here too. Schiller, in fact, seems to have had similarly ambivalent views towards music and to have seen its effect on the listener in almost identical, physical terms. Thus we find in the essay 'Über das Pathetische', in which Schiller examines the effect of tragic suffering ('Affekt') upon the spectator, sharp ridicule expressed about the state of emotional dependency induced in spectators by certain lachrymose forms of theatre (the 'bürgerliches Trauerspiel', possibly, or the 'comédie larmoyante'). Note the extreme language: 'Sie bewirken bloß die Ausleerungen des Tränensacks und eine wollüstige Erleichterung der Gefäße' (they—'melting emotions—merely promote an emptying of the tear-ducts and a voluptuous alleviation of the vessels).[45] The point is then extended to include contemporary music (one supposes that Schiller has in mind composers like C. P. E. Bach rather than Mozart and Haydn):'Auch die Musik der Neueren scheint es vorzüglich nur auf die Sinnlichkeit anzulegen' (even more recent music seem to be aimed primarily at sensuality).[46] Furthermore, Schiller observes worrying *physiological* reactions to the new emotional ('schmelzende') forms of music; at this point we are very much aware of the ex-medical student with his abiding interest in the mind–body question, as it was then understood. Ears, eyes, mouth, limbs, breath are all observed by the clinical gaze to be in a state of high excitation:

[44] GW xvii. 1010.
[45] Friedrich Schiller, 'Über das Pathetische', *Sämtliche Werke*, v, ed. Helmut Koopmann (Munich, 1968), 193.   [46] Ibid.

so wird plötzlich alles Ohr, wenn eine schmelzende Passage vorgetragen wird. Ein bis ins Tierische gehender Ausdruck der Sinnlichkeit erscheint dann gewöhnlich auf allen Gesichtern, die trunkenen Augen schwimmen, der offene Mund ist ganz Begierde, ein wollüstiges Zittern ergreift den ganzen Körper, der Atem ist schnell und schwach, kurz alle Symptome der Berauschung stellen sich ein (thus the audience is suddenly all ears when a melting passage is played. A sensual expression bordering on the bestial usually appears on every face. Drunken eyes swim, open mouths are all desire, a voluptuous trembling seizes the whole body, the breath comes rapidly and shallowly, in short all the symptoms of intoxication set in).[47]

This exaggerated piling up of responses suggests that perhaps after all the clinician has been replaced by a moralizing pedagogue whose disapproval of anything that detracts from man's higher faculties is as complete as that of Brecht. In another similar outburst against the principle of 'Verschmelzung', this time in the *Ästhetische Erziehung*, Schiller is able to examine the phenomenon within a broader philosophical framework, relating the effect of music upon the listener to that category of art which he terms 'schmelzende (as opposed to 'energische') Schönheit'. Once more possibly betraying his medical origins but also something of the interest of his age in such matters as aesthetic stimulation, Schiller establishes two, diametrically different, types of response: on the one hand, 'schmelzende Schönheit' leads to a kind of effete exhaustion: 'einem gewissen Grade von Weichlichkeit und Entnervung' (a certain degree of weakness and enervation).[48] It might, so Schiller believes, be useful for those people who are suffering from a one-sided emphasis on discipline, people who are, that is, 'unter dem Zwange entweder der Materie oder der Formen' (under the compulsion of matter or of form). But 'energische Schönheit' (energetic beauty) is no less one-sided, and since Schiller's main concern in this treatise is with the need to restore mental and spiritual equilibrium at a time in man's history when specialization of his activities was encroaching heavily on this terrain, 'schmelzende Schönheit' is dangerous indeed for those who are already, through the influence of the times, softened up, or disposed to self-indulgence and excess. For them a dose of 'energische Schönheit' is just what the doctor ordered! To hear both Brecht and Schiller discoursing on this theme, we might be forgiven

---

[47] Ibid. and p. 194.
[48] 'Über die ästhetische Erziehung des Menschen', *Sämtliche Werke*, v. 360.

for thinking that the whole of their contemporary culture was degenerate and in need of strong medication.

As in 'Über das Pathetische', Schiller once again goes into some considerable detail to register his anxiety about the harmful effects of 'schmelzende Schönheit'. His strong personal prejudice against music as an art-form surfaces when he states that even in its most respectable and intellectually demanding forms music, by its very nature, has deeper roots in sense perception than the other arts. Although this may accord with certain other eighteenth-century sources,[49] Schiller does not feel it necessary to support his assertions with any hard evidence and makes do with an elaborate rhetoric which may be his defensive counterpart to Brecht's invective: 'Die Ursache ist, weil auch die geistreichste Musik *durch ihre Materie* [Schiller's own italics] noch immer in einer größeren Affinität zu den Sinnen steht, als die wahre ästhetische Freiheit duldet' (this is because even the most intellectual music will always have a closer affinity to the senses because of its material than true aesthetic freedom permits).[50]

The music of which he approves—or would approve, since it is not clear that it even exists as yet—sounds desperately insipid and bland: 'die Musik in ihrer höchsten Veredlung', he asserts, 'muß Getalt werden, und mit der ruhigen Macht der Antike auf uns wirken' (at its highest level of nobility music must become form and must affect us with the powerful composure of Antiquity).[51] Schiller goes on, in this celebrated passage, to make similar stipulations to the effect that other art-forms should take over the best features of each other in what, as we look back, seems like an almost travestied version of the 'Gesamtkunstwerk'. Had he known of it, this might well have given added urgency to Brecht's attack on the hybrid form. It is not an encouraging prospect, nor one to which, thank goodness, German nineteenth-century composers paid much attention.

Like Brecht, Schiller develops an elaborate theory which attacks the idea—it was one which, as we have already seen, had been mooted by Lessing—of employing music to effect contrasts of

---

[49] Schiller's views on music should be read against the changing attitude towards the 'Affekte' in 18th-cent. aesthetics from Baumgarten's comparatively rationalistic approach to Herder's emphasis on 'expressiveness'. W. Seifert in C. G. *Körner: Ein Musikästhetiker der deutschen Klassik* (Regensburg, 1960) sees Schiller's friend as exemplifying a middle position between these two extremes.

[50] *Sämtliche Werke*, v. 378.   [51] Ibid. 379.

mood within a drama. Schiller will have none of this notion: he is concerned about the fact that music is capable of presenting transitions from one plane to another, for he sees this as an obstacle to detachment and rational reflection: 'wer uns unmittelbar nach einem hohen musikalischen Genuß zu abgezogenem Denken einladen ... wollte, der würde seine Zeit nicht gut wählen' (anybody seeking to invite us to participate in abstract thought after high-level musical enjoyment would not be choosing his time well).[52] Such generalizations reveal an inflexibility which is probably defensive: different minds respond in different ways to such stimuli and it is not inconceivable that an Einstein might be inspired to higher intellectual flights after some great aesthetic experience. Schiller's unwillingness to concede music's power to lead the mind from contemplation to action seems blinkered, though in fairness one could place it alongside the testimony of the young Thomas Mann, who maintained that after attending a performance of *Parsifal* he was incapable of constructive thought for two whole weeks.[53] Mann's statement must, however, be related to the context of his times, since auto-suggestion may have played a part during the wave of Wagnerian 'decadence' which swept Europe in the 1890s and contributed to states of deliberately cultivated neurasthenia. One notes that in both the examples quoted above Schiller proceeds from the premiss that as an art-form music produces a state of emotional dependency ('Leiden'); he believes that such a condition is one-sided and that it must be resisted in the appropriate manner (just as tragic suffering itself must be resisted by an act of conscious will on the part of the hero). The 'merely' physical (with which music is for him, as for Brecht, often associated) emerges as a rather primitive response on the very bottom rung of the ladder which leads up through 'aesthetic freedom' to a superior kind of freedom which is associated with man's highest faculty, 'Vernunft' (reason).

Brecht's equivalent to this condescending attitude towards the art-form of music is much less systematically grounded: it is not anchored in such an elaborate network of philosophical or aesthetic concepts. We already noted his tendency to short-circuit his terminology by means of a battery of slogan words like 'Rausch'

---

[52] Ibid. 378.

[53] Thomas Mann, letter to Kurt Martens (16 Oct. 1902), quoted in *Thomas Mann, Wagner und unsere Zeit*, ed. Erika Mann, (Frankfurt-on-Main, 1983), 11.

(cf. Schiller's 'Symptome der Berauschung', symptoms of intoxication), which is used interchangeably with the adjectives 'narkotisch' and 'hypnotisch'. It is interesting to find that the term 'Rausch' has now been stripped of all its Nietzschean–Dionysian associations of vitalism and plenitude of being; all that remains is the transient appeasement and satisfaction afforded by a drug. Like Schiller, Brecht stops to examine in detail the external physiological effects produced by such a craving, describing the responses of an audience in the concert-hall thus:

Ein einziger Blick auf die Zuhörer der Konzerte zeigt, wie unmöglich es ist, eine Musik, die solche Wirkungen hervorbringt, für politische und philosophische Zwecke zu verwenden [*this follows Schiller's point about the impossibility of making transitions between music and action*]—Wir sehen ganze Reihen in einen eigentümlichen Rauschzustand versetzter, völlig passiver, in sich versunkener, allem Anschein nach schwer vergifteter Menschen. Der stiere, glotzende Blick zeigt, daß diese Leute ihren unkontrollierten Gefühlsbewegungen willenlos und hilflos preisgegeben sind. Schweißausbrüche beweisen ihre Erschöpfung durch solche Exzesse (a single glance at the concert audience shows how impossible it is to use music that produces such effects for political and philosophical purposes— we see entire rows of people transported into an extraordinary state of intoxication, completely passive, self-absorbed, and, according to all appearances, doped. The gapes and stares signal that these people are irresolutely, helplessly, at the mercy of uncontrolled emotional urges. Sweating attacks indicate how exhausted they are by such excesses).[54]

Schiller regards such physical dependency as an obstacle towards freedom and the attainment of a harmony of being; Brecht talks of freedom too, but vaguely, and is more concerned to abolish what he regards as an obstacle to political and social enlightenment. The dependence which he believes he has identified spills over into the social and political mores of musical audiences. Lulling, hypnotic effects are, he believes, aided and abetted by naturalistic forms (Schiller, too, was declaring war on 'Naturalism') and styles of acting in which the actor identifies with his role (the Stanislavski method). That is another important reason why Brecht pays close attention to disjunctive techniques within his scheme for 'Trennung der Elemente': contrastive, interrupting, commenting devices and all the trappings associated with the so-called 'alienation effect' (Verfremdungseffekt) will prevent an audience settling for any

[54] Brecht, *GW*, xv. 480.

length of time into one particular mode of response. There is possibly a confusion of ends and means here, as well as a lack of evidence to confirm that the techniques employed to create 'Trennung' achieve anything like the effects intended. I would suggest that this may be because Brecht places so much emphasis on physiological and behavioural aspects of human response and so little on psychological aspects.

In the light of all this, then, Brecht's view in his 'high-didactic' period that music was the art-form which could make a major contribution to his new theatre and act as an antidote to narcotics looks very much like a bold attempt to fight the battle from within the enemy camp, so to speak. He does not, however, appear to embrace Schiller's principle of 'energische Schönheit' very thoroughly or successfully in his musical collaborations. One or two of the songs from the Weill contributions could perhaps be described thus, but again other examples such as the 'Alabama Song' (and various other parodies) seem, if anything, to correspond more to Schiller's category of 'schmelzende Schönheit'—at least if we, like many others, fail to identify the elusive 'Gestus'. As we trace the enthusiastic way in which audiences of the late 1920s greeted the 'culinary' offerings dished up in the *Dreigroschenoper* and *Mahagonny* we are left with the impression that Theodor Adorno[55] may have been one of the very few persons in the audience of those days who was disposed to react along the lines that Brecht wished and that Brecht was deluding himself when, looking back from the year 1937 at these operas, he felt able to make the claim: 'Und die Musik hatte die Aufgabe, das Publikum vor Trance zu bewahren. Sie übernahm nicht die Steigerung vorhandener oder angebannter Wirkungen, sondern brach solche Wirkungen ab oder manipulierte sie' (and music had the task of preventing the audience from sinking into a trance. It did not attempt to intensify effects already in existence or cast like spells upon it, but interrupted such effects or manipulated them).[56]

As is well documented and as I have already indicated, Brecht's hard-line position on emotional response to theatrical presentations started to show cracks, and already by the late 1930s was yielding some ground in the theoretical works. For the first time Brecht

---

[55] Theodor Adorno, 'Mahagonny', *Der Scheinwerfer*, iii (Essen, 1930), 12–15.
[56] Brecht, *GW* xv. 491 (redated to 1942, see Lucchesi and Shull, *Musik bei Brecht*, 204).

conceded that such effects are not to be completely expunged from his 'epic' theatre: 'Es ist ein oft auftauchender Irrtum, wenn behauptet wird, diese Art der—epischen—Darbietung verzichte schlechthin auf emotionelle Wirkung: Tatsächlich sind ihre Emotionen nur geklärt, vermeiden als Quelle das Unterbewußtsein und haben nichts mit Rausch zu tun' (it is a mistake which is often made to assert that this kind of epic entertainment can dispense completely with emotional effects. Actually the emotions are merely purified, avoid using the subconcious as their mainspring, and have nothing to do with intoxication).[57] This is especially interesting for the attempt to bring more precision into the cloudy area of 'emotional response'; in particular, the term 'klären', suggesting a purification and transformation of baser responses, is crucial. But it leaves much to be explained: for how can emotions be detached from their moorings in the subconscious ('Unterbewußstein') and what is the precise form of 'purification' to which they are subjected? One is, of course, put in mind of various Aristotelian-inspired eighteenth-century theories of 'Läuterung' (purification), notably those of Lessing and Schiller, who were both specifically concerned to anatomize the effect upon the emotions of tragic catharsis. It is interesting to compare Schiller's view of a direct emotional appeal which is subsequently 'processed' or 'refined' with Brecht's notion of 'klären'. For Schiller tragedy is concerned to arouse 'Leiden' but it is in the process of resistance to that suffering that truly aesthetic effects can be achieved. Unfortunately Brecht, with his characteristically laconic presentation of ideas, does not enlarge on the question of 'Klärung der Emotionen'.

Brecht and Wagner: The Role of Music as Commentary

Brecht's firm belief in music as a central pivot in the edifice of his 'epic' theatre could, perhaps, be seen as working against the natural grain of this particular art-form (and possibly, though this is more difficult to prove, against the natural grain of his own personality as well). However, it is clear that its central position in the theoretical frame is somewhat undermined in the later theory and

---

[57] Brecht, *GW* xv. 479.

especially in the 'Kleines Organon für das Theater', where other aspects of theatrical concern, hitherto somewhat neglected—like, for instance, choice of content—become more prominent. Was Brecht perhaps less keen on producing explicit, disjunctive effects? Or had he lost confidence in music as the central plank in his theory of 'Trennung der Elemente'? Had the need to polemicize against the evils of the 'Gesamtkunstwerk' become less overriding? These are matters about which we shall be in a better position to decide once we have made a detailed analysis of a number of Brecht's key dramas. But as far as Brecht's relationship with Wagner is concerned—I have stressed repeatedly that we cannot talk meaningfully of a 'reception' since apart from a few isolated references from his early Augsburg and Munich days to performances in which his first wife, the opera singer Marianne Zoff, took part, and a few parodistic 'tags' in the early dramas (such as the 'Ride of the Valkyries' scene in *Trommeln in der Nacht*), there is little evidence that Wagner impinged on Brecht's consciousness in anything but a vague and general way, and largely at second hand[58]—we are dealing once more with an example of Brecht's complete lack of insight into the historical determinants of his own thought processes and creative processes. This fact explains some of the more curious instances where Brecht claimed complete originality in areas where his ideas were as old as the hills.

Caught up in the tide of hostility towards all large-scale forms and all apparently pretentious artistry (Nietzsche's quip that Wagner's work was a 'polyp' was much quoted in the 1920s), Brecht was making common cause, as we can now clearly see, with the French composers known as 'Les Six' (e.g. Milhaud). These artists led the way in creating mixed and multidisciplinary forms, separated from each other in the distinctive, disjunctive manner outlined in Brecht's theory of 'Trennung der Elemente'. Jean Cocteau, another member of the group, had declared the sunken Bayreuth orchestral pit to be the trick of a 'hypnotist'. It is often said that Kurt Weill, Brecht's principal collaborator, fuelled the flames of Brecht's opposition to Wagner, but there may be some exaggeration in this since various essays written by Weill during the

[58] Marianne Kesting is surely overstating the case when she talks of Brecht's having taken over 'indirectly, the main techniques of Wagner's stage reforms' (auf indirekten Wegen die Hauptmodi der Wagnerischen Bühnenreform), 'Wagner/ Meyerhold/Brecht', 121.

1920s, for instance on the occasion of the first radio transmission ever of the *Ring* cycle, reflect a respectful, extremely informed, and incisive attitude towards the work, while on another occasion Weill's admiration and affection for *Die Meistersinger von Nürnberg* is freely and unequivocally expressed.[59]

While we bear in mind these mysterious workings of the *Zeitgeist* on Brecht and his contemporaries in the 1920s there are three points to note. First, there was a reaction abroad to the image of the 'decadent' Wagner, which had been so hysterically overworked during the period of the *fin de siècle*.[60] It is a view where 'Entartung' (degeneration) and 'Neuropathie' predominate, where eroticism and perversion luxuriate and on which Thomas Mann, in particular, drew so freely and so successfully in his artist-portraits (cf. Hanno Buddenbrook, Detlev Spinell, Gabriele Klöterjahn, etc.) Secondly, and not entirely separate from this phenomenon, was the Wagner cult; this manifested itself in a style of operatic production— and a reverential attitude—which was pretentious and easily lampooned. Brecht's own expressed reaction to the appearance of the singers at a Munich production of *Das Rheingold* in 1922[61] makes the point, albeit tastelessly. George Bernard Shaw, one of the most informed of early Wagner connoisseurs and Bayreuth habitués, conveyed the symptoms of the cult with a deadly irony.[62] An awareness of this 'cult' factor, together with a determination to keep Wagner the composer and Wagner the cult figure entirely separate in the mind is one advantage of our own historically distanced standpoint, and is absolutely essential for our under-

---

[59] Kurt Weill, *Ausgewählte Schriften*, 157–60. See also David Drew's observation that Weill's attitude towards Wagner was 'not at all negative like that of most of his young—and not so young—contemporaries' (keineswegs so ablehnend wie jene der meisten seiner jungen (und weniger jungen) Zeitgenossen), ibid. 14.

[60] E. Koppen, *Dekadenter Wagnerismus: Studien zur europäischen Literatur des Fin de siècle* (Berlin and New York, 1973).

[61] 'Ich mache *Das Rheingold* durch; ... Das Orchester leidet an Knochen-weichung, hier hat alles Plattfüße. Die Göttchen deklamieren zwischen sorgfältig ausgeführten Kopien von Versteinerungen der Juraformation, und die Dämpfe aus der Waschküche, in der Wotans schmutzige Herrenwäsche gewaschen wird, machen einem übel . . .' (I'm 'doing' *Rhinegold.* . . . The orchestra is suffering from structural degeneration; everything about it is flat-footed. The godlings declaim from amidst carefully executed copies of fossil formations in the Jura mountains, and the clouds of steam emanating from the laundry where Wotan's dirty male underwear is being washed give me a nasty turn). *Musik bei Brecht*, ed. Lucchesi and Shull, 102–3.

[62] G. B. Shaw, *The Perfect Wagnerite: A Commentary on the Niblung's Ring* (New York, 1967 (repr.)), 127 f.

standing of Brecht's theoretical position. I believe that Walter Hinck may have taken this point when, with reference to Brecht's continued attacks on the 'Gestamtkunstwerk', he points out: 'Diese Wendung gegen das "Gesamtkunstwerk" ist weniger auf Richard Wagners Theaterkonzeption als auf Max Reinhardts Inszenierungs-stil zu beziehen' (this turning against the 'Gesamtkunstwerk' has less to do with Richard Wagner's theatrical conceptions than to Max Reinhardt's style of production).[63] A final point to remember is that the young iconoclastic artists of the 1920s were aggressively establishing their own leaner, more athletic artistic styles in response to the exhilaration and excitement inspired by modern urban living and new technological advances. In such a context Wagner—or rather the Wagner with whom they had all been brought up—was bound to appear traditional and outmoded. Such injustices are, of course, an all too familiar feature of literary and cultural history.

Standing back from the fray, we can see important similarities in the respective positions of Brecht and Wagner. Applying our historical spectacles we realize that Wagner, as much as Brecht, was a revolutionary figure. Quite apart from his political involve-ments—and we should remember that these involved him in imprisonment and exile, penalties for radicalism which Brecht paid only in the second case—Wagner's attitude towards the reform of the opera was every bit as radical in its day as Brecht's towards that of the theatre over seventy years later. Wagner felt a burning desire to tackle the problem of music drama at a fundamental theoretical level and to give a 'state of the art' survey which would take into account all the most important developments in nineteenth-century philosophy and aesthetics. His theoretical insights were illuminated by a grandiose sweep of musical (Beethoven), operatic (Gluck, the French and Italian opera, Mozart), together with theatrical developments since the eighteenth century (but with glimpses far beyond that back to Ancient Greece). This was partly an attempt to clear his own mind about the new genre in which he planned to work before proceeding to the next stage of his development: *Oper und Drama* is partly a voyage of self-discovery and reorientation,

---

[63] *Die Dramaturgie des späten Brecht* (5th edn., Göttingen, 1971), 110. It may be, however, that in (correctly) relating Brecht's reactions to the workings of the *Zeitgeist* Hinck has chosen the wrong example: Brecht, as is well known, was fascinated by Reinhardt and learned much from him as a theatre-director.

these being the necessary prelude to the work on the *Ring*. Brecht likewise, having started out from an intuitive, richly anarchic foray into the medium of drama in a spirit of gay abandon which, at times, is reminiscent of the chaotic versatility of the young Goethe, found himself rigorously stock-taking after his reading of Marx in 1926 and set to with equally broad sweeps to survey past dramatic achievements and present a blueprint for new ones. A feature of both Brecht and Wagner—and it is a by-product of the very boldness of their sweeps—is the cavalier dismissal of many a worthwhile talent which is perceived as being not directly useful as ammunition for their own vision of where drama should be heading. Both Brecht and Wagner found themselves flying in the face of received opinions and orthodoxies and, more importantly, both possessed the talent and the creative drive to proceed to the work of giving their bold visions a tangible expression, producing creative works that reached the highest levels. But as practitioners of their respective art-forms who were also theorists, each laid himself open to literalists who were (and are) ever ready to pounce on any signs of deviation of theory from practice.

On the other side, Brecht's attempts to systematize differ from Wagner's in two radical respects: first, the tight Marxist strait-jacket which Brecht drew protectively around him inhibited severely any process of self-discovery via theoretical principles; secondly, Brecht's avoidance of all literary-historical contextualiza-tion—itself a by-product of his assumption of the classical Marxist framework of the class struggle and projection of a Utopian resolution for all conflicts—makes for a certain narrowness of vision and lack of insight into both the mainsprings of his own dramatic instincts and the extent to which these were participating in developments initiated by others and emanating from funda-mental requirements of the drama form itself. Thus we have the astonishing spectacle of Brecht's over-simplified claims for his new and 'original' 'epic' theatre in the notorious tables to which I have referred. The 'eureka' with which he hails the five cardinal principles of 'epische Oper': 'Vermittlung', 'Auslegung des Texts', 'Voraussetzung des Texts', 'Stellungnahme', and 'das Verhalten-Geben' sounds distinctively hollow when we compare these principles with the very similar functions which Wagner allocates to the orchestra in its deployment of the leitmotiv structure.

Admittedly, we had also taken note of the complexity of

Wagner's position: on the one hand, he seems to have enshrined the principle of perspectival commentary (which is the thread that binds Brecht's five principles together) in the orchestra; on the other, this same orchestra is relegated to the deep Bayreuth pit—a point which Brecht seems to have reacted to by placing *his* musicians under the most intense illumination on the stage. And we have seen, too, the ambiguity underlying the leitmotiv technique itself—the source of so much confusion among those people who have a vested interest in claiming Wagner's music drama as 'epic'. For the leitmotiv operates both *within* (i.e. at the level of structural integration) and *without* (i.e. at the level of contrast and 'disjunction'). According to Wagner's central idea of 'Vergegenwärtigung' it comes into being before our very eyes in its initial statement through the coming together of the melodic line (together with the attendant harmony, rhythm, and other musical textures) and the dramatic impulse (or 'Moment'). Thus it is from that point musically and dramatically fixed and grounded. When later the umbilical cord has been cut, it takes on independent life and may be subjected to an infinite range of metamorphoses and combinations, some musical, some semantic (as, for example, when two or more leitmotivs are combined). The leitmotiv can therefore operate on several planes simultaneously: providing reminders of and contextual associations with its moment of birth while also operating in a more general way, as a chorus or commentator would do, drawing threads together and pointing to the deeper mainsprings of the actions. The seemingly disjunctive status which some believe it thereby acquires must not be exaggerated, though, for such a commenting role as it may assume is seen as part of a process and cannot be divorced either from the leitmotiv's starting-point or from the various accumulated associations that it has acquired *en route*. Even while presented with individual examples of metamorphosed leitmotivs, for instance, we are still aware of the interlocking structure. A good example of this complex process can be found in the Prelude to Act III of *Siegfried* and has been lucidly analysed by Anthony Newcomb.[64] Certainly the mode of operation

---

[64] '*Siegfried*: The Music', ENO and Covent Garden Guides, 22: 'By combining, let us say, the melodic contours and rhythmic shape of one motif with harmonic changes of another, and overlaying the whole with a distinctive short figure extracted from yet another, one creates both a complicated new texture, in purely musical terms, and a psychologically complex musical reference ... Often, by just

is infinitely more complex than the rough slogans and provocative gestures with which Brecht's theoretical statements are peppered. The principle of commentary, however, is a powerful link that binds them.

Indeed, when one compares Wagner's methods of musical commentary with Brecht's 'gestische Musik' and use of musical interpolations or 'songs' as major devices to halt the flow of the action, one might seem to be moving on a different aesthetic plane. Both Brecht's ideas on music and his methods of implementing these ideas seem somewhat crude. This may be because he appears to invest music largely with a negative or purely contrastive function in his overall scheme; this in turn must represent a certain degree of downgrading or at least improverishment in terms of its expressive and technical capabilities—the reactions of both Kurt Weill and Paul Hindemith to such a role for their art is highly instructive. One may doubt the wisdom of tying music exclusively to an 'interruptive' role, since such an aim leaves no scope for much virtuosity. Interestingly, Brecht's notions of such a 'gestic' music do not look all that original either when we consider the popularity among eighteenth-century composers of the 'Singspiel', a kind of simple 'number' opera, in which arias are interspersed with spoken dialogue. Despite these abrupt contrasts and changes of tone the form reached a very high level of sophistication with Mozart (both *Die Entführung aus dem Serail* and *Die Zauberflöte* evolved from it) and the audience becomes accustomed to the constant changes of register, which in any case seem no more stylized than the many extravagant devices that characterize opera in general. The element of surprise, which for Brecht was such an important aim in the disjunctive and 'gestic' presentation of musical 'Trennung' wears off remarkably quickly—once more causing us to query some of the claims Brecht makes in his theory of 'Trennung der Elemente', a principle which, as we have seen, is neither deeply grounded at the theoretical level, nor, with the exception of an approving nod in the direction of Japanese and Chinese theatre, related historically to other long-established techniques.

Brecht and Wagner, then, do not touch explicitly at the theoretical level, but they can be said to have shared important

altering an orchestral colour or rhythmic detail in one motif, Wagner can effect such a combination with another, suggesting connections between psychological worlds that had previously seemed distinctly separate.'

common ground in their recognition of the importance for the drama of perspectival commentary. Brecht's unawareness of the importance of leitmotiv as a commenting device was entirely understandable; his dogmatic insistence on 'Trennung' and misunderstanding of the complexities of the 'Gesamtkunstwerk' blinded him to all such ambiguous and subtle possibilities and, in any case, had he known about it, the leitmotiv would have represented a threat to the battery of comparatively superficial theatrical devices which he found himself calling in to support his theory of 'Gestus' and 'alienation effect'. His cavalier and reductive attitude towards music once more obscured his vision and his relegation of its importance later in his career may reflect disappointment—for there is no evidence of his ever having retracted his overstated views—and explain the development in his dramas of alternative modes of creating perspective about which his theoretical works are silent. The fact that some of these alternatives have a more than superficial resemblance to Wagnerian leitmotivs is a highly intriguing paradox to which our attention must now be turned.

Introductory Note to
Chapters 4–7

It must be emphasized that Chapters 4–7 are not in any way intended to provide a comprehensive interpretation of any one of these works; far less do they represent—as, for example, Wolfgang Clemen's book in Shakespeare's imagery does for its author—an attempt to illustrate Brecht's development over the long period separating *Baal* from *Leben des Galilei*. They are intended to be 'exemplarisch', to provide, that is, illustrations of the many ways in which leitmotiv technique is employed by Brecht. Each text illustrates a different facet: thus the chapter on *Baal* shows how the technique can be used in predominantly lyrical context; that on *Lehrstück* examines how it operates in a work that is unequivocally didactic; that on *Die Heilige Johanna der Schlachthöfe* reveals a high level of virtuosity and something of a balancing act on Brecht's part in the way that 'gestic' parody is counterpointed with integrated motivic perspectives. The chapter on *Leben des Galilei*, finally, reveals the important part played by motivic patterns in pointing towards and concentrating our attention upon the nature of the paradox on which the drama rests, commenting and prefiguring in the strategic way that we may wish to associate with tragedy, identifying sources of impedance, both from within the protagonist and from without, that stand in the way of his altruistic aspirations. It is, of course, no accident that three of the particular works selected happen to be the most richly textured and therefore provide a treasure trove of examples. But the stark evidence offered in *Das Badener Lehrstück vom Einverständnis* acts as an interesting corrective since it might be said to occupy the other end of the spectrum as far as Brecht's use of motivic techniques is concerned. I leave it to others to explore; if they are so minded, the doubtless rich resources provided by such masterpieces as *Mutter Courage*, *Der Kaukasische Kreidekreis*, and *Der gute Mensch von Sezuan*, as well as those other dramas, less celebrated, which occupy positions between these extreme points on the scale.

4
Baal: Leitmotiv and Lyrical Drama

Probably there is no other drama of Brecht's with a more complicated genesis than this, his first substantial work, which was to follow the twists and turns of his prodigiously creative talents at their most impressionable stage. The four versions which have been singled out in the new edition from among the many reworkings of the drama are those of 1919, 1922, 1926, and 1955 (the latter, just to confuse, is based on a version of 1920, now lost); they reflect Brecht's increasing liberation from the drama's starting-point as a partly parodistic 'Kontrafaktur' to Hanns Johst's drama *Der Einsame*, which itself was based on the life of the historical literary figure Christian Grabbe. Though Brecht's natural predilection for parodistic forms often shows up the origins of his creativity to reside in a spirit of negation or rejection of other writers' efforts, it is true to say that the independence and originality of his invention in *Baal* dispels any sense of dissatisfaction or unease one might have about the nature of the process itself. It is obvious from the way he sought to update the work again and again—and there was even a *Lehrstück* version entitled *Der böse Baal der asoziale (Bad Baal the Antisocial One)* written around 1930—that the material had a special importance for him. Can this be because it possessed stronger autobiographical links than was customary?

It might not be surprising to find that his first drama had such personal significance. Baal's metamorphosis from bohemian poet to garage mechanic could well reflect Brecht's own changing perceptions of the poet-writer's role in society from one of staunch individualism and social aloofness to that of someone—now merely designated as '[des] Mannes Baal' (the man Baal)—with a fixed social status and position in a technologically based, working-class milieu. Set in such a world as this, Baal's bohemian escapades now acquire a distinctly ironical perspective. The work which has most in common with *Baal* is probably *Im Dickicht der Städte* (1927), of which the earlier version, entitled simply *Im Dickicht* (1923), brings to light a number of Baal-like impressions of the bohemian poet-artist—though now at an interesting remove, since the main protagonist, George Garga, aspires to such a life-style (which he identifies with the poet Rimbaud) without himself possessing any sign of those creative talents that Baal possesses in such abundance. We shall find some interesting overlap in leitmotivs with *Baal*, particularly in the thematic area of cosmic isolation—what we might term the drama's 'existential' dimension.[1]

Dieter Schmidt's pioneering study and comparison of the different versions of *Baal*,[2] together with his convenient edition[3] of three of these, is of inestimable value; doubtless the publication of further early versions (e.g. 1922) in the new *Grosse kommentierte Ausgabe* will yield more fruit for future Brecht scholarship (Brecht's method of working and reworking his texts creates a field-day for textual scholars and those who are interested in following the creative process). My own comparisons, however, will be strictly limited to the operation of the leimotiv structures within the drama, and for this purpose I shall select—somewhat arbitrarily—the 1922 version as my 'norm', while always bearing in mind the 1955 version (which probably is based chiefly on the 1920 version), since it is the one that is most familiar and easily accessible to all.

There are some factual details relating to the presentation of characters and situation to which it is first necessary to draw attention. First, a human dimension to the main protagonist which in the 1919 version had been provided by Baal's mother—this may have been partly a legacy from the Johst 'Vorlage' (model), since Grabbe's mother had played an important part in that drama—is dropped from all later versions. Likewise Baal's 'bourgeois' occupation as a clerk in an office is dropped, as is the somewhat Kafka-esque scene in which a messenger is sent from the office to his home to give him notice of dismissal. His imprisonment as a result of his failure to honour his financial obligations—which represented another aspect of his contact with society, this time in its punitive role—disappears likewise. The upshot is that Baal

---

[1] There is useful discussion of the 'existential dimension' of the drama in R. Speirs, *Brecht's Early Plays* (London, 1982), 22 f.

[2] Dieter Schmidt, Baal *und der junge Brecht* (Stuttgart, 1966).

[3] Baal: *Drei Fassungen* (1966) and Baal: *Der böse Baal der asoziale* (1968). Both Frankfurt-on-Main.

seems in the later versions almost to float freely and to have little in the way of social or domestic moorings; he is more radically, more unequivocally individualistic. To a certain extent the social status of his friend and companion Ekart grows more blurred as well: in the pre-1922 versions he appears as bohemian artist, a composer of symphonies and string quartets (a curious point, this, given Brecht's own expressed distaste for such forms of 'absolute' music);[4] but also more obviously as a tempter to Baal, appearing more frequently and in the role of *alter ego*, himself a self-styled drop-out who makes a powerful case to the effect that Baal too should cut loose from society and follow Ekart into the primitive world of nature (represented by the leitmotiv 'Wald') and the company of simple working people (the 'Fuhrleute', drivers): 'Geh mit mir, Bruder! Landstrasse, Heuhütte, Bauerndiele, Wald!' (Come with me, brother! Highway, hay-barn, farmer's joint, wood!) (1919, *GKA*, i. 32. 5–6.) The later Baal would seem to need less persuading. In the 1919 version, however, there is a much more highly developed conflict in Baal between these alternatives, and the urgent pleas of his friends—e.g. Johannes—that he should remain within the bounds of society have more force: 'Laß dich nicht verführen! Denk an deine Mutter und an deine Kunst.' (Don't be seduced! Think of your mother and your art.) (32. 15–16.) The latter phrase was missing from the earliest, 1918, version but returns to all subsequent versions. The effect of weakening these various sources of conflict for Baal is simply to heighten his individualism and to emphasize more strongly the lyrical aspects of the drama. Not that these are absent in the earliest versions, of course; on the contrary, the earliest of all (that of 1918) contains a large number of lyric interpolations with which we are familiar from the later collection of poems published under the title of *Hauspostille* (Domestic Breviary.) Whereas we can only talk of three major interpolations of this sort in later versions: 'Der Choral vom großen Baal' (The choral of Baal the Great), 'Vom ertrunkenen Mädchen' (The drowned girl), and 'Der Tod im Walde' (Death in the forest), the earliest version also contained in its complete form 'Die Legende der Dirne Evelyn Roe' (Ballad of Evelyn Roe). This may have been presented as an alternative to 'Vom ertrunkenen Mädchen', which does not make an appearance until the 1922

---

[4] See A. Dümling, *Laßt euch nicht verführen*, 13.

version (it could, however, have already existed in the now lost
1920 version, on which the final 1955 version is based).

Although it is a little difficult when reviewing the pattern across
so many different versions to establish a clear picture of the
changing relationship of the lyrical or balladesque elements, on the
one hand, and those providing some vestiges of dramatic conflict,
on the other, the point must be made that, whichever of the
versions between 1918 and 1922 one is talking about, the lyrical
dimension in *Baal* plays a very large role. When we examine the
poems (or 'Lieder', as Baal himself terms them) which have been
slotted into the text, it is immediately obvious that they perform a
very different function from the 'songs' which were later to become
such a distinctive feature of Brecht's dramas. They are by contrast
in no way introduced as disjunctive interpolations or deliberately
intended to break the flow of the 'action'.

In retrospect Brecht[5] attributed to them a 'naturalistische
Motivierung' (naturalistic motivation) and saw them as different in
kind from his later interpolated songs. This point has been well
taken by Gudrun Tabbert-Jones, who formulates the differences
between 'Lied' and 'Song' in terms of 'Distanz' and 'Zeigen'
pointing out[6] that in the former, 'der Gestus des Zeigens und
Vermittelns [ist] noch nicht besonders auffällig gemacht' (the
'Gestus' of pointing and interpreting is not yet presented in a
particularly striking manner). Interpolated 'Lieder' can make
general points about the human condition, to this extent creating a
measure of 'Distanz'. But if such interpolations are more obviously
integrated into their surroundings as the term 'naturalistic motivation' suggests, what, precisely, are these 'surroundings' in a work
like *Baal*? Here we have one of the loosest 'actions' of any Brecht
play (and if one must use such categories as Klotz's overworked
'open' and 'closed' forms, this would be the only drama of Brecht's
which, I believe, would conform in any meaningful way to the
category 'open'). We are dealing with Brecht's nearest approxima-
tion to the Strindbergian Ich-Drama, where a central character
provides the main—even sometimes the only—focus; where everything radiates from that source and where, correspondingly, other
characters and actions of any kind are strictly subordinated to this

---

[5] 'Über die Verwendung von Musik für ein episches Theater', *GW* xv. 472.

[6] Gudrun Tabbert-Jones, *Die Funktion der liedhaften Einlage in den frühen
Stücken Brechts* (Frankfurt-on-Main, 1984), 15.

end. And yet—and here the relevance of *Baal* for our main theme becomes clearer—this is a drama in which leitmotivic patterning exists on a scale which is quite remarkable. In the entire history of Brecht's dramas we only occasionally see its like again. How can this be reconciled with Wagner's demand that leitmotivs are basically dramatic in origin, that they are formed by the pressure or concentration of events or situations ('Momente')? These leitmotivs in *Baal* will not—indeed cannot—perform the function of perspectival commentary which was so central to Wagner's conceptions. In a work of such predominantly subjective colouring, where no action to speak of is 'presented' on stage, there can be nothing on which to comment. The motivs, instead, are at one and the same time action *and* commentary, they are an expression of the various facets of Baal's 'Weltgefuhl', which is basically static; they provide a mosaic picture, which is for ever being elaborated and enlarged, of this, in itself consistent and hermetic view of the world. They might also be said—and here one is put in mind once more of Klotz's theories (otherwise so misleading!) of the prevalence for motivic structures—to be employed as a kind of appliqué in order to hold together an otherwise chaotic, or disintegrating 'open' form.[7] A possible exception to this propostion might be the function which the 'Der Choral vom großen Baal' assumes as a kind of prologue. We shall deal with this matter at a later stage.

It may be helpful at this point to give a very broad survey of what I shall term the *Grundmotiv* patterning in *Baal*, while always bearing in mind the point just made about the necessary distinction between Wagner's postulate of a dramatic origin for this type of network and Klotz's suggestion that it is exclusively associated with looser structures, where it can impose a degree of coherence when this is otherwise lacking. Unfortunately, as we know,[8] Klotz sees this as the one and only function of leitmotivic structuring. For the time being *Grundmotive* will be understood as the broad, basic patterns, or groupings of motivic material which acquire precise associations through repetition and which themselves may contain smaller, subsidiary *Nebenmotive*. The first and by far the most

---

[7] Klotz, *Geschlossene und offene Form*, 106. On the structural use of motiv: diese Bilder und Motive [befreien sich] aus der Sphäre des Metaphorischen . . . Die ersprengte Handlung schließt sich auf einer anderen Ebene wieder zusammen' these images and motivs are removed from the sphere of the metaphorical . . . The shattered action is closed up again at another level).

[8] See Ch. 1, p. 19.

important of all these *Grundmotive* is the 'Himmel' (sky) group, which is clearly adumbrated as early as the Prologue, 'Der Choral vom großen Baal'. This group is extremely complex since, first, it has an antithetical strand which is subsumed under the motiv 'Erde' (earth, ground); and secondly, it possesses various colour associations (the influence of the French Symbolists, especially Verlaine and Rimbaud, but also that of the German Expressionists, is relevant here): 'violett', 'schwarz', 'gelb', 'blau' are some of the more frequently invoked colours. Thirdly, an important subsidiary component of 'Himmel' is the cloud, which is invariably white. Within this entire motivic configuration of 'Himmel' and 'Erde' the relationship between the two elements takes on, almost invariably, erotic overtones. The spatial relationship of 'oben' and 'unten' is frequently expressed in sexual terms: SOPHIE: 'und der Himmel ist über einem' (and the sky is above me) (1919 version, 'Nacht', 48. 23–4); BAAL: 'Wenn ich mich auf den Rücken legen, krümmt es sich hohl, so stark merke ich, dass die Erde eine Kugel ist und von mir bedeckt wird' (when I lie on my back, it assumes a rounded shape as if I were a hollow. I'm very much aware that the Earth is a sphere and is covered by me) (1919, 'Landstrasse, Sonne, Felder', 63. 17–20). The colour white—usually identified with the cloud motiv—represents, among other things, sexual innocence and desirability and as such presents a contant attraction and challenge to Baal's lusts (his ambiguous desire simultaneously to preserve and to destroy this innocence is a facet of his personality which is interestingly brought to light by the leitmotivs). Finally, further aspects of the 'Himmel' motiv are represented by the 'Geier' (vultures): its denizens are birds of prey which hover on high but are ready to swoop down in an instant to devour and physically destroy their victims. They represent possibly the only threat to Baal himself, the threat, that is, of physical destruction to which his human mortality renders him vulnerable. This sets up a slight element of ambiguity, since Baal appears in other respects to defy death, decomposition, and decay. It is simply a Darwinian survival instinct, then, which makes him take over the attributes of the vultures himself? In the 'Der Choral vom großen Baal' we find this leitmotiv presented programatically: 'Zu den feisten Geiern blinzelt Baal hinauf, | Die im Sternenhimmel warten auf den Leichnam Baal' (21. 1–2) (Baal looks up at the fat vultures in the sky, waiting among the stars for his corpse). We shall see presently how Brecht succeeds in combining the 'Geier' motiv with the motiv of 'Zähne' (teeth) which is identified with Baal's own animalistic and aggressive response to life.

To all these related leitmotivs—as well as to the secondary, non-erotic, existential significance of 'Erde' and 'Himmel', as suggested by the subsidiary motivs 'Planete' and 'Stern', we shall presently return. But first let us take stock of another two groups of primary motivs which, while not so pervasive as the first, nevertheless acquire a prominent status within the work's total organization: the 'Baum' (tree) group, for example, has this function. Especially important is the openness of the tree to elemental forces, such as wind and storm (we are obviously in the same world as the *Hauspostille* poems such as 'Vom Klettern in Bäumen', On climbing in trees). Erotic associations are foremost here too; the extensive root system of the 'Machandelbaum' (juniper tree), famous in folklore, as one recalls from the Grimms' Märchen,[9] is used to express in graphic terms this intimate relationship: 'Wie der Machandelbaum viele Wurzeln hat, verschlungene, so habt ihr viele Glieder . . .' (just as the juniper tree has many roots that intertwine, so you are many-limbed) (1922 version, 90. 17–19). Branches ('Äste') are seen to perform similarly amorous embraces ('um-klammern', 89. 36–8), while the wind represents the dominant force in such encounters: 'Und die Liebe ist . . . wie die Qual, vor der trunkene Baum knarzend zu singen anhebt, auf dem der wilde Wind reitet' (and love is . . . like the torment that causes the drunken tree to start its creaking song, as it is ridden by the wild wind). (91.3; 5–6). In addition, the motiv of 'schaukeln' (to sway) is used, once more as in the *Hauspostille* poems to convey the prolonged ecstasy of physical contact between the two forces.

If the 'Baum' group of motivs has a clearly vertical bias and in this respect closely follows the 'Himmel'–'Erde' configuration, another group—once again familiar to us from the *Hauspostille* poems—operates within horizontal parameters: this is the imagery associated with 'Wasser' (water), and in particular the surrender of self to the elemental forces of tide and current; 'swimming' might suggest a greater degree of control than this, but Brecht directs us away from such associations by often emphasizing the surrender of non-human (e.g. botanical) matter to the pull of tide, or else he

---

[9] Jakob and Wilhelm Grimm, *Kinder- und Hausmärchen*, 'Vom dem Machandel-boom'.

downgrades the human subject who is being 'carried' by the water to an inanimate corpse (the 'Ophelia' motiv) or a lower form of organism (e.g. a fish). We shall presently see how Brecht literalizes or concretizes this motivic imagery in *Baal* by making suicide by drowning not only a talking point among the young women characters (e.g. Sophie) who have been seduced by Baal and who fear the implications of pregnancy, but also by making it actually happen in the case of Johanna. Related to this motivic pattern of drifting downstream is Baal's vision of pregnant women as featureless polyps or sponges ('Schwämme', 90. 30) 'mit feucht klammernden Armen wie schleimige Polypen' (their arms damp and clasping, like slimy polyps) (90. 32–3). This network culminates —and I believe there is some sense of a progression here, however slight—in the very beautiful 'Ophelia' poem: 'Als sie ertrunken war und hinunterschwamm . . .' (when she was drowned and was swimming down river), a kind of transfiguration in poetic terms of many of the drama's otherwise shocking and repellent themes. Notice that the motiv of 'Tang' (weeds)—the tangled vegetation that drifts in rivers—is often associated with the higher 'poetic' register and contains an overlay of 'Jugendstil' decadence: 'Und die Liebe ist, wie wenn man seinen nackten Arm in Teichwasser schwimmen läßt, mit Tang zwischen den Fingern' (love is like when you let your bare arm swim in stagnant water with weeds between your fingers). (91. 3–5).

This survey of the main leitmotivs is presented simply as a rough guide for orientation and makes no claims for completeness. In particular, many subsidiary motivs have not been identified or presented. It is now necessary to give some attention to the relationship of the various leitmotiv patterns both to one another (i.e. as part of a cross-referential system) and to the development of the drama, which, as I have already stressed above, does not conform to 'normal' dramatic expectations. It would seem that the drama's momentum is produced from the interpolation of poems round which a very loose 'action' is draped, together with the interrelationship of the leitmotivic patterns themselves. If this impression is correct, then that is a unique feature of this work which is worth exploring in more detail.

I have already suggested that the 'Der Choral vom großen Baal' has a very special structural significance. Comparing the different versions, one notes a slight shortening over the years (the original

18 stanzas of the 1918 version are reduced to 14 in most of the subsequent versions, the only exception being the spartan and terse 'Lebenslauf des Mannes Baal' (1926) which manages to reduce them to 7). Of the leitmotivs already identified in this 'prologue' all major strands of the 'Himmel'–'Erde' complex are presented and, like the themes in a musical overture, they are presented in contrastive terms. Already as early as the 1919 version the erotic implications of this particular leitmotiv are made explicit:

> Was ist Welt für Baal noch?
> Baal ist satt.
> Soviel Himmel hat Baal unterm Lid
> Dass er tot noch grad gnug Himmel hat.

(What does the world hold for Baal? Baal is sated. He has so much sky beneath his eyelids that even when he's dead he'll have enough).

(21. 12–13).

While it is true that such a presentation must at this point in the work remain at the symbolic rather than the literal level, there is no gainsaying its usefulness as a programmatic and structural device. But one notices too that later in the work there is a tendency to concretize and integrate the imagery. This is chiefly done by linking the patterns repeatedly to the stage-directions. Much of the 'action' takes place out of doors (there is a Shakespearian ring to this—or is it Shakespeare out of Büchner?) and when it does not, the contrast with indoor settings is significant. Thus: 'Landstraße, Sonne, Felder' (highway, sun, fields), 1919; 'Landstraße am Getreidefeld' (highway by a cornfield), 1919; 'Bäume am Abend' (trees at evening), 1919 and 1922; 'Ebene, Himmel, Abend' (plain, sky, evening, 1919 and 1922; 'Hölzerne braune Diele, Nacht, Wind' (brown wooden bar, night, wind, 1919 and 1922; 'Braune Landschaft, Regen' (brown landscape, rain, 1919; 'Ahorn im Wind' (maple in wind), 1919 and 1922; 'Landstraße, Abend, Wind, Regenschauer' (highway, evening, wind, shower of rain), 1919 and 1922; 'Wald, Eine Bretterhütte' (wood, a wooden hut), 1919 and 1922; 'Grünes Laubdickicht, Fluß dahinter' (green thicket with river behind), 1919, 1922. These are remarkable directions, and almost Expressionist in their insistent concentration on the essentials of natural scenery; but far from being abstract, they are saturated with dense concentrations of meaning because of their direct relationship with the textually situated leitmotivs. Possibly they are even starker in the 1922 version where, for example, Brecht can achieve added intensity by juxtaposing two tree-scenes: 'Gekalkte Häuser mit braunen Baumstämmen' (white-washed houses with brown tree trunks) and 'Mainacht unter Bäumen' (May night under trees). This version also contains new tree-scenes featuring a variety of species, e.g. 'Grüne Felder, blaue Pflaumenbäume' (green fields, blue plum trees) and 'Junge Hasel-sträuche' (young hazel bushes). It is interesting that the scene between Sophie and Baal which in the 1919 version had been placed indoors ('Kammer') is relocated in 1922 to the open air ('Mainacht unter Bäumen'). The strong flavour of the outdoors is an unmistakable feature of the 1922 version and the effect is to ground the leitmotivs even more firmly in their surroundings and to make them take on more and more the appearance of an imaginative substitute for a conventional dramatic action.

Turning again now to examine in greater detail the 'Himmel' configuration of leitmotivs we notice that this is almost invariably mentioned within the dialogue in conjunction with Baal's various erotic entanglements, e.g. Baal to Emilie, 'Branntweinschenke' (brandy bar), 1922; Baal to Johannes and Johanna later in the same scene; Baal to Sophie, 'Baals Dachkammer' (attic room), 1922; Baal to Sophie, 'Mainacht unter Bäumen', 1922. These are only a few examples; scarcely a scene goes by without our being made aware of this imagery. More intermittent are its component strands e.g. 'Geier' (vultures) and 'weiße Wolken' (white clouds). We would scarcely expect to find them concretized; they are more in the way of elaborations or offshoots from the main line, which itself has been firmly established. They become—especially the 'weiße Wolke' (itself so reminiscent of the ballad 'Erinnerung an Marie A', Recollection of Marie A.)—a short-hand device, in this case for Baal's sexual fantasies, which repays further close analysis. As in the poem, the meaning of the 'weiße Wolke' is deepened by its association with a lack of individual identity: the 'ich' of the poem cannot remember the precise features of his partner, but he *does* recall instead the cloud which is passing overhead. Since clouds are constantly changing shape and lack all fixed contours, it is tempting to believe that it is just this lack of clear definition which attracts the ever-inconstant, infinitely exploitative male who has no wish to be tethered or forced into any permanent alliance. The scene between Baal and his friend, the sexually inhibited Johannes, brings out very clearly this problematical aspect of Baal's sexuality. Baal titillates Johannes, altering the remote and more poetic 'weiße Wolke' to the more basic 'weiße Wäsche'. But Baal has to concede that even this appealing prospect fades and degenerates when the conquest has been made and the full consequences—in the form of pregnancy—turn what once was a romantic male fantasy into a revolting reality (note the idea of physical deformation which is suggested by the term 'schleimige Polypen'). There is an adolescent fascination here with the causality behind the natural process—a naïve incredulity, almost, that one thing can lead to another, together with a rejection of these consequences which is, para-doxically, almost puritanical: 'Aber die Liebe ist auch wie eine Kokonuß, die gut ist, solange sie frisch ist, und die man ausspeien muß, wenn der Saft ausgequetscht ist und das Fleisch überbleibt, welches bitter schmeckt' (love is like a coconut. As long as it's fresh it's fine. When the juice has been squeezed out and the bitter-tasting flesh remains, it must be spat out) (29. 18–21).

This element of physical revulsion in the face of biological processes is a not entirely consistent feature of the thinking of Baal and the young Brecht. As I have stated earlier, it cannot easily be reconciled with his apparent acceptance of the processes of putrefaction and decay as they are presented in 'Vom ertrunkenen Mädchen'. Does something of the 'Ekel', or nausea, so often exprssed by Nietzsche's Zarathustra[10] when contemplating the existential position of man, attach to Brecht's thinking as well? I believe the identification of such an existential dimension in Brecht's first drama is a feature which is not always given as much weight as it deserves in the secondary literature; a fuller awareness of the leitmotiv structure must therefore form an essential ingredient in any interpretation that claims completeness. The combination of different motivs, such as the 'Geier' and human Zähne', which is part of this wider 'Himmel' pattern, presents further complexities for the interpreter. The birds of prey, which possibly symbolize man's vulnerability and mortality, are the only creatures which cause Baal fear: doubtless because they represent a threat to his own physical well-being. Baal's response is an

[10] Nietzsche, *Zarathustra*, ed. P. Pütz (8th edn., Munich, 1989), Zarathustra's response to his 'Überdruß am Menschen' is 'Ekel! Ekel! Ekel!', p. 179. Brecht's knowledge of Nietzsche is beyond dispute.

interesting one which reflects the combative rather than the passive
spirit exhibited elsehwere in *Baal* (e.g. in the wind and water
leitmotiv); it is the spirit which one associates with a healthy animal
which is caught up in the struggle for survival: 'Man muß Zähne
haben, dann ist die Liebe, wie wenn man eine Orange zerfleischt,
daß der Saft einem in die Zähne schießt' (you have to have teeth
and then love is like devouring an orange so that the juice squirts
into the teeth). (90. 37–9). This ruthless and sadistic streak in Baal
has been noted by several commentators;[11] it must be viewed,
however, within the context of an existential indifference on the
part of Nature to man and of man's need to adopt strategies of
cunning and even violence in the struggle for survival. This
complete amoralism is sharply nuanced by means of the leitmotiv
patterns.

It is evident that by following these patterns we are taken straight
to the heart of the drama's meaning. Given the degree to which
subconscious preoccupations predominate in *Baal* and the absence
of inhibition with which themes such as male sexuality are
expressed, one is scarcely surprised to find this. However, the point
of major interest is that all these effusions are more or less
uncensored by their author. In other words, an analysis of the
'Himmel'–'Erde' pattern—together with the 'weiße Wolke'—does
not bring to light any hierarchical perspectival organization,
according to the principles of leitmotivic commentary expounded,
for example, by Wagner. Again this is an indication that a tailoring
of the leimotivs to meet dramatic—or other—needs simply does not
take place; this will emerge as the most distinctive feature of their
treatment in *Baal*. But we must pursue the point with a further
analysis of 'Himmel'–'Erde' patterns, this time veiewed with their
other contextual associations in mind, that is with the existential
problem at the fore instead of with the more obvious and
provocative erotic associations that characterize this particular
pattern. Interestingly, it is the 'Erde' angle of the antithesis which is
uppermost here; its counterpart is, furthermore, less strictly
'Himmel' and more the entire cosmos along with the other planets
in the solar system. This complex is announced in the earliest extant
version (1918), in which the 'Choral vom großen Baal' appears as
an end-piece rather than as a Prologue; it reappears in the 1919

[11] Ronald Gray, *Brecht the Dramatist* (Cambridge, 1976), 28 f.

version, but the relevant stanza is dropped from what, as we have seen, has now virtually become a Prologue:

> Torkelt über den Planeten Baal
> Bleibt ein Tier vom Himmel überdacht
> Blauem Himmel

(Baal lurches over the Planet and is covered like an animal by the sky, all blue)

(19. 26–7).

The extension of spatial imagery to include the entire planetary system is significant, although the full meaning is not yet made explicit. It becomes so, however, in the important scene, already meantioned, between Baal and Johannes (Baals Dachkammer), where Baal comments on the relative insignificance of the planet Earth when it is viewed in relation to the entire solar system 'Wenn man nachts im Gras liegt, ausgebreitet, merkt man mit den Knochen, daß die Erde eine Kugel ist und daß wir fliegen und daß es auf dem Stern Tiere gibt, die seine Pflanzen auffressen. Es ist einer von den kleineren Sternen' (when you lie stretched out, at night, on the grass, you're aware in your bones that the Earth is a sphere and that we're flying and that there are animals on the planet that devour its plants. It is one of the lesser planets) (89. 26–30). A picture of biological interdependency throughout the length and breadth of the cosmos emphasizes in turn the relative unimportance of the 'Erde' (and by implication, human life) and could be seen as offering some explanation for Baal's exaggerated and possibly rather self-conscious 'Diesseitigkeit' (this-worldliness). Commentators on Brecht's poetry of this period are reluctant to use the term 'metaphysical' but there are times when one is tempted to do so here, so long as it is recognized that there is no transcendence, just vestiges of an existential *Angst*.

The anticipation of the cosmic imagery in *Leben des Galilei* is not the least remarkable feature of this group of leitmotivs in *Baal*. But the motiv of earthly insignificance will find another interesting application in Brecht's drama *Im Dickicht der Städte*, where it is combined with a new theme, namely the insigificance and inadequacy of all verbal means of communication. There the hero, George Garga, relativizes all knowledge in the following terms: 'Was für Dummheiten! Worte auf einem Planeten, die nicht in der Mitte ist.' (What rubbish! Words on a planet that's not at the centre.) (*GKA*. i. 594. 3–4.) In *Baal* different consequences are drawn from

this basically identical awareness of the Earth's relative insignificance: namely Baal's cult of impersonality in all his relationships. It
is as if this is a logical consequence of man's dethronement in the
cosmic scheme of things (again this links up with the idea of
survival of the fittest and the downgrading of man to the animal
level). Baal goes so far in his cult of impersonality that he makes a
direct statement, unembellished with imagery this time, which is
unusual: 'Ich bin ein Liebhaber ohne Geliebte' (I'm a lover with
nobody to love) (1922, Baals Dachkammer, 3: 101. 33–4). And in
the poetically 'transfigured' context of the 'Ophelia' poem transformation *and* depersonalization of the drowned girl—who in life
might have been identified with Baal's victim, Johanna—go hand in
hand. Gradually the decomposing body loses any vestiges of human
individuality and becomes indistinguishable from the plant and
animal life surrounding it:

> Tang und Algen hielten sich an ihr ein
> So daß sie langsam viel schwerer ward
> Kühl die Fische schwammen an ihrem Bein.
> Pflanzen und Tiere beschwerten noch ihre letzte Fahrt

(water weeds and algae clung to her body, so that she slowly became much
heavier. Coolly fishes swam around her legs. Animal and plant life
obstructed her final journey)

(126. 15–19).

An interesting and complex perspective is opened up by the
following lines:

> Als ihr bleicher Leib im Wasser verfaulet war
> Geschah es, sehr langsam, daß Gott sie allmählich vergaß:
> Erst ihr Gesicht, dann die Hände und ganz zuletzt erst ihr Haar

(as her pale body decayed in the water, it happened (very slowly) that God
gradually forgot her. First her face, then her hands and last of all her hair)

(126. 25–7).

References to the negligence of the Almighty abound in the
Hauspostille poems and have been mostly construed to be ironical.
However this may be, the fact that Brecht again and again links
human and earthly insignificance and cosmic isolation to such a
theological scapegoat is interesting. Ekart, too, uses this perceived
absenteeism as an explanation for his particular form of response—
an opting out of all social ties and a Rousseauistic escape into the
primitive world of nature (for which the 'Wald' stands as a *chiffre*).

This radical way of dealing with such monumental indifference—the 'giving like for like' approach, which is comparable to Baal's game with the 'Geier'—is urged by Ekart on his friend: 'Und zu den Wäldern, wo das erzene Schallen oben ist und man das Licht des Himmels vergißt: Gott hat einen vergessen' (let's to the woods, where the echo of metal is above one and one forgets the sky's light: God has forgotten us) (1922: 94. 35–6; 1955). Both Baal and Ekart connect God's 'forgetfulness' with acceptance and affirmation of man's physicality, and his animal qualities. It is almost as if the characters were trying to prove something to the deity thereby!

It would be wrong to treat this leitmotiv complex relating to 'Erde' as if it were wholly divorced from the erotic. Indeed the two spheres cannot in the end be kept apart, as the intricate interweaving of the motivic groups indicates. The frenetic need for constant physical gratification—without any kind of social commitment—is itself closely interwoven with the theme of cosmic isolation and human insigificance; indeed it is the overwhelming recognition of the latter which determines the other. It is as if the sexual act becomes a means of drowning out a truth which, however philosophically Brecht and his characters may pretend to accept it, drives them on obsessively to achieve their insignificant alternative. Baal himself does not voice such opinions, however; his degree of self-knowledge is not large and his responses are instinctual rather than analytical. Sophie Dechant, on the other hand, does perceive things thus, though the realization does not cause her anguish, but rather pleasure 'Es ist gut, so zu liegen, wie eine Beute und der Himmel ist über einem und man ist nie allein' (it's good to lie as if one were a piece of prey and the sky is above one and one is never alone) (106. 18–19). This draws the existential and the erotic threads tightly together. Perhaps it is no accident that this scene ('Mainacht unter Bäumen', May night beneath trees) is juxtaposed with another: 'Gekalkte Häuser mit braunen Baumstämmen' (whitewashed houses and brown tree trunks), which shows a beggar putting forward the Christian message to Baal during a Corpus Christi procession. It is almost as if Sophie's statement is a bold, uninhibited answer to the beggar's drunken reminder of an orthodox Christianity. Sophie's remark also has its counterpart is another quotation from *Im Dickicht der Stadte*, one which this time is not presented in leitmotiv form but in the form of direct statement (we have to recall that the early version of this drama, *Im*

Dickicht, was written before 1923 and its genesis therefore overlaps with later versions of *Baal*). Almost at the eleventh hour of the play, which presents a conflict between the two protagonists Garga and Shlink that has been explicitly described as motiveless by Brecht, Shlink surprisingly reveals all, informing Garga, as the lynch mob closes in on him, that his pursuit of his adversary—and one observes the aggressive, sadistic motiv again in this very conflict—was really an attempt to overcome his existential *Angst* through physical contact: 'Ich habe die Tiere betrachtet. Die Liebe, Wärme aus Korpernähe, ist unsere einzige Gnade in der Finsternis! Aber die Vereinigung der Organe ist die einzige, sie überbrückt nicht die Entzweiung der Sprache' (I've watched the animals. Love, the warmth of bodily contact, is the only mercy we find in the darkness. But the union of our organs is the only union and it fails to bridge the rift caused by language) (*GKA* i. 491. 22–5).

To investigate the implication of the incipient 'Sprachkritik' (critique of language) which underlies Schink's statement would take us too far from *Baal*. I shall merely point to the higher status—or rather the unquestioned status—of poetic utterance in the earlier drama. The large number of lyric interpolations bears witness to this; apart from the expected opposition to his works from polite society, Baal's status as poet is upheld by all (and it is praised by the common folk, e.g. the 'Fuhrleute'), even though the form this appreciation takes may be rather unusual (like hanging his poems in the toilet). Brecht had clearly further to go along the way of radically dismantling and uncovering human cosmic insignificance, and it was evidently not one of the aims of this otherwise anarchic drama to subvert poetic language. The mantle of the French Symbolists, especially Rimbaud and Verlaine, still hung around Brecht's shoulders. However repellant Baal may seem as a human being—and possibly precisely because of this repellant quality—the poet in him is surely asserted by his creator (though not without irony and sarcasm). One could though—and this inconsistency has been laid bare by analysing the leitmotivs—point to the unresolved problem of reconciling the significance of poetic utterance with the complete insignificance of man. At this stage at least it would appear that Brecht could still hang on to a few traditional shreds to cover his nakedness!

Because of the lack of a perspectival or commenting role for the leitmotiv structure in *Baal* to which I drew attention above, it is difficult to define a hierarchical pattern other than in terms of magnitude (*Grundmotive*, or primary motivs, being larger units which contain smaller, subsidiary motivs, *Nebenmotive*). In other words, such a relationship does not here—as it would, say, in Wagner's theory and practice and in the practice of dramatists (e.g. Kleist and Grillparzer) who make extensive use of the technique— set up different levels of authority by means of which the dramatist can steer the readers or audience towards an overarching and persuasive (though not necessarily dogmatic or univalent) inter- pretation and fitting together of the component parts of the drama. It is not clear, for instance, whether the poet-hero's naïve *un*- awareness of an existential *Angst* is more exemplary, or meant to carry more weight than Sophie's frank statement about cosmic isolation.

Alternatively, of course, it could be the result of Baal's refusal to acknowledge his *Angst*. In order to seek further clarification about Brecht's treatment of the existential theme, it might be useful at this point to consider a group of leitmotivs which are set in contrast to the motiv of whiteness. For the pervasive imagery of dirt and pollution might seem on the face of it to signal unpalatable aspects of the human condition such as might inspire attitudes of nausea or revolt à la Büchner. The leitmotivs obviously link up with those expressing decay ('Verwesung') such as appeared, though in 'transfigured' form, in the 'Ophelia' poem. But in its cruder form this imagery was more prominent in the 1919 version than in any other before or after. One of the stanzas later omitted from the 'Choral vom großen Baal' presented the motiv as the obverse to that of virginal purity:

> Und wär Schmutz dran, er gehört nun doch einmal
> Ganz und gar, mit allem drauf, dem Baal!

(And if there was dirt on it, then that is quite fitting for Baal—dirt and all it entails).

(20. 36–7).

References to human excrement and bodily functions are not altogether expunged from the final version, as is revealed by the retention of the 'Abort' (Water-closet) poem, which, however, has a distinctly comic flavour, Baal seeming to take a kind of schoolboy delight in trying to shock members of polite society by allusions to such unacceptable matters:

> Wenn ihr Kot macht, ist, sagt Baal, gebt acht
> Besser noch, als wenn ihr gar nichts macht!
> (producing dirt, says Baal, is better, mark you, than producing nothing)
>
> (86. 6–7).

However, possibly the most revealing example of all—and this one *was* dropped from all later versions—connects the physically repulsive and the existential. Baal (1919, Nachtcafé, 52. 36) gives expression to the idea of a polluted Creation: 'die Welt ist ein Exkrement des lieben Gottes' (the world is a piece of God's excrement). It is a thought worthy of Büchner and it is something of a puzzle to the theologically minded. Has a creative spirit been at work, then, after all (as in the poem, 'Vom ertrunkenen Mädchen': where we hear that 'Gott sie allmählich vergaß') and has He only succeeded in producing filth and decay?

One should not, possibly, exaggerate the Büchner connection since, in Brecht's post-Nietzschean world, expectations about God have been considerably lowered. The response to material decay etc. is less one of revolt than one of acceptance and accommodation to circumstances: 'Anpassung' (one way of describing Baal's philosophy of 'giving as good as you are given'). Brecht's tacit acceptance of the order of things is worth comparing both with Büchner's non-acceptance and his [Brecht's] own later rejection of the social and political status quo and his repeated calls to 'change the world'—it needs it!' The reversal of position cannot be ignored or its importance underestimated.

Reviewing the basic leitmotiv structures in *Baal*, we must recognize the following points: First, the patterns are mainly static, that is, it is not a matter of vital importance *at which point* in the drama they occur. Baal's numerous adumbrations of erotic 'Himmel'–'Erde' imagery, together with the inevitable 'weiße Wolke' do not develop. This is not surprising, since his own relationships themselves do not develop. Exactly the same can be said about the 'Baum'–'Wind' configurations. Only when we examine the 'Wasser' pattern are we aware of anything like a deliberate 'placing' of motivs and even then this is not precise. Virtually the only strand of 'action' in the drama concerns the Johanna episode, which is given particular attention at the beginning of the work and then followed through in some detail to its calamitous outcome. The placing of the poem 'Vom ertrunkenen

Mädchen'—which is generally, but not specifically, matched to Johanna's fate—is certainly dramatically and structurally significant, for although widely separated from the suicide itself (which is reported in Baal's Dachkammer; Baal's Attic, 2 (1922), it is placed fairly near the end (Landstrasse, Weiden; highway, willows, 1919), and in this final position acquires significance as a means of drawing various threads together, both in terms of leitmotivs and in terms of action. One can compare its earlier placing and much more vestigial form in the 1919 version (Hölzerne braune Diele, Nacht, Wind):

> Schwimmst du hinunter mit Ratten im Haar
> Der Himmel drüber bleibt wunderbar

(as you swim downstream with rats in your hair, the sky above remains magical)

(62. 7–8).

In this form it is presented by Baal not as an open-ended 'poetic transformation' of Johanna's fate, but more as a taunt in reply to the grotesque character Maja (the stage-directions suggest that the tone is 'brutal'). It would not be wise to make too much of the Johanna–Ophelia motiv, since the poem is so very generalized, but one has a sense of the rightness of the placing in the later versions. Secondly, one can say that the anchorage of the leitmotiv patterns in the various stage-settings or 'Bühnenbilder' (e.g. Himmel, Bäume, Weiden) certainly integrates them into the whole work. But such integration is at a static and descriptive level only; one could say that, in its unconcentrated, spread-out form, it operates horizontally, rather than vertically within the drama. It is scarcely ever—the Johanna action is the exception—related to any retrospective movement of dramatic anticipation (cf. Wagner's 'Erinnerung' and 'Ahnung').

The structuring of the leitmotivs—as we saw, scarcely to be regarded as hierarchical—might nevertheless seem to operate by antithesis or contrast. Thus the oppositions 'Himmel'–'Erde'; 'Weiße'–'Kot'; 'Bäume'–'Wind'; 'Wasser'–'Fische', etc. present an apparent conflict or structural dynamic. But such rudiments of a dialectic are instantly cancelled out by the meeting up of opposites through the all-pervading force of transience and the all-unifying principle of erotic experience, this being regarded as the only viable means by which man can overcome his cosmic isolation and drown out any *Angst* which might still be lurking. It is arguable whether the drama form is ideally suited to such an all-transcending view of the world and whether it can really work effectively without a more rigorous development of conflict. We have seen how potential sources of such conflict such as family ties—Baal's mother—and social frictions—his position as an office-worker—together with the possibilities lying inherent in the character of Ekart for clashes and oppositions were all systematically and ruthlessly expunged from the later versions, leaving Baal in a kind of splendid isolation. And we are made aware of the work's tendency towards the monologue form of drama which had been pioneered by Strindberg, whom the young Brecht considered to be one of the great 'educators' of the New Europe around 1920.

What we have, then, is the unusual situation of a drama which is largely sustained and held together by its dense network of leitmotiv patterns which are purely self-referential and do not point either beneath—to underlying meanings already present but requiring evaluation—or above, to an external set of criteria which are being imposed upon the work (this, as we shall find in a later chapter, would apply to didactic commentary). To some extent, *Baal* resembles an extended poem—it comes close to the genre of 'lyrisches Drama'—and the leitmotivs could be regarded as a mainstay of the poem itself, part of its very 'language'. It also resembles a 'Rollengedicht' (role-poem) and one is put in mind of Goethe's many experiments, at a similar point in his career, with lyrical monologue and lyrical drama: forms, that is, which seem to occupy an area *between* the genres. And if it can truly be said that Brecht's first inclinations (and maybe his true loyalties, though this would be more difficult to prove) were lyrical—and that he had to turn himself, *faute de mieux*, into a dramatist—then this lyrical bent had been much assisted and fostered by his reading of the French Symbolist poets, especially Rimbaud (the similarities between 'Vom ertrunkenen Mädchen' and 'Le Bâteau ivre' have frequently been noted)[12] and Verlaine (the similarity in the physical appearance of Baal and Verlaine as depicted by Caspar Neher was emphasized by Brecht himself).[13]

A dramatic structuring of leitmotivs, then, is almost completely

[12] See, for example, D. Schmidt, Baal *und der junge Brecht*, 130.
[13] Neher's mongoloid sketch of a distinctly Verlainian-looking Baal is reproduced as frontispiece in Dieter's Schmidt's (1966) edition of *Baal: Drei Fassungen*).

absent from *Baal*, but not entirely, if one considers the role of the Choral as a Prologue. In the earliest extant version (1918)—which, as I have already pointed out, contained a larger range of *Hauspostille* poems, this Choral was arbitrarily stationed about mid-way through the work. From 1919 onwards, however, Brecht removed it entirely from the 'action' and established it at the beginning. It is not, of course, a prologue in the traditional sense (cf. *Wallensteins Lager*), where factual, expository material can be slipped in by way of preparation for a complex dramatic action. Perhaps it is more like the 'Vorspiel auf dem Theater' to Goethe's *Faust*,[14] where the dramatist's aim is to present at the outset a very definite perspective, in that case disarming the public, persuading them to discard conventional views and to redirect their attention to the higher poetic flights rather than merely popular attractions. Brecht's 'prologue' does have a 'Gestus'—and a much clearer one than we find elsewhere in *Baal*: it is one of ironic distancing towards the 'hero'. Unlike Baal's other poetic interpolations—and presumably we have to see the Choral as one of his own poetic works—this one refers to him throughout in the third person and does so with much wit and irony (notice, for instance, how the name 'Baal' recurs in almost every stanza, often more than once). The mock-heroic emphasis comes across very clearly and it is obviously important for Brecht's purpose that the reader or spectator catches this nuance before he is plunged into the outrageous chronicle of Brecht's antics. Like the parodistic framework to the *Hauspostille* itself with its injunctions and tongue-in-cheek caveats, the 'Choral vom großen Baal' invites us not to take the forthcoming proceedings too seriously. Since the leitmotiv structure itself is not, as we have seen, employed to such an end for perspectival purposes (as it will later be by Brecht) and since it functions instead as a neutral, explanatory, and elaborative technique, the Prologue is all that we are given in the way of authorial perspective—which is not a great deal by comparison with the other dramas which will be the subject of attention in future chapters.

[14] For a comparison between Goethe's and Schiller's Prologues see F. J. Lamport, '*Faust-Vorspiel* und *Wallenstein-Prolog* oder Wirklichkeit und Ideal der weimarischen "Theaterunternehmung" ', *Euphorion* 83 (1989), 323–36.

5

Das Badener Lehrstück vom Einverständnis: Leitmotiv and Didacticism

In its earlier (1929) version simply called 'Lehrstück' this work belongs to the group of short didactic pieces ('teaching plays') with music which present exemplary situations in the form of quasi-judicial interrogations followed by 'verdicts', or solutions to problems which, in their harsh and uncompromising logicality, often entail violence or sacrifice on the part of the 'learning subject'. *Das Badener Lehrstück vom Einverständnis* is generally regarded as one of the most austere of all this group: the celebrated 'clown scene' in which the limbs of a giant clown are systematically sawn off to illustrate the indifference of human beings towards one another—an extreme example of attitudes which Brecht had already explored in his 'city' poetry, the collection entitled 'Aus einem Lesebuch für Städtebewohner' (Primer for City-Dwellers)—caused such a furore at the first performance that missiles were hurled on to the stage. Theo Lingen, the celebrated actor who was taking the part of the clown, Herr Schmitt, recalls looking out upon a seething auditorium where people were milling around excitedly—all, that is, with the exception of an august personage sitting in dignified silence amidst the hubbub: 'einen würdigen, weißhaarigen, vollkommen ruhig dasitzenden Herrn, der an dem Skandal überhaupt keinen Anteil zu nehmen schien' (a respectable white-haired gentleman sitting there quite peacefully, taking absolutely no part in the scandal).[1] It was none other than Gerhard Hauptmann, himself a veteran of lively first nights (his own *Vor Sonnenaufgang* was particularly notorious). Another anecdote concerns Brecht's composer-friend Hanns Eisler, who noted that a critic sitting next to him had fainted. When this was later reported to Brecht the

---

[1] Quoted in Dümling, *Laßt euch nicht verführen*, 253.

latter's reply was 'Das ist zu dumm, der Mann wird doch nicht ohnmächtig in einem Sinfoniekonzert, wo doch immer gesägt wird, nämlich die Geigen . . .' (that's really too daft. Surely the man doesn't faint in a symphony concert, where there's always a lot of sawing—in the violins).[2]

In its original form, *Lehrstück* was a work of partnership between the two leading avant-garde artists in their respective fields: Brecht and Paul Hindemith. We have already noted the importance which music had acquired for Brecht's theory in the landmark essay of 1930, 'Anmerkungen zu Mahagonny'.[3] Both men were keenly interested in 'interdisciplinary' approaches, and particularly in bringing the art-forms of music and drama together;[4] they had in fact long been eyeing one another up with a view to a possible future collaboration, even before the Baden-Baden Festival eventually brought them together, first on the partial collaboration over *Der Lindberghflug*, where Kurt Weill was responsible for over half of the music, Brecht cunningly keeping the two composers in tandem, then on *Lehrstück*, for which Hindemith wrote a complete score. This collaboration did not survive long and ended in much acrimony, only narrowly avoiding litigation (of which Brecht, but not Hindemith, was inordinately fond). In a preface to the final, much expanded version of the text, now shorn entirely of its music, and entitled *Das Badener Lehrstück vom Einverständnis*, Brecht blamed himself for having allowed the experimental, open-ended approach adopted by Hindemith to give too much prominence to the music (as is clear from his preface to the score, Hindemith allowed for a high degree of musical flexibility in the form of ad-libbing and rearranging the musical score in response to the tastes and requirements of the performers). Although, as we have already seen, in theory Brecht was in favour of allowing music to enjoy a prime position, when faced with the reality of a collaboration with a composer who held his own particular art-form in such high

---

[2] Hanns Eisler, *Materialien zu einer Dialektik der Musik* (Leipzig 1976), 234.

[3] See discussion above, Ch. 3, p. 72.

[4] On Hindemith's collaboration with Brecht and the 'misunderstanding' between them, see Dieter Rexroth, 'Paul Hindemith und Brechts "Lehrstück', *Hindemith Jahrbuch*, 12 (1983), 41–52. The 1929 version which Hindemith set consists of seven sections as against eleven in the (unscored) version of 1930. There are contrapuntal orchestral sections, sections for individual singers and for chorus and orchestra, interspersed with sections for speakers alone (usually introductory). The clown scene is structured around a slapstick dialogue which alternates with a 'dead-pan' orchestral refrain, very much in the vein of 'gestic' commentary.

esteem as did Paul Hindemith, Brecht had his bluff called and could only register his discontent by applying to Hindemith's score the Marxist smear-term 'formalist'. Thus assailed, the relevance of Hindemith's score for 'den Menschen unserer Zeit' (contemporary man) could be seriously questioned and undermined. Already an ideological gap had opened up between Brecht and Hindemith which was to prove unbridgeable: on the one hand, we find a view of art as a human activity which finds its own centre from within, even though social interaction may be perceived as part of this aesthetic; on the other hand, a view where the nature of the content has to be closely defined and where social and political aims take clear precedence over forms themselves. Later, when the political going had become much tougher even than in 1930, in a now celebrated letter[5] Brecht was able to make more capital out of the fact that Hindemith's refusal to accept the principle of the politicization of art had led to his own disgrace and downfall at the hands of the Nazis (the famous 'Hindemith Affair'). Although our primary concern here is with genre-related questions rather than with political differences between Brecht and his composer-collaborator, the extent of Brecht's inflexibility on these matters is instructive and makes the *Lehrstück* a particularly good model for illustrating the 'hard-line' austerity that characterizes his high-didactic stance, when he is prepared to reject a musical contribution in which his own central doctrine of 'Gestus' is so well served (e.g. Hindemith's extremely apt and witty music for the clown scene).[6] Brecht's gesture of recasting the text for exclusively dramatic, non-musical purposes smacks strongly of pique and makes his earlier theoretical statements about the respective roles of music and drama, to say nothing of his stipulations for musical 'Gestus', look hollow.

Given this unpromising background for artistic endeavour, it is all the more surprising to discover that Brecht's texts—and both of them at that—shed some new light on our central theme: Brecht's use of leitmotiv. In its original, shorter form (the text, that is, which was written to receive a musical score) *Lehrstück* focuses attention

---

[5] The text of Brecht's letter is reproduced in full in *Musik bei Brecht*, ed. Lucchesi and Shull, 147–9.

[6] Theoretically, as we have already observed (see Ch. 3 above, p. 90), the notion of 'Gestus' was certainly not intended to have an exclusively political definition. In practice it generally had.

on the single crashed airman, a character based on the historical French aviator Charles Nungesser, and makes no mention of the crew (which plays an important part in the final version). Since as a genre the *Lehrstück* is 'epic' theatre in its most undiluted and uncompromising form, one might reasonably expect it to employ exclusively exhortatory (and thus disjunctive) forms of commentary or prescription. Indeed at first sight, this is what we appear to have: two choruses, one 'trained', the other 'to be trained' ('die Menge'), confront the audience from a podium. Deliberately and patiently they expound the doctrine of 'self-overcoming' which is implied in the notion of technological advance which has not kept pace with social and political revolution. In this early version the aviator ultimately accepts the doctrine and the dialectical opposition is resolved; in the later version he remains obdurate and it is the 'collective', i.e. the crew, which provides the audience or reader with exemplary behaviour.

Despite the austerity and unconcealed didacticism of all this, it is remarkable to discover outlines of definite leitmotiv patterns in both versions of the work. There is, first of all, an implied allusion to the Icarus motiv, that potent expression of man's over-weening pride and hubris ('sich erheben') in relation to his environment.

> Aber wir haben uns erhoben.
> Gegen Ende des zweiten Jahrtausends unsrer Zeitrechnung
> Erhob sich unsere
> Stählerne Einfalt
> Aufzeigend das Mögliche
> (But we raised ourselves up.
> Towards the end of the second millennium in our calendar
> Our steel simplicity
> Raised itself up
> Showing what was possible).

> > (*GKA* iii. 27. 30–4)

This is developed into contrasting primary motivs (*Grundmotive*) of vertical movement (flight and the conquest of gravity), on the one hand, and falling ('Der Sturz', scene 2: 28 ff.), on the other; at a later point a horizontal pattern also occurs, though this motiv is much reduced in the second version (the 'river' motiv and the allied motiv of 'swimming' denote compliance with eternal natural laws):

Du bist aus dem Fluß gefallen, Mensch,
Du bist nicht im Fluß gewesen, Mensch
(You have fallen from the river, man,
You have not been in the river, man).

(44. 13–14)

Finally, and this is more starkly emphasized in the early version, the conquest by science of space is projected beyond the material plane and into a metaphysical dimension with almost Faustian overtones: 'das Unerreichbare' (the unattainable). This motiv seems to have reflected the concerns of Hindemith rather than Brecht;[7] at any rate, as if to expunge any suggestions of an other-worldly, or mystical dimension to human life, Brecht ostentatiously altered 'das Unerreichbare' to 'das noch nicht Erreichte' (the not yet attained), drawing attention to the change in a footnote (27. 37–9).

The remarkable scene (scene 6) in which the 'subject' contemplates and confronts death, which in the first version is entitled 'Betrachtet den Tod' (Contemplate death) but later changed into the more concrete 'Betrachtung der Toten' (Contemplation of dead people), brings to light a process of inner rehabilitation after the individual has fully acknowledged his own insignificance:

dann lerne ich:
was ich tat war falsch
denn jetzt lerne ich,
daß der Mensch
liegen soll und nicht
sammeln Höhe noch Tiefe
auch nicht Geschwindigkeit
(then I learn
that what I did was wrong
for now I learn
that man
should lie prostrate and not
gather heights or depths
nor even speed).

(*Lehrstück* fragment,
Deutsche Kammermusik,
Baden-Baden, 1929)

---

[7] These tendencies are also reflected in Hindemith's collaboration with Gottfried Benn over the oratorio *Das Unaufhörliche* (1931).

This personal insight and admission of 'guilt', which is almost reminiscent of the insights of a Classical hero, is later replaced with a recalcitrant refusal to comply with the principle of consent ('Einverständnis') whereas the aviator's colleagues willingly comply with the injunctions of the control chorus. A different, but equally important leitmotiv pattern to that of spatial relationships ('oben'/ 'unten'; 'schwimmen'/'Fluß') is suggested by imagery of size ('die kleinste Größe', the smallest magnitude); this motiv is developed fully in scene 7, where a number of exemplary postures to be adopted in the face of the elements (the Storm) are presented, all of which entail acceptance of human insignificance and smallness of stature: 'In seiner kleinsten Größe überstand er den Sturm' (in his smallest magnitude he overcame the storm) (38. 21).

While all these leitmotiv patterns are suggested—and they are patterns which are already familiar to us from *Baal* and which we shall find in other dramas of Brecht's as well—it must be noted that they are only lightly indicated, scarcely developed, and at times even seem to hover curiously between the level of imagery and that of abstraction. It is as if they remain exclusively at the level of primary or *Grundmotive* and are not allowed, as in the other works, to proliferate or diversify or to extend into the sphere of the tangible or concrete. The leitmotivs cannot be said to serve a dramatic purpose or to be 'vergegenwärtigt' (actualized) because there is no action as such in *Lehrstück* and the whole piece is in the nature of a reconstruction of the 'crash' of the aircraft and an analysis of its implications. The patterns do, however, operate as a structurally unifying device in the same way as they might, say, in an epic poem. Thus, in scene 2, the horizontal and the vertical patterns are succinctly combined to form a kind of prelude:

> Der niedere Boden
> Ist für euch
> Jetzt hoch genug
> (The lower ground
> is now for you
> High enough).

> (28. 7–9)

Throughout the first few scenes this spatial imagery dominates. Then the emphasis shifts from the conquest of physical forces like gravity ('die Gesetze der Erde', the laws of the Earth) to the non-physical, or moral implications of 'Sturz' ('das Grundgesetz', the basic law). This, the didactic core of the work, relies heavily on direct exhortatory statement or Biblical-sounding precepts which relate to the principle of 'Einverständnis': 'Wer aber den Wunsch hat, einverstanden zu sein, der hält bei der Armut' (but he who wants to acquiesce, must remain poor) (38. 30–1). It is as if the images—or *Grundmotive*—themselves require strong reinforcement. At the same time, though, a new and potent motiv—the storm—emerges as a natural force far stronger than the technological achievements of aviation. It may be that this motiv also carries with it social and political overtones, being regarded as an instrument for radical change or revolution. The aviator's confrontation with physical death represents the first step in the process of achieving 'Einverständnis' and gradually this abstract notion concentrates around the motiv pattern of 'die kleinste Größe'. Inconspicuousness, a trimming down of all individuality to the tiniest quantity, is symbolic of a death of self and an admission of human insignificance in the face of eternity, identified with the 'new' pattern of horizontal imagery, the river; 'aus dem Fluß fallen' signifies a defiant individualism, possibly akin to the Schopenhauerian principle of individuation, while 'im Fluß sein' and 'schwimmen' denote the suitably unpretentious compliance in which identity is engulfed in something larger (this idea is closely akin to imagery in certain poems of the *Hauspostille* (e.g. 'Vom Schwimmen in Seen und Flüßen' on which I commented in the chapter on *Baal*). Slightly later (scene 11: 45. 12), the 'Fluß' turns out to be the 'Fluß der Dinge', a motiv which carries Classical overtones (Heraclitus' doctrine of flux). In the final version vertical *Grundmotive* return (scene 9: 42. 33–4):

> Tausend Jahre fiel alles von oben nach unten
> Ausgenommen der Vogel
> (For a thousand years everything
> Except the bird fell downward from above).

In the light of what has been suggested above about the 'abstract' quality of the imagery, it is perhaps significant that almost exact repetition is used rather than the metamorphosis to which we are accustomed in a 'normal' Brechtian leitmotiv pattern.

Aber wir haben uns erhoben.
Gegen Ende des zweiten Jahrtausends unserer Zeitrechnung
(But we raised ourselves up.
Towards the end of the second millennium in our calendar).

(27. 30–1)

The sense of 'erheben' has, however, itself now altered from the physical to the moral level of response to man's limitations, and this gives the work (in its final version) a distinctly triadic structure which is nicely accentuated by the motivic patterning. Thus the first phase of *Grundmotive* signals 'erheben' followed by 'Sturz'; the second, the vertical 'Fluß' and 'schwimmen', denotes 'Einverständnis', while the final 'erheben' points to the moral triumph attendant on facing death and accepting limitations; this in turn leads to the possibility of a return to technological aspirations, but tempered this time with suitable humanitarian and social-cum-ethical perspectives. This pattern might be compared to a dialectic of thesis–antithesis–synthesis.

As I have already suggested, the motivic patterning strikes a rather abstract note because these leitmotivs are not anchored within specific dramatic situations or 'Momente'. All the same the network does have a dynamic impetus and a generative function in so far as the things they refer to may themselves be transposed; to a certain extent the motivs, even though themselves unchanging, become markers for the forward movement of the dialectic. One is most put in mind of similar abstract techniques in the 'Denkspiele' of Brecht's older contemporary, Georg Kaiser: in the *Gas* dramas, for example, a sustained dialectic is enlivened by equally pervasive leitmotivic patterning (as well as a powerful rhetoric).[8] It is interesting that Brecht's collection of poetry ('Aus einem Lesebuch für Städtebewohner'), written at approximately the same time, relies on a more unvarnished, less metaphorical language than even the austere *Lehrstück*. This might point to interesting genre-related differences: even the skeletal drama form of *Lehrstück* promotes a degree of concentration and structural organization with which the 'lyric' form may dispense. In the light of Brecht's later employment of very similar leitmotiv patterns in *Leben des Galilei* (e.g. gravitational imagery), it will be interesting to examine the extent

---

[8] For discussion of motivic patterns in Kaiser's dramas, see E. Schwerer, *Metapher, Allegorie und Symbol in den Dramen George Kaisers*, diss., Yale, 1966 (University Microfilms, 1974).

to which, in the later, dramatically much more expansive work, Brecht is interested in tethering or integrating the leitmotivs more completely to their context, as well as allowing for their proliferation and development along lines which more closely resemble Wagner's notions.

To conclude, Brecht's natural predilection for such motivic forms and patterns does not seem to have abandoned him, even in this somewhat unpromising and austere context. The comparison to which I have already alluded with the situation in *Baal* operates in terms of the basic subject-matter of the *Grundmotive*: 'oben'/ 'unten'; 'schwimmen'/'Fluß'. But, as was seen, *Baal* offers a leitmotiv network which is presented in a unique lyrical profusion. Also, unlike *Baal*, the *Grundmotive* in *Das Badener Lehrstück vom Einverständnis* relate to their surroundings in a manner which is more akin to dramatic orthodoxy, being closely integrated into the 'action' (even if, as we have just seen, 'action' here could better be described as a 'dialectical argument'). At no point are these motivs disjoined; they are presented 'straight' and without any framing 'Gestus', and this feature links both the musical and the non-musical texts. They become, however, major bearers of the work's didactic meaning, alongside the unliterary device of direct, exhortatory statement; indeed they enliven some of the most memorable formulations in this somewhat unapproachable, but austerely beautiful work.

6

Die Heilige Johanna der Schlachthöfe Leitmotiv and Parody

Is it a coincidence that this—the indubitable, though not yet fully appreciated, masterpiece of Brecht's entire creative output up to the time of his exile in 1933[1]—happens also to be a drama which is second only to that other masterpiece, *Leben des Galilei*, in its presentation of a complex, densely ramified network of leitmotivs? What we are about to examine is a drama which demonstrates such a degree of virtuosity in this particular area that it bears comparison with that of some of the most illustrious practitioners from the tradition of German Classical drama and can even stand its ground in the company of the most exuberant practitioner of all, Shakespeare, whose achievements in this sphere have been so ably analysed by Wolfgang Clemen.[2] A second question, however, immediately poses itself: is there some connection between these densely interlocking motivic systems and the form of parody which itself provides the largest single ingredient contributing to the drama's 'Grundgestus'? We shall certainly want to establish the relationship between leitmotiv and parody in this drama, but in order not to prejudice our results, it will be prudent first to proceed to establish, present, and analyse the patterns and their own internal relationship to one another and their contribution to the

---

[1] Among the most perceptive analyses I would single out those of Peter Wagner Bertolt Brechts "Die Heilige Johanna der Schlachthöfe" ', *Jahrbuch der deutschen Schillergesellschaft*, 12 (1968), 493–519; Helfried Seliger, *Das Amerikabild Bertolt Brechts* (Bonn, 1974); Rainer Pohl, *Strukturelemente und Entwicklung Pathosformen in der Dramensprache Bertold [sic] Brechts* (Bonn, 1969), 107–15; Uwe-K. Ketelsen, 'Kunst im Klassenkampf; "Die Heilige Johanna der Schlachthöfe" ', *Brechts Dramen: Neue Interpretationen*, ed. W. Hinderer (Stuttgart, 1984), 106–24. All these writers emphasize the work's importance, a typical remark being the following: 'Vom artistischen Standkpunkt aus betrachtet, bedeutet das Stück einen Höhepunkt im Schaffen Brechts' (from the artistic point of view the piece represents a climax in Brecht's creative output) (Seliger, p. 183).

[2] *Shakespeares Bilder* (Bonn, 1936).

perspectival structure of the work as a whole. Only when we are armed with such information shall we be in a position to address the other issue and to seek answers to questions like: to what extent can the leitmotiv network itself be regarded as part of the 'Klassikerparodie' (parody of the Classics) which, ostensibly, is such an important element in the work? Is its extensive use and application to be explained in terms of the form in which it is presented, a form which contrasts so strikingly with the sparse and austere *Lehrstücke* which Brecht was developing as a genre with considerable single-mindedness at exactly the same period (i.e. 1929–31)? The proposed method of procedure would also seem appropriate in that the 'Klassikerparodie' was not an original feature of the conception and that, moreover, there is clear evidence to show that some of the parodistic material was suggested to Brecht by his co-workers.[3]

At least three groups of extremely pervasive patterns of primary leitmotivs (*Grundmotive*) can be discerned in *Die Heilige Johanna*. First, there is the comparatively abstract vertical imagery of 'oben' and 'unten' (top/bottom; above/below) which for Brecht provides a basic frame for image-patterns which he can subject to infinite variations from one drama to the next. In this basic form it can be identified in *Baal*, as we have seen;[4] it is present also in *Das Badener Lehrstück vom Einverständnis*[5] and will be prominent too in *Leben des Galilei*.[6] Secondly, there is the secondary leitmotiv pattern that clusters around the leitmotivs of the 'Bau' (structure) or 'Gebäude' (building); here the structure implied is Capitalist society, which is seen in terms of a (man-made) edifice which, depending on one's point of view, may seem impregnable or flimsy, either in need of remodelling, or entirely satisfactory for present requirements. The third group of leitmotivs derives from the very title and subject-matter of the drama itself: the 'Schlachthof' (stockyard) which produces two quite different aspects: firstly, the animal motiv (which, since the days of Aesop, has afforded many possibilities for oblique commentary on the human condition); secondly, the notion of 'Schlacht' or 'Kampf' (battle), which,

---

[3] As with other works of this period, Brecht called on the services of a 'collective' (consisting of assistants like Hermann Borchardt, Emil Burri, and Elisabeth Hauptmann). Their role seems to have been mainly one of collecting material and making suggestions which Brecht himself would then 'edit' rigorously. See *GKA* iii. 452.

[4] See above, p. 114.

[5] See above, p. 133.

[6] See below, p. 181.

applied to the Capitalist sphere, culminates in the 'Börsenschlacht' (stock-market battle)[7] and to a spectacular stock-market crash, and when applied to the Salvation Army, produces gestures of almost equally ruthless militancy in the name of religion. It may be interesting to note at this point that the first group of leitmotivs revolves very much around Johanna herself and is subjected to various elaborations and modifications which reflect the heroine's own development. Whether this development is purely a function of the standard 'development' of the Classical tragic heroine, and thus a function of the parody, remains to be seen; what is incontestable is the fact that it is a fundamental and self-conscious feature of the work and can, for once, be 'taken as read'. The second group relate specifically to Mauler, while the third has more application to general issues, such as organized religion, economics, and social conditions. Since these correspond closely to the three main strands of the drama which have been identified by commentators using other (e.g. thematic) methods of analysis,[8] it is possibly significant that the leitmotiv patterning takes this particular form. Thematic and leitmotivic overlap is very much a feature of *Die Heilige Johanna*. But in addition, the primary leitmotivs and their off-shoots overlap with each other, which adds to the work's complexity.

The vertical pattern of leitmotivs—'oben' and 'unten'—has many complex strands, both in its religious and its political applications. In the former application it appears as an antithesis between man's higher spiritual aspirations and his lower urges and physical needs (these are usually equated with bodily functions, especially eating); the apparent dualism between mind and body is, of course, parodistically reminiscent of Schiller's categories and his particular treatment of the theme.[9] There is a further extension of the latter leitmotiv into the animal sphere (the word 'fressen'—to eat, of animals—when used of human beings provides a useful bridge between the two levels). Thus Johanna, operating at the start

---

[7] Scene 9 ('Viehbörse') and Graham's 'report' of the battle (scene 10).

[8] See, for instance, Wagner, 'Bertolt Brechts "Die Heilige Johanna" ', 497–8, who divides the drama into three distinct actions: 'Die Johanna-Handlung', 'Die Mauler-Handlung', and 'Die Handlung des Proletariats'.

[9] The persistent dualism in Schiller's thinking can be traced back as far as his years of medical training, as the title of his successful dissertation indicates: 'Über den Zusammenhang der tierischen Natur des Menschen mit seiner geistigen'. See the illuminating editorial discussion *passim* in F. Schiller, *Medicine, Psychology and Literature*, ed. K. Dewhurst and N. Reeves (Oxford, 1978). There has been some discussion of this dualism in relation to audience response above, Ch. 3, p. 95.

of the action as a committed member of the Salvation Army, whose
job is to save souls, mouths many a platitude, while trying to direct
the thoughts of the poor away from earthly and physical matters
(such as the provision of free meals in the Salvation Army soup
kitchen) and on to a higher plane. Those waiting in the soup
kitchen are accordingly told: 'Oben streben und nicht unten
streben. Oben sich noch einen guten Platz anstellen und nicht
unten. Oben der erste sein wollen und nicht unten' (work for a good
position up above, not here below. Want to be the first man up, not
the first man down) (*GKA* 135. 8–10). The hollowness and
hypocrisy of these words is already laid bare by the materialistic
and competitive terms (they would be described as 'kleinburgerlich'
in Marxist terminology) which amount to the adage: 'aim at getting
the best for yourself and outdoing your fellow-men'. At this point,
therefore, Brecht has framed the 'oben/unten' primary leitmotiv
with a contradictory or adversative 'Gestus'.

Another form in which the spiritual dimension implied by 'oben'
is expressed occurs later (scene 5), the scene in which Johanna
upbraids the meat-packers for their callous behaviour. She uses a
phrase which had tripped lightly off her tongue at the point when
she was preaching to the poor about their lack of all 'Sinn für das
Höhere' (scene 2: 135. 28 ff.). These wretches are still at the later
point regarded as being bereft of these higher promptings, and
Johanna acknowledges this, employing the leitmotiv, but she is now
sufficiently awakened to the causes of their moral degeneration to
see that their material plight must first be improved if they are ever
to be able to afford the luxury of higher aspirations: this is, of
course, another version of Brecht's celebrated maxim: 'Erst kommt
das Fressen, dann kommt die Moral' (first comes eating, then
comes morality). The earlier display of indifference to 'higher
things' (in the form of the Church's message and doctrines) which
Johanna had so deplored in the unemployed masses appears
retrospectively to her as understandable:

> Lebend von Minute zu Minute unsicher
> Können die sich nicht mehr erheben
> Vom niedersten Boden
> (Living from minute to minute, uncertainly
> They can no longer raise themselves
> From the lowest ground).
>
> (137. 39–138. 2)

Other members of the Salvation Army had likewise dismissed them as useless layabouts:

> Nur mit Niedrigem
> Ist ihr Sinn angefüllt! Faulenzer sind es!
> Gefräßig und arbeitsscheu und von Geburt an
> Bar jeder höheren Regung
> (Their minds are stuffed
> With low ideas! They're lazybones!
> Gluttonous, shirkers, from birth onward
> Void of all higher impulses!)
>
> (138. 29–32)

The connection which Johanna has made between physical deprivation and lack of human higher aspirations is succinctly nailed down by following through her various modifications to the 'oben' (often synonymous with 'das Höhere') and 'unten' motivic patterns. Thus, for example, she explains to Mauler the new insight she has achieved into the situation of the poor, whom he has kept

> In solcher Armut . . .
>   daß sie
> Gleichermaßen entfernt sein können von jedem Anspruch
> Auf Höheres als gemeinste Freßgier, tierischste Gewöhnung
> (In poverty like this . . .
>   that they
> Can be just as far away from any claim
> To higher things than the lowest gluttony, the beastliest habits).
>
> (169. 29–32)

One could cite numerous other examples scattered through the drama which fix these meanings and associations in our minds, enabling us to make connections and comparisons which act as perspectival lattices through which we can approach the inner meaning of the work. The most striking of these is undoubtedly the clear connection that is established between the leitmotivs and the character of Johanna herself. But there is one occasion when it is tellingly applied to Mauler. This is towards the end of the drama (scene 10), when the 'meat-king' for a brief interlude acts upon his often expressed disillusionment with the commercial, Capitalist world and throws himself upon the mercies of the Salvation Army—only to be rejected by them, since he is now bankrupt as a result of his speculations which had led to the great 'Borsen-schlacht'. Picking up the leitmotiv which had earlier been used by Johanna tendentiously, Mauler equally sanctimoniously declares his rejection of all materialism and embraces spiritual values:

> Doch nicht deshalb, weil wir nicht mehr mit irdischen
> Gütern gesegnet sind—das kann nicht jeder sein—
> Nur weil wir kenen Sinn für Höheres haben.
> Drum sind wir arm!
> (But not because we are no longer blest with earthly
> Goods—not everyone can be that—
> Only because we have no feeling for higher things.
> That's why we're poor!)
>
> (213. 22–4).

It would almost seem as if this deliberate link with Joanna in her early—i.e. pre-enlightened—phase points to an ironic reversal of roles; that is, at the point in the action when she has long since abandoned her naïve idealism and has outgrown the leitmotiv of 'oben'/'das Höhere' altogether, Mauler appears to have developed to the very same point from which she started out. We would almost seem to be dealing with a double development of the two major characters. One is from idealism to 'enlightenment' (cf. Johanna's often repeated phrase 'ich will's wissen', I want to know), which, however, finally brings disillusionment (Johanna). The other is from ruthless, exploitative Capitalism (tinged occasionally, however, with the hypocritical bad conscience that often accompanies this) to rejection of materialism and adoption of spiritual values (Mauler). But not quite, since Brecht has further surprises up his sleeve and seems to enjoy the possibilities which a 'Classical' action provides once in a while for manipulating the plot and providing unexpected twists and turns. This is Mauler's rejection by the Salvation Army together with the opportunistic arrival of another of those 'letters' from his business associates in New York—advising him how to extricate himself from what appeared to be a hopeless financial situation. A certain ambiguity lingers around this near-conversion of Mauler. His recognition of man's desire for 'higher things' (cf. Johanna's phrase 'der Sinn für das Höhere', a sense of higher things) which she had applied to others, i.e. the downtrodden workers, Mauler applies to himself and his ilk ('wir'). This ambiguity is deliberately left open by Mauler's adoption of a leitmotiv which Johanna has outgrown, but the link thus established between the two characters enables the reader or spectator to make the necessary cross-references (which connect the earliest part of the work to the latest) in a way that is both economical and effective. By bringing the two examples into juxtaposition, we can more clearly observe the paradoxical nature of an action in which the two main characters move and develop in opposite directions.

Probably even more significant than the religious (or perhaps one should say 'moral') resonances of the 'oben'/'unten' leitmotivs is the political meaning that Brecht skilfully builds into the main frame. The two thematic branches of association are interconnected: it is no accident that the political level takes over after Johanna's 'erster Gang in die Tiefe' (first Descent into the depths)—I shall comment on this particular branch itself shortly—and one could say that for Johanna it soon replaces the spiritual and moral levels of association altogether. Indeed, this is one of the tangible signs of the heroine's development, which is in the nature of a political awakening. As we shall see, this branch of the leitmotiv network has some bearing on Mauler too, who links the political implications of mass movements with his fear of their revolutionary potential. Johanna's involvement with the stock-market bosses—she is strongly warned against getting entangled by her Salvation Army superior, Major Snyder—opens her eyes to the gulf between the haves and the have-nots and she quickly starts to refer to the former as 'ihr da oben' (you up there). An important stage in her development and grasp of political and social realities comes later (scene 9) when she not only registers the gulf between 'oben' and 'unten' in terms of an opposition, but also connects the two by using the very expressive series of subsidiary leitmotivs which suggest the available routes that link the two spheres. First there seems to be a clearly defined route ('ein Weg') between them; then, on closer inspection, it turns out to be merely a plank stretching from the depths to the heights; then, in a third attempt, Johanna hits on precisely the correct leitmotiv to express the unequal relationship: the see-saw on which large numbers of people are gathered at the bottom end in order that the rest (the few) may be hoisted up aloft:

> . . . Da sitzen welche, Wenige, oben
> Und Viele unten, und die oben schreien

Hinunter: Kommt herauf, damit wir alle
Oben sind; aber genau hinsehend siehst du was
Verdecktes zwischen denen oben und denen unten
Was wie ein Weg aussieht, doch ist's kein Weg
Sondern ein Brett, und jetzt siehst du's ganz deutlich
's ist ein Schaukelbrett, dieses ganze System
Ist eine Schaukel mit zwei Enden, die voneinander
Abhängen und die oben
Sitzen oben nur, weil jene unten sitzen
Und nur solang jene unten sitzen, und
Säßen nicht mehr oben, wenn jene heraufkämen
Ihren Platz verlassend, so daß
Sie wollen müssen, diese säßen unten
In Ewigkeit und kämen nicht herauf
(. . . Some, a few, sit up above
And many down below, and the ones on top
Shout down: 'Come on up, then, we'll all
Be on top', but if you look closely you'll see
Something hidden between the ones on top and the ones below
That looks like a path but is not a path—
It's a plank, and now you can see it quite clearly
It is a see-saw, this whole system
Is a see-saw, with two ends that depend
On one another, and those on top
Sit up there only because the others sit below
And only as long as they sit below;
They'd no longer be on top if the others came up
Leaving their place, so that of course
They want the others to sit down there
For all eternity and never come up).

(197. 23–38)

This particular example of gravitational imagery, which is presented in the form of a paradox, is a notable feature which has developed from the somewhat abstract 'oben'/'unten' framework into an extremely concrete, expressive, and visually sharp and memorable formulation, one which is at the same time so concentrated as to shed light on the most salient aspects of the class struggle: the mutual dependence of the two different spheres, or more precisely, the parasitic relationship of the 'few' to the 'many' on whose exploitation they rely; the mutually exclusive relationship of the two, i.e. the 'either–or' aspect which makes it impossible in the interests of the maintenance of the present spatial arrangements or hierarchy that the disadvantaged folk at the bottom of the see-saw will ever gain access to the upper level.

And yet, as one knows from the see-saw principle itself, this present configuration of forces, unlike the rain from Heaven, *need not* be immutable, although it may seem so for the time being. The ends of a see-saw can, after all, be reversed; it can also be brought into equilibrium by external agencies. Brecht's subtle choice of leitmotiv is brilliantly suggestive. Furthermore, the leitmotiv has the strategic function of underlining Johanna's crucial role as a potential controller of the fulcrum: she appears as the agent of moderation between two seemingly irreconcilable spatial levels. She herself appears to realize this as her transformation of the vertical pattern into a suitably Biblical horizontal equivalent makes clear. Thus, when she drives the meat-packers from the Salvation Army Hall (scene 7, a deliberate parody of Christ's expulsion of the money-changers from the Temple in John 2: 13–16), she expresses the business of mediation as a (futile) running from one extreme point (i.e. the stock-market) to the other (the workers): 'Ich lauf von Pontius zu Pilatus und mein: wenn ich euch da oben half, dann ist denen unter euch geholfen' (and I run around from pillar to post, thinking: 'If I help you people on top, the people under you will also be helped' (176. 38–9; 177. 1). Even as she says this, she is aware that such attempts at mediation are fraught with difficulty: 'Wer denen, die da arm sind, helfen will, der muß ihnen, scheint's, von euch helfen' (if a man wants to help folks that are poor it seems he'd better help them get away from you) (177. 2–4). A similar realization, though couched in much more brutal terms, is expressed by Major Snyder of the 'Schwarze Strohhüte', acting almost in the role of a chorus, when he expresses the relationship betwen the two extreme points in terms of an unbridgeable *horizontal* opposition:

Arme Unwissende!
Was du nicht siehst: aufgebaut
In riesigen Kadern stehn sich gegenüber
Arbeitgeber und Arbeitnehmer
Kämpfende Fronten: unversöhnlich.
Laufe herum zwischen ihnen, Versöhnlerin und Vermittlerin
Nütze keiner und gehe zugrunde
(Poor simpleton!
You're blind to this: set up in huge formations

The givers and the takers of work
Confront one another:
Warring fronts: irreconcilable.
Run to and fro between them, little peacemaker, little mediator—
Be useful to neither and go to your doom)

                                                          (179. 1–8)

This generalizing statement bears a close relationship to the horizontal pattern, but takes this forward in a significant manner which could even be described as 'gestic' by virtue of its more explicit bearing upon the entire leitmotivic structure. As in Classical tragedy it serves as a foreshadowing device, since Johanna's continued attempts to effect changes in the hierarchical arrangement of society ('oben' and 'unten') are indeed, as Snyder indicates, doomed to failure and will bring about the downfall of the main protagonist ('gehe zugrunde'). But that still leaves open the question of how such a 'downfall' is to be evaluated.

The overarching function of this example—I mean in the way it underlines the impassable gulf between spatial extremes—is not, however, definitive; it will turn out to be merely one more biased perspective and its playful, parodistic statement of futility and immutability is meant to be read dialectically—that is, as an exaggeratedly hopeless view of the social hierarchy of 'oben' and 'unten' which is seen to imply inherent contradictions that are incapable of any resolution by 'do-gooders' like Johanna. Depending on the extent to which this development of the pervasive leitmotiv pattern is perceived by the reader or spectator as a merely relative rearrrangement rather than a definitively overarching one, room will be left in the ultimate perspectival structure for the implied alternative: namely a genuine coming together of the hitherto separated spheres of interest. The Communist agitators who wish to counteract the drastic gulf in society and bring the 'oben' and 'unten' together can only conceive of this *rapprochement* in terms of violent revolution. The leitmotiv thus becomes a focal point for what emerges as the most powerful theme of the drama: the question of peaceful attempts at mediation and change (Johanna's way) versus bloodshed (the workers). And in performing this function it inevitably throws the spotlight on to Johanna herself and on the way she comports herself in her state of increasing enlightenment about the impossiblity of her task, and on her particular way of approaching a solution. The extremities of the see-saw become yet wider (note Brecht's remarkable ability by his use of hyperbole to refashion and transpose the imagery) as she herself observes:

> Denn es ist eine Kluft zwischen oben und unten, größer als
> Zwischen dem Berg Himalaja und dem Meer
> (For there is a gulf between top and bottom, wider
> than between Mount Himalaya and the sea).

> (222. 29–30)

As we shall presently see, Brecht draws on a host of further devices to reveal the conflict within Johanna and these produce further complexity in an already complex text since some of these indubitably engage our sympathies for her as a courageous individual whose personal crusade touches our hearts and imagination, even though we are well aware of its doom-laden dimensions.

This brings us inevitably to consider the final stage of the drama, when Johanna's full awareness ('ich will's wissen') is achieved, a point of 'self-knowledge' which, of course, also characterizes Classical, Aristotelian tragedy. Aware now—after her own failure and betrayal of the workers—of the wholly intractable nature of the class-system, Johanna, to use the terms of the leitmotiv patterning, sees no further possibility of peaceful mediation between 'oben' and 'unten', or specifically of reversing the position of the see-saw:

> Und was oben vorgeht
> Erfährt man unten nicht
> Und nicht oben, was unten vorgeht.
> Und es sind zwei Sprachen oben und unten
> Und zwei Maße zu messen
> Und was Menschengesicht trägt
> Kennt sich nicht mehr
> (And what goes on above
> Is not found out below
> Or what happens below, above.
> And there are two languages, above and below
> And two standards for measuring
> And that which wears a human face
> No longer knows itself).

> (222. 31–7)

At this crucial point in the drama Brecht, through a chorus of cattlemen and slaughtermen, uses the 'oben'/'unten' frame to emphasize an iniquitous hierarchical structure, the seemingly unassailable edifice of the Capitalist system:

> Soll der Bau sich hoch erheben
> Muß es Unten und Oben geben.
> Darum bleib an seinem Ort
> Jeder, wo er hingehört
>
> .   .   .   .   .   .
>
> Unten ist der Untere wichtig
> Oben ist der Richtige richtig
> (Top and bottom must apply
> For the building to be high.
> That's why everyone must stay
> In the place where they belong
> Underdogs have weight below
> The right man's right when up you go).

(223. 1– 10)

(I shall be considering the 'Bau' leitmotiv presently). In what appears like a dialectical exchange Johanna counters the implications of inviolability with a reiteration of the unacceptability of the division and with a new insight which turns the previous associations of 'oben' and 'unten' upside down:

> Und der Oberen Niedrigkeit ist ohne Maß
> Und auch wenn sie besser werden, so hülfe es
> Doch nichts, denn ohnegleichen ist
> Das System, das sie gemacht haben:
> Ausbeutung und Unordnung, tierisch und also
> Unverständlich
> (And the lowness of those above is measureless
> And even if they improve, that would be
> No help, because the system they have made
> Is unique; exploitation
> And disorder, bestial and therefore
> Incomprehensible).

(223. 20–5)

In such a reversal of the 'normal' spatial parameters, it is those 'above' who now become identified with inhuman (= animal) qualities. This exchange between Johanna and the representatives of Capitalism, which is sustained largely by means of the leitmotivs of 'oben' and 'unten'—interpreted and used variously, according to the perspective of different interest-groups—is in its almost dialectical structure at times reminiscent (as, too, was *Das Badener Lehrstück vom Einverständnis*) of Georg Kaiser's vigorous ding-dong exchanges within dialogue. But there is no sign in Brecht's *Johanna* of the desired synthesis or *rapprochement*: the see-saw remains:

> Die aber unten sind, werden unten gehalten
> Damit die oben sind, oben bleiben
> (But those who are down below are kept below
> So that the ones above may stay up there).

> (223. 17–18)

This is simply a confirmation, a restatement of a position after all effort at altering the balance has failed. The world continues to function in its unsatisfactory way:

> Wieder laüft
> Die Welt die alte Bahn unverändert
> (Again the world runs
> Its ancient course unaltered).

> (221. 18–19)

It will already have become apparent that Brecht is not satisfied to leave the spatial/vertical leitmotivic patterning on a purely abstract level. As elsewhere, he fixes and concretizes it by linking the leitmotiv network to Johanna's own progression from a state of ignorance to one of enlightenment, a progression which is instigated and punctuated by her three 'Descents' or 'Gänge in die Tiefe'. Of course, it is difficult at this point not to anticipate discussion of the 'Klassikerparodie' (parody of the Classics) by referring to Faust's descent to the Mothers or seeing echoes of Classical mythological sources (e.g. Orpheus, Aeneas). But Johanna's 'Descent' makes sense within the drama's own terms of reference, particularly the 'oben'/'unten' pattern, and independently of any parodistic 'Vorlage' or model. Johanna's 'first Descent' (scene 2: 132 ff.) shows her confronting the masses at the slaughteryards; her second (scene 4: 148 ff.), takes the form of a conducted tour around the yards by Slift, Mauler's chief henchman, ostensibly to observe the 'Abschaum der Welt' (scum of the world), as Slift describes the grasping and desperate actions of Frau Luckerniddle and Gloomb, both of whom are quite prepared to sacrifice all higher principles—like exposing the injustice done to the former's

husband by his employees or, in the case of the latter, being
prepared not to press the lack of adequate safety precautions in
return for further employment prospects, or simply food. But at the
end of this laying bare of apparent human iniquity and lowness
Johanna, looking more closely beyond the obvious level of
appearances, has observed the total dependence of these people on
those in positions of power and influence:

> Nicht der Armen Schlechtigkeit
> Hast du mir gezeigt, sondern
> *Der Armen Armut*
> (Not the wickedness of the poor
> Have you shown me, but
> *The poverty of the poor*).
>
> (154. 10–12)

In other words, she is well on the way to an analysis of the
fundamental causes for the existence of the spatial/hierarchical
order.

The third 'Descent to the depths' (scene 9: 196 ff.) is the decisive
one, in which Johanna's involvement with the plight of the
unemployed culminates in her failure to discharge the duties with
which they had entrusted her and which she had willingly accepted.
At this stage it would be relevant to talk of her moral 'decline': we
note her bad-tempered outburst when she suffers physical deprivation in the freezing weather conditions. She herself will refer to this
decline, of which she is well aware, in terms of physical weakness:
'Sagt: "Es war zu kalt" ' (Say: it was too cold) (202. 21–2). Again
Brecht's preoccupation with the centrality of man's physical needs
and their priority over higher aspirations is hammered home.
Johanna's grasp of these priorities is gained only as a result of direct
personal experience and privation. The comfort of a cushioned
bourgeois upbringing together with the mental attitudes that this
inculcates is shown to be a useless yardstick of measurement. The
three 'Descents' imply the urgent need for movement away from
familiar starting-points: from an apparently elevated position
downwards:

> Dreitägig ward in Packingtown im
> Sumpf der Schlachthöfe
> Gesehn Johanna
> Heruntersteigend von Stufe zu Stufe

.   .   .   .

... Dreitägig abwärts
Schreitend, schwächer werdend am dritten und
Verschlungen vom Sumpf am Ende
(For three days Joan was seen
In Packingtown, in the stockyard swamps
Going down, downward from level to level

. . . .

... Three days walking
Down the slope, growing weaker on the third
And finally swallowed by the swamp).

(202. 14–20)

In such ways Brecht is able to suggest the idea of an entrenched class structure and the obstacles in the way of the heroine's own ability to surmount this, particularly in her role as mediator between 'oben' and 'unten'.

The counterpart to Johanna's three 'Descents to the depths', which represent important constituent parts of the drama's action, is the attempt by all and sundry at the end to place the heroine on a moral pedestal, a transfiguration which is expressed—parodistically—as a transportation upwards and heavenwards, 'towards higher regions' (the concluding scene of *Faust*, Part 2, 'Bergschluchten', is never far from our ears or minds). Significantly this 'elevation' is strongly urged by adherents of the Capitalist system, who have long sensed the political advantage of allying themselves to the morally respectable Black Straw Hats—a camouflage to hide their true purposes which should serve to maintain the status quo for an indefinite period. Brecht's ironical 'Gestus' in these closing phases of the drama is clear and unmistakable as the hypocritical Salvation Army leader, Major Snyder, urges Johanna ever upwards:

Erhebe dich, Johanna der Schlachthöfe
Fürsprecherin der Armen
Trösterin der untersten Tiefe!
(Rise, Joan of the stockyards
Champion of the poor
Comforter of the lowest depths!)

(220. 35–7)

Significantly, Johanna herself is not disposed to be wafted aloft like this, aware of her kinship with the more familiar 'Depths' to which she had thrice descended: 'Welch ein Wind in der Tiefe' (What a wind in the depths!) (220. 38.) With the wisdom of hindsight she would have preferred to have delivered the letter to the workmen toiling 'below' and not to suffer the ignominy of betrayal of the cause. The 'rosy glow' which suffuses the stage at the moment of her death is a highly ironical parody of the apotheosis of Schiller's celebrated heroine. At this point I should merely like to point out the insistent parodistic framing of the 'oben'/'unten' leitmotiv in the closing scene, a feature which was not evident to nearly the same extent in the various earlier examples which we have examined. A supplementary observation is that the pattern itself, in all its diverse transformations and metamorphoses, persists from beginning to end, permeating even the syntax and the rhythms of the verse. The mercurial instability of the stock-market share index—an amusing offshoot of this motivic pattern of 'oben' and 'unten'—produces a 'Klassikerparodie' (this time Hölderlin's *Hyperions Schicksalslied*) in which the enjambment neatly and almost visually encapsulates the motion of falling itself:

> Den Preisen nämlich
> War es gegeben, von Notierung zu Notierung zu fallen
> Wie Wasser von Klippe zu Klippe geworfen
> Tief ins Unendliche hinab
> (for unto prices it was given
> To fall from quotation to quotation
> As water hurtles from crag to crag
> Deep down into the infinite).

> (211. 37–9)

There are other examples in the drama of a similar echoing of sense through rhythm.[10]

I believe it is clear from the above examination that the leitmotiv pattern of 'oben' and 'unten' provides important perspectival commentary on the main protagonist and her development within the drama. It is now time to examine how such patterning is used to illuminate the role of her adversary, Pierpont Mauler. Despite his glaring faults, Mauler nevertheless presented for Brecht a pheno-menon of almost mythical proportions: the embodiment of the power-drive which spurred many a self-made tycoon within the Western Capitalist system and which was most fully exemplified by

---

[10] 'Dreitägig ward in Packingtown im | 'Sumpf der Schlachtohöfe | Gesehn Johanna | Heruntersteigend von Stufe zu Stufe | Den Schlamm zu klären, zu erscheinen den | Untersten', *GKA* iii. 202. 14–18. (Quoted above, p. 152–3).

certain prominent American millionaires of the early twentieth century.[11] Brecht has chosen, however, to present Mauler in a more complex light than this would suggest: the successful tycoon also aspires to philanthropy, which is not in itself, perhaps, so unusual, given the abiding need experienced by those who have gained their ascendancy by ruthlessness to assuage a guilty conscience. But Brecht adds a more ambiguous personal facet to Mauler's character—and does so despite all his frequently stated renunciation of individual traits in his characterization. This is Mauler's genuine fascination with Johanna's innocence, her unworldliness, her courage and her persistence, her disinterested, totally unegotistical desire to penetrate behind appearances in an effort to try to understand the economic and human problems posed by the Capitalist system.

In examining the leitmotivs used in connection with Mauler I shall attempt to demonstrate how Brecht manages, despite all his stated prejudices against psychological analysis, to expose the deeper layers of character and motivation. For in arguing his own case and trying to stand his ground against his troublesome but persuasive adversary, Mauler is forced to analyse and defend the mainsprings of his own behaviour in ways he would not otherwise have done. Thus, in scene 8, entitled 'Pierpont Maulers Rede über die Unentbehrlichkeit des Kapitalismus und der Religion' (Pierpont Mauler's speech on the indispensability of capitalism and religion), his long speech expounding the rationale of Capitalism—which he is still at this stage able to defend with a fair degree of conviction— is dominated by a leitmotiv pattern which is to be of considerable significance. Capitalism is presented as an edifice which, as he admits in his long peroration about money, is not without its problematic aspects: 'dieser Aufbau! . . . Sehr schwierig herzustellen immerfort und mit Gestöhn | immerfort hergestellt' (what a structure! . . . Very hard to set up, continually set up | With many a groan) (183. 26, 30–1), an allusion, presumably, to its exploitative character and to the necessary hardships this brings to the have-nots in society. But nevertheless it is an edifice, a system, which he

---

[11] It is well known that Brecht was much taken by the work of Gustavus Myer, entitled 'Geschichte der großen amerikanischen Vermögen' (1916), which featured tycoons like J. D. Rockefeller and John Pierpont Morgan (father and son); also a German edition of George Lorimer's 'Briefe eines Dollar-Königs an seinen Sohn' (1904).

regards as possessing almost an existential significance: 'aber doch unvermeidlich | Abpressend der Ungunst des Planeten das Mögliche, wie immer | Dies sei' (but still inescapably | Wresting the possible from a reluctant planet | However much or little that may be). (183. 31–3). This latter subsidiary letimotiv, the planet, is familiar to us from *Baal* and *Im Dickicht der Städte*.[12] Even more telling is what we might term the 'infrastructure' underlying the 'Bau' that is Capitalism. Mauler's edifice is created, it would seem, as a bulwark against chaos, being a kind of insurance policy against the random workings of Chance:

> . . . Bedenk die Wirklichkeit und
> Platte Wahrheit, vielleicht nicht angenehm, aber doch
> Eben wahr, daß alles schwankend ist und preisgegeben
> Dem Zufall beinah, der Witterung das menschliche Geschlecht
> (consider the reality
> The plain truth, not pleasant maybe, but still
> True for all that: everything is unsteady and the human race
> is exposed to luck, you might say, to the state of the weather).

$$(183. 20–4)$$

This is a fair point and could be seen as a defence of, or as an explanation for, nearly all the endeavours of civilized man: it is certainly an argument which commanded respect with the young Heinrich von Kleist as he set to work to construct a 'Lebensplan' (life's plan) for precisely the same reasons.[13] What is lacking, of course, in Mauler's exposé is the dimension of human responsibility and concern. Survival of the fittest has never been one of mankind's most uplifting doctrines: 'Geld, aber ein Mittel, einiges zu verbessern, und sei's | Für einige nur' (But money's a means of making some improvement—even if only | For certain people) (183. 25–6), even if there is a general consensus that 'alles ist schwankend' (everything is unsteady) or that the planets are not attuned to human requirements. Mauler spins a subsidiary motiv

---

[12] See discussion above, p. 121.

[13] '. . . und der Zustand, ohne Lebensplan, ohne feste Bestimmung, immer schwankend zwischen unsichern Wünschen . . . ein Spiel des Zufalls . . . würde mich so unglücklich machen, daß mir der Tod bei weitem wünschenswerter wäre' (and the condition produced by living without a plan for one's life, without clear purpose, always dithering between vague desires, a plaything of chance, would make me so miserable that I would far prefer to die), Heinrich von Kleist, *Sämtliche Werke und Briefe*, ed. H. Sembdner (Munich, 1965), ii. 490.

within the main leitmotiv structure to suggest the puny power that one mere individual like himself possesses to alter the system—a mere 'fly', as it were, trying to stem a landslide:

> Denn sieh, wenn ich
> Der viel dagegen hat und schlecht schläft, auch
> Davon abgehn wollt, das wär, als wenn eine
> Mücke davon abläßt, einen Bergrutsch aufzuhalten. Ich würd
> Ein Nichts im selben Augenblick und über mich weg ging's weiter
> (Just think, if I—
> Who have much against it, and sleep badly—
> Were to desert it, I would be like a fly
> Ceasing to hold back a landslide. There and then
> I would become a nothing and it would keep on going over me).

$$(183. 35-9)$$

Why a landslide, one might ask? Is this a tell-tale suggestion that deep down Mauler suspects that the forces governing society *are* in the last analysis uncontrollable and irrational? Mauler goes on at this point in his speech to develop the 'Bau' leitmotiv as he poses the (for him) hypothetical question of an alternative architectural structure to the present one, a model which like the existing one would help to stave off disaster and chaos and yet at the same time would produce a radically different social hierarchy. A destruction, then, of the existing structure ('Sturz'), leading to a *tabula rasa* and a new beginning. But such a revolutionary blueprint is immediately dismissed by Mauler, who speculates about what would happen if he were to relinquish his present defensive, holding operation.

> Denn sonst—müßt alles umgestürzt werden von Grund aus
> Und verändert der Bauplan von Grund aus nach ganz anderer
> Unerhörter neuer Einschätzung des Menschen
> (For otherwise everything would have to be overturned
> And the architect's design fundamentally altered
> To suit an utterly different, incredible, new valuation of man).

$$(184.1-3).$$

Not only would this constitute a quatum leap in prevailing attitudes, but it would once and for all and quite unceremoniously dispense with any further need for organized religion or for the Almighty, 'der Abgeschafft würd, weil ganz ohne Amt' (who would have no function left | And be dismissed accordingly) (184. 5–6). The alternative architectural 'Bau' is therefore quite impracticable for Mauler, although by expressing his character's awareness of such an alternative Brecht produces a formal 'Gestus' which signals the viability of a process of reconstruction, even while the character himself is denying it. One could suggest a cross-referential parallel here with Johanna's see-saw leitmotiv, where we discovered that the possibility of additional interpretations—going beyond the character's own limited perspectives—was likewise left open.

One can see that many strands of meaning are woven into this configuration: there is the idea of creating stable social structures, irrespective of the cost in human terms, as a means of staving off chaos and dispelling personal feelings of *Angst*: 'Denn sieh, wenn ich | Der viel dagegen hat und schlecht schläft . . .' (Just think, if I—Who have much against it, and sleep badly) (183. 36–6). Then there is the defensive reaction to change, even though the reasons for maintaining the status quo are not rational; above all, Mauler's neurotic fear emerges as a strong source of resistance and takes on almost pathological proportions. Behind the façade of ruthless and forceful exploitation lurks a fear-ridden, insecure man who is hard put to it to expound a credible case for Capitalism, least of all when he reaches for a suitable leitmotiv to convey its nature and, by extending a subsidiary motiv (the landslide), reveals more than he can possibly have intended.

Mauler's deep-seated insecurity finds further expression after the stock-market crash, when he goes out to the stockyards in search of Johanna. A strong sense of disillusionment, bordering at times on nihilism, is now conveyed by a further transformation of the 'Bau' leitmotiv into something sordid and disgusting. The material components of the structure are revealed to be base indeed:

> Und was das Ding aus Schweiß und Geld betrifft
> Das wir in diesen Städten aufgerichtet haben
> (And as for the thing made of sweat and money
> Which we have erected in these cities).

> (203. 36–7)

The edifice looks imposing, despite these sordid pre-conditions, however:

> 's ist schon, als hätt einer
> Ein Gebäud gemacht, das größt der Welt und
> Das teuerste und praktischste
> (It already seems as though a man

> Had made a building, the largest in the world and
> The most expensive and practical).
>
> (203. 38–204. 1)

Yet its pretentious exterior cannot conceal these disgusting raw materials of which it is composed:

> aber
>
> Aus Versehen und weil's billig war, hätt er benutzt als
> Material Hundscheiß, so daß der Aufenthalt
> Darin doch schwer wär und sein Ruhm nur der
> Am End, er hätt den größten Gestank der Welt gemacht
> (but
> By an oversight, and because it was cheap—he used dog-shit
> As its material, so that it would have been very difficult
> To live in and in the end his only glory was
> that he had made the biggest stink in the world).
>
> (204. 1–5)

Not only does Mauler's new treatment of the leitmotiv reveal the extent to which he himself is now capable of distinguishing between appearance and reality, it also allows room for the expression of feelings of nausea experienced by anyone such as himself who has participated in such a revolting—and in his now revised view—indefensible institution:

> Und einer, der aus solchem Gebäud herauskommt
> Der hat ein lustiger Mann zu sein
> (And anyone who gets out of a building like that
> Should be a cheerful man).
>
> (204. 6–7)

This presentation of the leitmotiv seems almost to take on a confessional aspect, but such an impression soon needs correction as Mauler lapses into self-satisfaction, almost as if he were surmounted by a moral halo, as he reaches for a version of the 'oben'/'höhere'–'unten' primary leitmotiv:

> Den Niedrigen mag das Unglück niederschlagen
> Mich muß es höher, in das Geistige tragen
> (Bad luck may crush the man of humble size;
> Me it must waft to spiritual skies).
>
> (204. 10–11)

This self-conscious stylization—which once more serves the characterization by underlining the instability within Mauler's make-up—

is economically conveyed by the now well-established leitmotiv pattern.

Mauler's final application of this pattern further underlines his critical detachment from the present structure of society and his increasing powers of awareness. His ruthless exposure of the base motives of other interest-groups such as the Black Straw Hats in trying to make common cause with Capitalism is now also laid bare: 'Ich seh, ihr wünschtet euer Haus zu bauen | In meiner Schattenseite' (I see you would like to build your house | In my shade). (209. 18–19) Note here the felicitious extention of the 'Bau' leitmotiv which conveys the notion of clandestine secrecy which must accompany all efforts of the Church to lean parasitically on Mammon. The close, interdependent relationship between the two institutional 'structures', Church and Capitalism, in Mauler's new analysis can only be regarded as an association of weakness. To match, or 'shadow' the intrinsically dubious basis of the structure which is Capitalism, representatives of the Church acquire no more intrinsic strength than straws—and straw is hardly a robust building material; as such they can afford protection to the already grossly incapacitated members of society or the enfeebled, such as drowning men, providing no answer at all to the human problems created by Capitalism.

> Doch auch
> Wenn Mensch nur das hieße, wem geholfen wird
> Wär's auch nicht anders. Dann braucht ihr Ertrinkende.
> Denn euer Geschäft wäre dann
> Strohhalme zu sein
> (But even
> If man were only what is helped
> There would be no difference. Then you'd need drowning men
> For then it would be your business
> To be straws for them to clutch at).

(209. 21–5)

A parallel building project between Capitalism and the Church such as Mauler believes to have been confirmed signals reciprocity and an accommodation between the two: 'So bleibt alles | Im großen Umlauf der Waren wie der Gestirne' (So all remains | Within the mighty orbit of wares, like that of the stars) (209. 25–6), an ironical equation from a now disillusioned man who is well aware that his recent financial crash has made him unattractive to the Church bosses (as ruthless, it seems, as their stock-market counterparts), precisely at the point when he wished to renounce material values and embrace the spiritual life.

I have already commented on the way that the various primary leitmotivs such as 'Gebäude' and 'oben'/'unten', for example, are explicitly drawn together at the conclusion in a summarizing commentary. Thus the entrenched forces of Capitalism in the shape of the packers and the stockbreeders rhapsodize about raising and extending the 'Bau', but emphasize that such an extension is dependent upon a strict maintenance of the existing gulf between 'oben' and 'unten':

> Soll der Bau sich hoch erheben
> Muß es Unten und Oben geben
> (Top and bottom must apply
> For the building to be high).
>
> (223. 1–2)

This neatly draws the political threads together. Another summarizing application of the 'Bau' structure was presented in the stage version of 1931 but was then subsequently removed by Brecht. This is perhaps a pity, since the device of suddenly directing the audience's attention at the very last minute to the precise nature of the social structure by showing that the stage itself—or 'Bühnenbau'—is supported, held aloft entirely by the amorphous mass of working folk which had featured so prominently in the action could be regarded as a stroke of genius: 'Während der letzten Strophen ist das Fundament sichtbar geworden, auf dem alle stehen. Die ganze Bühne wird von einer dunklen Masse von Arbeitern getragen' (during the last stanzas the foundations on which all are standing become visible. The entire stage is supported by a dark mass of workers) (234. 27–8). To the attentive reader who has been following the 'Gebäude' network on its course this visual representation or concretization of a leitmotiv which has been so strongly and consistently presented could only be regarded as a dramatic gain, since it both anchors the otherwise metaphorical network in the action and makes a striking visual impact on which to close. Even those who find its political implications harsh or unpalatable must surely appreciate the virtuosity and ability shown by Brecht in sustaining motivic patterns over the entire drama. One might also be inclined to view this example of collective load-bearing alongside the leitmotiv used by Mauler to characterize his own role within the self-same structure. Not without pathos and self-stylization does the 'pre-enlightened' Mauler refer to himself in scene 6 in a manner almost reminiscent of Heine, as the strong man of Classical mythology, Atlas, who holds aloft the entire world on his muscular shoulders. The mismatch between image and actuality is deliberately gross here and one is strongly aware of the parodistic 'Gestus':

> O Slift, was hab ich da gemacht!
> Slift, ich hab mir aufgeladen das ganze Fleisch der Welt.
> Gleich einem Atlas stolpere ich, auf den Schultern
> Die Zentnerlast von Blechbüchsen, gradenwegs
> Unter die Brückenbögen
> (O Slift, what have I done!
> Slift, I've loaded myself with all the meat in the world.
> Like Atlas I stumble, cans by the ton on my shoulders
> All the way down to join the people who sleep
> Under bridges).
>
> (168. 2–6)

But how telling the contrast between this ludicrous distortion of the true nature of the social hierarchy and the real truth which is so startlingly revealed at the end of the stage version. Again one may regret Brecht's decision to lop off this particular limb of 'Bau' imagery. Did he, perhaps, not wish to make the social situation too explicit? But that would point to a conscious decision on his part to allow other focal points, such as the sympathetic presentation of the main protagonist, to assume the foremost position.

In order to discover whether that kind of character-emphasis might indeed best accord with Brecht's intentions, we shall now turn to the third major group of *Grundmotive* (primary leitmotivs), that relating to the 'Schlachthof' itself, which, as I indicated above, encompasses two separate facets, or subsidiary strands (*Nebenmotive*): first, an active function, according to which men are the agents of brutality against animals (the latter being simply another metaphor for fellow humans); second, there is the passive form of victimization, in which again the animal motiv is central as the target for exploitation and aggression. Given the predominantly social and political emphasis of this network, it is not surprising to find that this too is linked to the 'oben'/'unten' configuration (as, for instance, through such a phrase as 'von oben nach unten brüllenden Menschheit', humanity bellowing from the heights to the depths). Not surprisingly either, since the animal terminology is class-determined, it is the language used by superiors ('ihr da oben', you up there, as Johanna eventually describes them) towards their inferiors. In Mauler's parlance, though, it takes on an ambiguous flavour, as we shall see. The leitmotiv of the 'Schlachthof' reflects both the subject-matter of the drama and its symbolic and metaphorical significance, a Brechtian principle which is certainly not exclusive to *Die Heilige Johanna der Schlachthöfe*.[14] This function is made clear in the programmatic, almost prologue-like introductory speech with which Johanna makes her first appearance:

> In finsterer Zeit blutiger Verwirrung
>
> . . . .
>
> In solche Welt, gleichend einem Schlachtaus
> (In gloomy times of bloody confusion
> Into such a world, a world like a slaughterhouse).

> (132–3. 35–8)

Note that this speech is repeated substantially, but without the 'Schlachthof' leitmotiv, by Mauler in a kind of deliberate rounding off in the penultimate Section (10) of the drama (215. 35–216. 4). Having made the point so clearly, Brecht can then allow the metaphorical implications to develop freely, without having recourse to a heavy-handed or allegorical spelling out of the meaning. Capitalism in this configuration is inevitably associated with 'schlachten' (slaughter) and thus, as we have already noted, the active implication of the motiv is a matter of hypocritical regret for stock-market tycoons like Mauler ('O tierisches Geschäft', O bestial business; 'unser Geschäft ist blutig', our business is bloody, etc.—where he actually confuses the two functions of slaughterman and victim). This could be another example of Brecht's use of the Freudian slip as Mauler's feelings of guilt and insecurity are unconsciously revealed. It is not self-evident to Mauler as it is to the more hard-bitten Capitalists that the qualities which the ruling classes attribute to their 'inferiors', the workers, may more aptly be applied to themselves. The lines 'es sind zu viele, die | Vor Jammer brüllen, und es werden mehr' (There are too many people howling

---

[14] Cf., for instance, *Im Dickicht der Städte* or *Der Flug der Lindberghs*, where title and leitmotiv material are similarly interwoven.

with pain | And they are on the increase) (166. 12–13) immediately transfer the leitmotiv from the animal to the human sphere and expose the unpleasant reality of suffering and exploitation which the employers would dearly like to cover up.

A robuster view of the 'Klassenkampf' which is enshrined in the 'Schlachthof' leitmotiv is expressed and concretized in the 'Börsenschlacht' (stock-market battle). This is presented in two parts: first, directly in the three stock-market scenes (9, Livestock Exchange) in which first Mauler himself, then his delegated assistant, Slift, drives the share prices ever upwards until finally the market collapses. Even more effectively, the final stage of this process—which Mauler avoids because of his squeamishness—is presented in the (parodistic) form of a teichoscopic report of a battle (scene 10): 'Erinnere, Mauler, dich ...' (Remember, Mauler) (210. 20), to which Mauler replies 'So, Slift, so hast du mir den Kampf geführet? (So, Slift, that was how you managed the fight?) (216. 6). The ruthlessness of this battle is matched by the militant demeanour of the Church in its form of an army—the Black Straw Hats. In their songs they frequently employ the 'Schlacht' (or 'Kampf') leitmotiv to express an aggression which Brecht identifies as the same spirit that governs the world of Big Business:

> Man muß marschieren
> Und kümmern sich um nichts und helfen gehen
> Und auffahren Tanks und Kanonen
> (You've got to march
> And leave your cares and help with might and main
> And bring up tanks and cannon too).
>
> (159. 9–11)

By employing such militant tactics and terminology it is suggested that succour for the poor will be attained:

> Und Flugzeuge müssen her
> Und Kriegsschiffe über das Meer
> Um den Armen einen Teller Suppe zu erobern
> (And airplanes there shall be
> And battleships over the sea
> All to conquer a plate of soup, brother, just for you).
>
> (134. 21–3)

When finally the 'battles' are over—when, that is, the 'Börsenschlacht' has subsided and given way to a resumption of Capitalist activity—the significance of the double 'Schlacht' and 'Kampf' imagery and the interdependent relationship of the two has become fully apparent.

As far as the passive or 'animal' aspect of the leitmotiv is concerned, 'Tier' and 'tierisch' are used as a kind of short-hand device to stress moral inferiority or social deprivation. We have pointed already to its importance as a means of establishing attitudes towards the human condition and mentioned Mauler's typical ambivalence. On the one hand, he identifies the wretched plight of the working masses in these terms ('armen Leute, schlecht, und tierisch', poor folk, wicked, and brutish: 147. 9) but, on the other, is soon found making distinctions prompted by the change wrought in him by Johanna. Thus 'tierisch' (brutish) ceases to have for Mauler the association of 'despicable' and 'beneath contempt' which it has for the other meat bosses; instead it elicits from him compassion and humanitarian feelings (how genuine and un-trammelled by sentimentality these are is another matter): 'es sind zu viele, die | Vor Jammer brüllen' (There are too many people howling with pain) (166. 12–13), or else in a combination of 'oben'/'unten' and animal leitmotivs:

> in dem Sturz der
> Von oben nach unten durch Jahre
> Ohn Unterlaß zur Hölle fließenden
> Brüllenden Menschheit . . .
> (in the downward rush
> Of howling humanity,
> Surging towards hell without respite).

> (167. 2–6)

On the other hand, Johanna herself with her clear-sighted, entirely genuine humanitarianism makes a distinction between animal and human; she is not to be found confusing the two levels or manipulating them. Instead she upbraids the meat-packers, while incidentally pointing out that their ruthless behaviour could conceivably lead some people (not herself) to regard *them* 'nicht mehr als Menschen . . . sondern als wilde Tiere' (no longer as human beings but as wild animals) (177. 6–7). She believes distinctions should be made: 'mit Menschen soll man nicht umgehen wie mit Ochsen' (human beings shouldn't be treated like steers) (177. 14–15), the implication being that such identification of the human and the animal reflects the possibility of a certain brutalization, thereby turning the attribute back on those employing it themselves.

A very interesting new application of the animal leitmotiv occurs just before the end, when Johanna—despite all her scrupulous attempts earlier to keep the animal and the human categories separate[15]—now associates *herself* with an animal:

> Hätte ich doch
> Ruhig gelebt wie ein Vieh
> Aber den Brief abgegeben, der mir anvertraut war
> (If only I had lived
> As tranquilly as a cow
> And yet delivered the letter that was entrusted to me).

(221. 5–7)

This new configuration of associations reflects a complex development. Johanna's self-hatred and sense of having betrayed the workers' cause reaches a high pitch of negativity and disillusionment. The hypothetical self-identification with a 'Vieh' (beast, such as a cow) is out of character with the earlier Johanna and is presented as a kind of hyperbole to reflect the lengths to which she would have been prepared to go—in fact to have foregone all her most human qualities of intelligence, kindliness, and perseverance in order to have carried out her political task. It is a strange thought indeed, since the possession of such qualities as she has shown must surely come across as so much more appealing than the automatic, unquestioning, instinctive behaviour which she now presents as the alternative.

From an analysis of the major group of leitmotivs it can be seen how firmly anchored the patterns are within the progression of characters and events which is such a distinctive feature of this work. The extent to which they serve to define, reveal, and underpin the characterization is, possibly, surprising when one considers that the drama's genesis overlaps with the writing of several of the *Lehrstücke*, works in which characterization as such is pared down to an austere two-dimensionality. We shall look more closely at this phenomenon when we turn to consider the question of parody and the extent to which the traditional features which appear in *Die Heilige Johanna* must be regarded as wholly

---

[15] Implied in her earlier insistence on man's 'higher' aspirations, see above, p. 142.

conditional upon that form, but before proceeding to that matter, I should like briefly to survey some other leitmotivs which are not quite so pervasive as the primary patterns but are nevertheless important in the hierarchical configuration. There is, for example, a group of leitmotivs which is specific to the *masses*; the comparatively low-key status of these is perhaps significant, and certainly Marxist critics have not been slow to criticize the apparent insignificance of this crucial element in the class struggle.[16] However, it is also true that it is this area of association which elicits one of the most remarkable and eloquent passages in the entire drama, in which the leitmotiv patterning plays a crucial role. This is Johanna's dream (scene 9: 185. 28–39; 186. 1–30,) in which in vivid, even visionary terms, Johanna sees her role as mediator on the fulcrum of the see-saw transformed into something much more expressive and compelling; sees herself metamorphosed magically into many different selves ('in vielfacher Gestalt') leading the vast procession of poor and downtrodden through the city streets, changing their surroundings on their course ('alles verändernd, was mein Fuß berührte', changing whatever my foot touched: 186. 12). This is a highly concentrated, complex configuration of leitmotivs and when one examines it closely it can be seen to contain many of the major primary motivs: 'oben'/'unten'; 'Bau'; the idea of the 'Kampf', here modified into a rousing crusade. It is as if the major elements had been taken up and transcend into a higher register, the Utopian aspect being unmistakable. This special function and fusing of the leitmotivs marks the section out as a classic exemplification of the term 'Zwischenbilanz' (interim survey) invented by Emil Staiger— thence to be modified by Volker Klotz into 'integration point'—to identify structurally crucial points in drama in which the hero or heroine is able to stand back, draw the threads of the action together, and achieve for both himself and the audience a deeper clarification and understanding of an action which has hitherto appeared mysterious and puzzling.

In this instance the instrument of change and transformation is brilliantly and economically expressed via the leitmotiv pattern: it involves a change of *physical* state. Thus, whereas the 'Bau'/ 'Gebäude' pattern had implied a rigid structure and even the see-saw appeared to be permanently fixed; whereas animal traits had

---

[16] See Schumacher's still illuminating study: *Bertolt Brecht: Die dramatischen Versuche 1918–1933*, 434–93.

overlapped with human at every point in the inexorable 'Schlacht' or 'Klassenkampf', in the bright new vision this entire ossified and degraded structure is at one fell swoop transformed from the solid into the liquid state. Key words here are 'Klumpen' (bunch or clump) and 'fließen' (flow). At first the marching masses represent a physically dense, solid entity (this being virtually a concretization of the term 'solidarity', one feels). This gigantic, seemingly hazardously constituted physical mass consolidates into a kind of panting inchoate monster (possibly traces of the animal leitmotiv linger on here): 'und jetzt hing | Der Klumpen übern Rand, einen Augenblick | Festhaltend, in sich pulsend ... (And the bunch was suspended on its edge, holding fast | A moment, quivering) (185. 36–8). Then suddenly, magically, it seems, though evidently in response to a word from their leader (later identified as Johanna herself), this once so solid mass is changed into a liquid state and pours unstoppably through the city streets, its former inertia now utterly changed into a driving, purposeful self-propulsion forwards and onwards. One notes the not negligible role played here by the leader herself, around whom the 'Schlacht' leitmotiv, much altered, crystallizes:

> An eurer Spitze sah ich stumm mich schreiten
> Mit kriegerischem Schritt, die Stirne blutig
> Und Wörter rufend kriegerischen Klangs)
> (I, silent, saw myself striding at your head
> With warlike step and bloodstains on my brow
> And shouting words that sounded militant).
>
> (186. 4–6)

The point of greatest significance here is the new awareness of the necessity for violence and destruction as an accompaniment to successful revolution: 'Tugend und Schrecken' (virtue and terror) almost smack of French Revolutionary slogans; 'unmäßige Zerstörung bewirken' (causing measureless destruction) is unequivocal and uncompromising. The remarkable thing is that already at this point Johanna is able at the subconscious level to accept the principle of violence as a necessary concomitant of radical change. However, her conscious actions continue—until just before her death—to be governed by the principle of nonviolence. The dream therefore anticipates clearly the direction in which Brecht wishes the problems explored in the drama to be resolved. When she is at her lowest ebb (scene 9, Stockyards) and overcome with cold and hunger, Johanna will be prepared to renounce the Utopian vision which earlier she had so eloquently articulated: 'so kalt war's nicht in meinem Traum' (it wasn't as cold as this in my dream) (198. 30).

Another important facet of this richly textured motivic pattern in the dream vision relates to the transformed masses who are now pouring like molten lava through the streets of Chicago, destroying and changing everything in their path. The anonymity and facelessness of such a mass phenomenon is significant: first as a 'Klumpen', then as a 'Fluß', the almost elemental power of this force resides in its very composite nature and in the abandonment of all the individual features which had distinguished its component parts. At various points this renunciation of individual qualities is presented as a desideratum or as a source of defensive fear, depending on the standpoint of the observer. Mauler's detective, sent by him to track down Johanna, who has joined the waiting workers in the snow, registers amazement. 'Ohne jedes Gesicht oder Namen sitzt das und wartet' (the mob sits there and waits, without a face or a name) (194. 21). The allied leitmotiv of snow is another means of expressing the idea of the obliteration of all individual traits and also occurs in the dream vision where its positive, protecting and blanketing features are stressed:

> so zog der Zug, und mit ihm ich
> Verhüllt durch Schnee vor jedem feindlichen Angriff
> (So the procession moved, and I along with it
> Veiled by snow from any hostile attack).
>
> (186. 16–17)

It will have a less positive meaning for Johanna, however, when she is subject to physical cold and has to learn suffering at a fundamental level. Thus the leitmotiv signifies at the lower level a physical trial, at the higher level the necessary featurelessness and renunciation of individuality which is a pre-condition of revolutionary change. For Mauler, no less than for Johanna, it becomes a force to be reckoned with: 'und wenn es schneit, dann | Schneit's auf sie, welche du kennst' (and if it snows | it will be snowing on the girl you know) (185. 19–20). Does that, possibly, reflect Mauler's fears that the individual features characteristic of Johanna (to which he is deeply attached) will be expunged and that she will thus be removed by snow from his ken, possibly even merged with the masses whom he fears? For Mauler, then, the referential status of 'Schnee' is basically negative; for Johanna, as we have seen, it is positive in the dream vision but in her hour of direst need she appears unable to meet the austere and spiritual challenge entailed by 'Schnee':

> O Wahrheit, helles Licht! Verfinstert durch einen Schneesturm zur Unzeit!
> Nicht mehr gesehn werdend fürderhin! Oh, von welcher Gewalt sind Schneestürme
> (O truth, shining light! Darkened by a snowstorm in an evil hour!
> Lost to sight from that moment! Oh, how violent are snowstorms!)
>
> (205. 25–8)

But that application still leaves open those positive associations of transfiguration through 'Selbsterkenntnis', self-knowledge (which in Brecht's terms mean self-obliteration) such as the Communist agitators are urging. The 'Schnee' leitmotiv can thus be seen to be an admirably flexible instrument and Brecht shows considerable mastery of the technique in the manner in which he concretizes the image, in itself simple, and invests it with a wide range of meanings.

As we move towards an elucidation of the complex interrelationships of the different leitmotiv groups, we cannot ignore any longer the role of the parody. It is, of course, not confined to Schiller's *Die Jungfrau von Orleans*; Goethe's *Faust*, Schiller's *Wallenstein*, Hölderlin's *Hyperions Schicksalslied*, and many another Classical work provides Brecht with additional ammunition. There are two aspects of his application of the parodies to which I should like to draw attention. Firstly, there is the extent to which the 'Klassikerparodien' are disjunctive in function, operating as 'gestic' devices. Secondly, it is important to discover the extent to which the adoption of the broader elements of parodistic imitation fit in, e.g. twists and turns of the plot (which, for once, is based on the Aristotelian model), traditional forms of characterization, together with the adoption of attendant features like 'tragic guilt' (Johanna's transgression in failing to deliver the letter with which she is entrusted), the 'divided personality' (Mauler's 'zwei Seelen', two souls); all of which devices, being in themselves ambiguous, may boomerang against the author and at times elicit readings along more traditional lines than Brecht's stated intentions might have suggested. Such possibilities, as on other occasions, point to the likelihood that subconscious processes, which otherwise would be under strict censorship, may be operating at the point of creation. There seems to be some tangible evidence of this in *Die Heilige Johanna*; certainly the Behaviourist model with its mechanical view of human personality is abandoned in favour of some highly effective characterization. It has to be said, too, that parody proves to be a two-edged sword. It may indeed, and is clearly intended to, operate disjunctively, to play up the discrepancies between form and content, to suggest a ludicrous mismatch. It depends, though, on the playful laying bare of similarities *and* differences between the work, or sections of it, and its parodistic 'Vorlage' or model. Unless a kinship through similarity exists, however, the differences cannot be appreciated; in fact the attraction for the reader resides in a careful balancing of like and unlike. Take, for instance, Frau Luckeniddle's lament about the ever-recurring need of human beings to eat:

> Das ist die Grausamkeit des Hungers, daß er
> Wenngleich befriedigt, immer wieder kommt
> (That's the awful thing about hunger: no sooner
> Is it satisfied than back it comes again).

> (175. 32–3)

The success of this parody depends on our recognizing the *Wallenstein* tag:

> OCTAVIO. Das eben ist der Fluch der bösen Tat,
> Daß sie, fortzeugend, immer Böses muß gebären
> (The curse of evil deeds is that, multiplying,
> They needs must breed yet more).

The technique of parodistic substitution ('Hunger' instead of 'böser Tat'; 'Grausamkeit' instead of 'Fluch'; 'immer wieder kommt' for 'immer muß gebären') also involves trivialization, a common feature of parody. The same technique applies to the 'Börsen-schlacht'–*Hyperion* parody, already mentioned.

These sporadic examples of pardody certainly contribute to the general ironical and distanced tone with which much of the drama is pervaded. Also, in so far as the parody sometimes overlaps with the leitmotiv structures analysed above, it can serve a distancing, 'gestisch' function (Mauler's use of the 'Atlas' leitmotiv, for example, or the *Faust* 'Bergschluchten' parody at the end with its incorporation of the 'oben'/'unten' leitmotiv are cases in point). The letter-device (one of which Schiller could be said to have been rather fond) is another amusing way in which the contrived, irrational workings of the stock-market are suggested. But frequently the leitmotiv structuring seems to operate separately from the parodies—or above and beyond them. When one considers the lateness of their introduction, that may not be so surprising, for they do not seem to be all that deeply rooted in the context, although it is not unusual for Brecht to 'hitch' them on to existing leitmotiv patterns. While many a leitmotiv may itself originate in Brecht's almost unstoppable ability to pull out another Classical allusion—the 'Bau' for instance, may, as has been suggested,[17] have been derived from Schiller's ballad, 'Die Glocke'—they take on a life of their own and soon acquire contextual meaning from their surroundings. When such a process has gone a certain distance, they start to look more like any other 'source material' which the author, as is customary, develops along new lines, and less like pure parody (this is a grey area, as Brecht must have been well aware, since his notorious 'piratings' of the Ammer Villon translations had led to a celebrated court case over *Die Dreigroschenoper*). I see little difference myself between an author's referring parodistically in one literary work to another and his doing so in other ways, whether by allusion, comparison, or whatever.

There is little doubt, however, that Brecht's imitation of Classical or Aristotelian drama often acts as an overarching device, subsuming the individual 'Klassikerparodien', many of which were rooted out by Brecht's assiduous co-workers and set on top of the piece like icing on a cake. It tends to operate, significantly, in the broader areas of characterization and plot, where one's awareness of similarities between text and 'Vorlage' may loom larger than the observed differences. The character of Johanna is one of Brecht's finest portraits, whatever his intentions may have been, and it has been rightly observed that she stands at the beginning of a line which leads straight on to Mutter Courage, Shen Te, and Grusche.[18] Of course, we are tempted to see Johanna's dream

[17] See, for example, Gudrun Schulz's valuable study, *Die Schillerbearbeitungen Bertolt Brechts* (Tübingen, 1972), 140 f.

[18] F. Ewen, *Bertolt Brecht: Sein Leben, sein Werk, seine Zelt* (Hamburg and Düsseldorf, 1970), 225. (English version: *Bertolt Brecht: His Life, his Art, and his Times* (New York, 1967).)

vision as a parodistic counterpart to Joan of Arc's voices and to enjoy recognizing the connection. But there the resemblance ends, and we are immediately caught up in the memorable projection of the vision of a new society which, one has to admit, has brought out the best of Brecht's gifts for linguistic and rhetorical expressiveness and his subtle manipulation of complex motivic material. That becomes, surely, the decisive point, while the other fades into insignificance. Brecht persuades us to grapple with the issues of the drama in terms of the time-honoured theme of an idealism which falls foul of reality—a theme which, paradoxically, lies at the heart of the greatest dramas of the dramatist whose work he is parodying as well. Because of the complex and ambiguous way in which he builds up associations through leitmotivs we are put in a position where we can view Johanna's 'failure' as much in terms of the personal dilemma of a leader as in terms of socio-economic forces which are only comprehensible in terms of Marxist analysis.

It is, finally, relevant to bear in mind the extent to which 'action' in the Aristotelian sense may serve to interact with the impressions and associations built up through the leitmotivs. Again this is an intentional function of the parody. The action takes on definite features such as peripeteia: confused tidings in the wake of the 'Börsenschlacht', for example, give credibility to the rumour that Mauler is going to open the stockyards again; this would weaken the case for a general strike and helps to motivate Johanna's refusal to take part in violent retaliatory measures which have been planned on the basis of the opposite assumption. Likewise, Mauler's repudiation of his 'crimes' and desire to embrace religion and the spiritual life is foiled by the (mistaken) assumption of Major Snyder that his financial viability is once and for all finished, thus rendering him useless to the ever-impoverished Church. This 'rejection' simply leads him back to the stock-market (making us doubt the sincerity of his original decision) and to the setting up of new Big Business ventures. Such twists and turns in the action—and they are most noticeable at the end—are possibly introduced to emphasize the extent to which irrational forces—like rumour, for example, or half-understood and incomplete information—can produce results which, as in the case of Johanna's 'transgression', are out of all proportion to their cause. I do not think, however, that this is how it comes across in the drama. Instead, we are given a convincing and credible display of perfectly familiar half-truths and imperfect sources of information on which so many human decisions and actions have, of necessity, to be based. We recognize this, in short, as a feature of life itself—not just of Classical tragedy—and acknowledge the element of 'blindness' which, especially in Johanna's case, carries with it strong empathatic signals.

The question of responsibility for her actions, given such a reading, seems less clear-cut; it is not self-evident that she could have acted in any way other than the one she chooses, a situation which is typical of Classical tragedy (and a point of overlap, as we shall see, between this drama and *Leben des Galilei*). We may tend to see her dilemma as that of the individual who is struggling for enlightenment ('Wissen') and humanitarian values against the entrenched forces of a monolithic system. We may note the Schillerian theme of the limits and entanglements that beset those who try to implement ideals in an imperfect world.

In the last analysis, then, a tension is set up between the leitmotiv patterns, on the one hand, in which the call for revolution comes across strongly and clearly and, on the other, the overarching parodistic effect whereby we tend to identify the heroine, in terms of her 'guilty' behaviour at least, with her model, Schiller's Maid, who likewise transgresses because of weakness of the flesh. Which of these 'perspectives' carries the greater authority? Which, as it were, 'overarches' the other? The answer is surely plain: the richness of the leitmotiv texture, the impressive way in which Brecht reaches again and again through the leitmotiv network for a resolution of the fundamental dichotomies of 'oben'–'unten', and, above all, the sheer poetic power with which he raises many of these motivs into a higher register of revolutionary idealism must tilt the balance emphatically towards the cause of the masses and the desire for social and political change as expressed through the medium of the leitmotivs. But, because of the rather different signals coming through the other channel, there is no overall resolution within the drama itself and no one perspective commands total support. An ambiguity remains, as well as a greater ironic complexity than we find in Schillerian drama.

7
Leben des Galilei: Leitmotiv and Paradox

This drama—to some people's minds Brecht's greatest—exhibits a complexity in the handling of perspectival techniques unparalleled elsewhere in his work, even the richly endowed embodiment of leitmotiv parody, *Die Heilige Johanna der Schlachthöfe.* For the first time Brecht is able to allow his innate dramatic instincts full rein and this has the consequence of removing the drama even more thoroughly from the strait-jacket of his theory of 'epic' theatre. It is to this drama above all others that the theory of leitmotiv developed by Wagner can be most profitably applied, although as I have pointed out it is largely *faute de mieux* that we are forced to adapt a critical tool which was designed in the first instance for music rather than for word drama. The drama is crucially important too in charting Brecht's own development over a period of just less than twenty years and unique in that it is the only large-scale work to be available in three distinct versions, one of which is in English. At last, since the advent of the *Große kommentierte Berliner und Frankfurter Ausgabe,* we are in a position to compare these in full and no longer have to rely on snippets of information and extracts from scenes. This is not the place for a full-scale comparison between the Danish version (1938/9), the American version (in English, 1947), and the Berlin version (1955/6), but it will at certain points be useful to draw attention to changes affecting the perspectival techniques. In very general terms, the American version tends to be more concise; this feature—which may well have something to do with Charles Laughton's influence—produces a somewhat leaner texture. The final version was completed not long before Brecht's death and thus only briefly exposed to his own personal direction at the Theater am Schiffbauerdamm; although it shows a much surer and far more succinct handling of dialogue than the Danish version (not the American, however, which is quite brilliant), this is not achieved by cutting down on the dense webs of leitmotivic imagery. Indeed, if anything, these are extended and reinforced to add further depth and concentration to the texture.

The material for the drama had a very special personal significance for Brecht and it is interesting to find that already in the early 1930s the figure of Galileo had started to attract his attention, a process which was prompted naturally enough by the increasing stranglehold of Fascism upon all cultural and intellectual life and institutions in Germany and the countless signs of repression. Paul Hindemith, Brecht's composer for the *Badener Lehrstück*—and, like Brecht, one of the victims of Fascism—had sought in his opera *Mathis der Maler*, by focusing on the struggles of a late medieval painter, Matthias Grünewald, to express the fundamental and potentially tragic conflict between conscience and authority in his own age—and such a conflict must have seemed almost a commonplace to artists at the time. Brecht, on the other hand, was typically drawn to a more practical hero and to practical issues, finding in the great seventeenth-century physicist, forced out of an intellectual ivory tower by the Church, a wonderfully powerful and suggestive figure in whom all kinds of ramifications and ambiguities inherent in both the situation and the character could be explored in the greatest possible depth. Although Brecht would have argued that the attraction exerted upon him by Galileo was due entirely to the issues that were raised by his actions and that Galileo was in fact to be regarded as an *exemplary* case, along the lines of the *Lehrstücke*, it is clear from the various reworkings to which he subjected the material that character and characterization itself had moved into the foreground of his drama. Since the days of *Baal* this had been ruthlessly and most successfully relegated, partly as a result of Brecht's avowed lack of interest in the psychological dimension of human behaviour, partly in response to his concern to give political and social issues pride of place (the case of *Die Heilige Johanna* illustrates the conflict and contradictions which such a programme set up, especially in comparison with the contemporary *Lehrstücke*). The collaboration with the character actor Laughton in Hollywood could only enhance this feature further. It is scarcely surprising that this unmistakable shift to character drama brought in its train important changes in the dramatic structure and presentation as well. The comparative absence of aggressively 'epic' features is especially apparent. Of the four great 'exile' dramas

Leben des Galilei stands out very prominently in this respect: *Mutter Courage*, its nearest equivalent, still retains an important 'epic' dimension through its songs; as does *Der kaukasische Kreidekreis* through its framework and its omnipresent 'Sänger', who even reports the innermost thoughts of Grusche to the audience; while *Der gute Mensch von Sezuan* adopts the aggressively disjunctive feature of split characterization. *Leben des Galilei*, by comparison with these, is relatively unaffected by manipulative devices.

Before we proceed to analyse the remarkable network of leitmotivs by means of which Brecht creates a complex texture of perspective to match the demands of the material, we must first take note, however, of those other perspectival devices, most of them disjunctive, of which he still avails himself. This brief review will concern itself exclusively with the textual evidence; matters such as stage-production will not be taken into consideration. In all three versions Brecht relies on his now familiar summarizing prefaces (they might be termed 'mini-prologues') which take their place before each scene. Mainly these contain factual information such as dates and the anticipated outcome of the action contained in each, this being Brecht's surprisingly naïve method of attempting to eliminate emotional involvement on the part of the audience, an involvement which he felt must necessarily follow upon their being surprised by events. The two later versions of the drama show some development of the technique to include short, introductory verses, spoken or sung by a 'Sänger' (singer), which go beyond the strictly factual and expository to take issue in a pithy, 'gestic' fashion with the forthcoming action. Often this will reflect an authorial stance which is humorous, ironic, and even somewhat affectionate towards Galileo. It might be of interest to reflect how these interpolations bear a certain resemblance to the musical prologues and transitional devices sought by Lessing and implemented by Richard Wagner. But, of course, they appear to contain none of the accumulative elements—leitmotivs linking past and present and anticipating the future—which are such a feature of Wagner's practice. Brecht seeks to detach each scene from the preceding ones; he does not wish for any carry-over of accumulated impressions, nor should there be any buildup to a climax at the end, which might present difficulties for the audience in adjusting to contrasting moods. Brecht's 'mini-prologues' are, therefore, not transitional but they *are* prospective and anticipatory within the scene itself and they establish a tone—which is surprisingly even throughout the work—as well as terms of reference by means of which we are enjoined to approach the action.

Brecht makes extensive use of the related devices of sententiae and stichomythia in *Galilei* and this performs an additional perspectival function. Partly, Brecht is 'historicizing' and developing the disputational element in seventeenth-century scholastic and scientific discourse and dialogue. Occasionally Galileo's statements seem unequivocally bald, e.g. 'Die Wahrheit ist das Kind der Zeit, nicht der Autorität (truth is born of the times, not of authority) (222. 35) and again 'als Wissenschaftler haben wir uns nicht zu fragen, wohin die Wahrheit uns führen mag' (our duty as scientists is not to ask where truth is leading) (223. 5–6). The status of such a seemingly universal remark is, however, deceptive and it will be sharply modified by the repentant old scientist at the very end, whose sense of wrongdoing is such that he comes to acknowledge the need for responsibility in the pursuit of knowledge: 'Hätte ich widerstanden, hätten die Naturwissenschaftler etwas wie den hippokratischen Eid der Ärzte entwickeln können . . .' (had I stood firm the scientist could have developed something like the doctors' Hippocratic oath 284. 27–9). It is not self-evident that this new perspective gained by the hero is necessarily definitive either, however. Stichomythic generalizations can be regarded as a kind of extended use of sententiae and occur frequently in the form of biblical proverbs, as, for example, in the crux scene between Barberini and Galileo (this exists only in the second and final versions, where it appears as scene 6, 2 and scene 7 respectively). This is a virtuoso passage and anticipates our later discussion of leitmotivic imagery since the first biblical quotation (from the book of Proverbs) already contains elements of the imagery of movement: 'Die Sonne geht auf und unter und kehret an ihren Ort zurück' ('the sun also ariseth, and the sun goeth down') (236. 23–4). This is followed by a series of stichomythic exchanges—again from the book of Proverbs—in which the implications of a fearless pursuit of knowledge are debated. The 'gestic' element which comes over strongly here is Barberini's expression of political caution and expediency, which contrasts totally with Galileo's unconditional demand for the pursuit of knowledge, a clash which will bear important fruit later in the drama when Barberini as Pope consents to Galileo's being brought before the Inquisition and to his thus being forced into recanting his teachings and sacrificing his principles.

Another fairly familiar example of 'disjunctive' commentary is the use of the ballad-singer (scene 10) to convey the sense of Galileo's impact on the thinking of the common people. In bold and blunt terms Galileo's theories are presented in 'potted' form and their social, political, and theological implications are spelled out for the benefit of the common folk in mocking and anti-authoritarian terms:

> Und es begannen sich zu kehren
> Um die Gewichtigen die Minderen
> Um die Vorderen die Hinteren
> Wie im Himmel so auf Erden
> (So the circles were all woven:
> Around the greater went the smaller
> Around the pace-setter the crawler
> On earth as it is in heaven).
>
> (260. 2–5)

Here one senses the deliberate anachronisms typical of Brecht's Marxist approach to history: such an expression of class-consciousness as the Sänger provides could scarcely have been possible in the context of the seventeenth century, even if it had been tolerated by the authorities (which is unlikely). Notice that once more, while reaching for a device—the ballad—which is one of the stock-in-trades of his 'epic' theatre, Brecht is careful to link the Sänger's imagery (it is the familiar imagery of movement) and the accompanying pantomime (representing the principle of the Earth moving round the Sun) to a pattern which pervades the entire drama. We shall return at a later point to the function of the ballad-singer's verses in the context of the leitmotiv structure and commentary.

Possibly also belonging to the sphere of 'disjunctive' commentary is an interpolated anecdote, present in the first version (scene 8: 72. 23 f.), but thereafter dropped. The Keunos story is clearly meant to provide a parallel situation to Galileo's (the Greek philosopher seemingly complies with authoritarian demands upon him, but wins out in the end). It is a situation with which Galileo can identify without his having to make a direct or explicit statement, and it represents one possible attitude towards the problem of repressive authority which is Galileo's own. The reason it was dropped relates to Brecht's rather drastic reappraisal of his hero's behaviour under pressure. The earlier conception still has something of Brecht's 1930s view of the politically deft, cunning intellectual who is prepared to play along, even adopt a posture of servility, in order to ultimately triumph over the forces of repression, as the Keunos does towards the authoritarian Agent. That would conform to Andrea's first reaction at the very end to the news that Galileo has kept his work on the *discorsi* going, for he sees this as a ruse adopted by Galileo whereby his recantation would seem to have been part of a studied plan. Of course, in Brecht's revised and more severe view of the hero and his problem such (laudable) tactical behaviour by which the end would justify the means is revealed to have been far from Galileo's intentions. Although the device of the parallel interpolation is a familiar one in Classical drama (Goethe is especially fond of it, as we see from *Torquato Tasso*)[1], it is somewhat uneconomical as a form of oblique commentary and it finds no counterpart in the taut construction of the two later versions.

If this diffuse type of perspectivism later seems irrelevant to Brecht's purposes, another seemingly long-winded device does find favour and in the final version alone. This is the presentation of a section of Galileo's own *discorsi* (scene 13) just after the climactic moment of his recantation (274. 31–9; 275. 1–7). A section is quoted—and Brecht is relying here on a close translation of the original—in which a general scientific principle is stated on the basis of a number of disparate examples. The subject-matter refers to the respective vulnerability of larger and smaller organisms in the face of danger, and the applicability of the principle—the smaller are resilient whereas the larger are endangered—to Galileo's own situation is spelled out so clearly as to make this serve as an internalized image and paradox. As such, it will be examined in greater detail below.

---

[1] The Prinzessin's susceptibility to excessive emotional and artistic (in her case, musical) stimulus is presented as a partial parallel to Tasso's similar sensitivity. The parallel creates a special bond between the two characters. The Prinzessin, of course, controls her weakness by a policy of reuniciation ('Entsagung') which she unsuccessfully enjoins upon Tasso. Goethe, *Werke* (Hamburger Ausgabe), v, ed. L. Blumenthal and E. Haufe (9th edn., Munich, 1981), 1801–16 (p. 122).

We can see from the above, therefore, that many of the perspectival devices in *Leben des Galilei* have lost that sharp edge associated with a disjunctive presentation which was a characteristic feature of the notion of 'Trennung der Elemente' in the heyday of Brecht's 'epic' theory and the application of 'Verfremdungseffekt'. The disjunctive and the integrated modes of perspectival comment-ary are indeed sometimes hard to distinguish. In the notable absence of 'songs' which would continue to break up the dialogue within the individual scenes, the additional reduction in the number and variety of purely 'text-external' techniques seems fairly drastic and leaves a great deal of scope for new or more highly developed alternative forms of perspectival commentary to appear.

To these we shall now turn our attention. First let us take stock of the general position, identifying a number of leading, or *Grundmotive*. Pride of place must go to those which can be grouped together under the general label of 'laws of motion', motivs, that is, relating to the principles governing movement of astral bodies (scenes 1, 4, 6, 8, 9 and 14). These derive from the very physical laws and forces which are the subject of Galileo's research. The constituent images are diverse since Brecht is able to exploit their spatial ramifications: circular movement, for example, is very prevalent, movement of one heavenly body around another, but there is also a vertical implication: the contrasted levels of 'oben' (above) and 'unten' (below), and from this notion there also comes the idea of distance or 'Abstand' (scenes 7 and 9) and of relative size (scenes 3, 12, and 13). A further offshoot is developed from the notion of flexibility and freedom of bodies which are no longer seen as functioning within a hierarchical framework. Such 'freedom' can be interpreted negatively when it is seen to remove long-established and fixed props in which people have since time immemorial placed their trust (scene 3). In all these major groups of leitmotivs social, theological, and political associations are hinted at, which has the effect of opening up a deeper layer of interpretation and perspectival commentary. Because of the constant repetitions, development, and transformation of the motivs over a large number of scenes it is, I believe, appropriate to regard them as operating in a fashion akin to the leitmotiv networks with which we are familiar from studying Wagner's theories. Slightly different, perhaps, from these are what I shall term 'secondary' motivs (*Nebenmotive*). An example of these is the chess imagery, which almost qualifies as a leitmotiv in that it recurs in scenes 1 (11. 18) and 7 (55. 31) of the Danish version. However, its status is reduced in the final two versions to a single appearance in scene 7, although it might not be too difficult to argue for its wider extension into other scenes through the allied motiv of constriction ('Enge') and its contrastive counterpart of unfettered breadth ('Weite').

A leitmotiv which receives a pantomimic rather than the more usual textual presentation is the mask. Its first appearance is in the crucial scene between Barberini and Galileo (Haus des Kardinals, scene 7: 234. 36–40; 235. 1–2). The motiv—which in this respect resembles the chess motiv—is actualized here too by its being anchored in the pantomimic material established in the stage-directions, from which we learn that a masked ball is taking place. Later in the scene the two cardinals, Bellarmin and Barberini, appear wearing the masks of a lamb and a dove respectively (representing Christ, the sacrificial victim, and the Holy Ghost). The mask enables Barberini, the keen amateur mathematician, to express his views about the implications of Galileo's work in a much franker fashion than normally; on the other hand, Galileo himself is significantly unmasked, which suggests his vulnerability. The later example is in scene 10, the Carneval, which forms a striking contrast to the earlier example, not only in social terms (ragged common folk replace Church dignitaries) but also in terms of the frankness and boldness of the utterances expressed. Masks in this context, it would seem, do not denote dissembling or dishonesty.

The way in which the 'movement network' operates as a perspectival device in the drama is extremely complex and it is fascinating to observe how Brecht turns the bare bones of a scientific theory—the revolution of the Earth around the Sun—into a literary technique capable of infinite nuances and flexibility. An especially brilliant stroke is the pantomimic demonstration of the theory of rotation itself by means of a simple experiment on stage (scene 1) in which Galileo moves the boy Andrea, together with chair on which he is sitting. Is it too fanciful to suggest that the process of grounding and visibly demonstrating the principle underlying what is the most pervasive and wide-ranging of all the *Grundmotive* in this drama is akin to the process of 'Vergegen-wärtigung' (actualization) by means of which Wagner sought, theoretically, to establish his leitmotiv patterns? Supporters of Brecht's theory would doubtless point to the 'deictic'[2] element in such a scientific demonstration, and if this were the only reference to the principle in the entire drama I believe they would be right. But the fact of the matter is that this 'demonstration' has a clarifying function which operates far beyond the confines of Andrea's education and assists the reader or spectator in his understanding and appreciation of all the many later repeated examples of motivs relating to movement. This crucial fact makes the first 'demonstration' appear quite similar to the Wagnerian model. For example, the stage-directions in the second scene of *Das Rheingold* present before our eyes and in a most conspicuous fashion the splendour of Valhalla, an image which remains fixed in our minds for ever afterwards, as the Valhalla leitmotiv weaves in and out of the action of the tetralogy and is subjected to an infinite number of transformations and permutations with other leit-motivs.[3] Is Brecht not establishing a motivic structure, as Wagner is here, even if we are not dealing in the latter case with scientific principles and even if the substance of the image itself is monumental and static? Intentionally or unintentionally, Brecht succeeds also in effectively combining the didactic and the poetic/literary possibilities inherent in the imagery and thereby also—perhaps inadvertently?—locates, even integrates, the motivic ingredients into the 'action' in a manner which scarcely accords with the tenets of 'Trennung' or 'epic' disjunction or 'Verfremdung'.

The dramatic—or literary—implications of the scientific principle of circular movement of the heavenly bodies ('rollen') are chiefly social/political and theological, but because of Brecht's deliberately anachronistic, and Marxist-tinged viewpoint, according to which the arguments against God have once and for all been settled, it is the first two which really predominate in the drama. For fairly obvious reasons the fullest revolutionary implications can only be drawn out in closeted circumstances. For much of the action Galileo is forced to adopt a policy of caution towards the authorities of Church and State (and, as Brecht made clear in the

---

[2] The element of 'pointing', often through non-verbal means, identified as an important aspect of dramatic representation by certain theorists. See Ch. 1, p. 6.
[3] 'The daybreak illuminates with increasing brightness a castle with gleaming battlements which stands on a rocky summit in the background': *Das Rheingold* (ENO and Royal Opera Guides; London and New York, 1985), 54.

Preface to the American version, it is the political role of the Church, the Church as 'Obrigkeit', authority, with which he is mainly concerned).[4] This has an important effect on the presentation and structure of the 'movement network' which could well be compared with the dramatically conditioning factors that operate in traditional drama, as well as in Wagner's music drama.[5] Thus it is only among his pupils and intimates that the revolutionary spirit of his teaching can be expressed without fear or favour. Right at the beginning of the drama in a long peroration in scene 1 Galileo can almost programmatically spell out the significance of his discoveries 'Denn die alte Zeit ist herum . . . Und die Erde rollt fröhlich um die Sonne, und die Fischweiber, Kaufleute, Fürsten und die Kardinäle und sogar der Papst rollen mit ihr' (because the old days are over . . . And the Earth is rolling cheerfully around the Sun, and the fishwives, merchants, princes, cardinals, and even the Pope are rolling with it) (190. 21; 191. 35–7). Ostensibly all this is for the child Andrea's benefit, and conforms to Galileo's role as teacher. One can possibly envisage this great speech as a kind of Prologue: the carefully constructed rhetoric (e.g repetition of the phrase: 'denn die alte Zeit ist herum') and the prophetic tone of 'Ich sage voraus, daß noch zu unseren Lebzeiten auf den Märkten von Astronomie gesprochen werden wird' (it is my prophecy that our own lifetime will see astronomy being discussed in the market-places) (191. 25–6) all suggest an appeal to a wider public than the 6-year-old child. But the interesting point is that Brecht has *not* chosen the unambiguously disjunctive route and has preferred to combine the two levels of appeal, specific and general, thus tethering the motivic element to a certain extent.

---

[4] Bertolt Brecht, *GW* xvii. 1110.

[5] By 'dramatically conditioning' factors I understand situations which 'relativize' the statements of characters, rendering them less than satisfactory as objective perspectives upon the action. The term 'character voice' (cf. 'authorial voice') is sometimes used to describe this. Thus, for example, Saint-Just's powerful statement about the inexorable march of history (Georg Büchner, *Dantons Tod*, *Sämtliche Werke und Briefe*, i, ed. W. Lehmann (Hamburg, 1967 ff. 46), is conditioned by the fanatical style in which it is couched (a form of 'gestus' really, betokening inhumanity). As for Wagner, to take an obvious example, Sieglinde's narrative concerning the appearance of the Wanderer at her wedding and his implanting of the Sword in the tree (*Die Walküre*, Act I (ENO and Royal Opera Guides, London, 1983), 62–3) betrays only partial knowledge of the full meaning of this act and its perpetrator; it is left to the orchestra to enlighten the listener about the true identity of the Wanderer through reference to Wotan's leitmotiv.

The only comparably unfettered expression of the egalitarian and anti-authoritarian implications of this leitmotiv come in the ballad-singer's version (scene 10) to which reference has already been made. Here the existing hierarchical social and political structure is heavily satirized:

> Und um den Papst zirkulieren die Kardinäle
> Und um die Kardinäle zirkulieren die Bischöfe
> (Around the Pope the cardinals
> Around the cardinals the bishops).

(260. 6–7)

We have noted already the anachronistic overstatement of views which at the time could not have been so boldly expressed, not even at the level of Bänkelsang, and we have to concede that on this occasion, possibly, the disjunctive presentation is more perceptible, the raw expression of the subversive implications of Galileo's theories less credible in purely contextual terms. Nevertheless the picking up of an important element in the leitmotiv structure, which by this time has become so well established in the reader's or spectator's mind that he is inclined to see its cross-referential implication as much as—or even more than—any contextual significance does, I would suggest, produce an overarching effect of structural integration, although this could be more akin to the looser integration which adherents of 'epic' (e.g. Klotz) have identified than the 'dramatic' implications of leitmotiv structure which I have identified with Wagner. In the case of Brecht's *Galilei* I believe we shall find evidence of both levels of integration.

Other applications of the 'movement network' are more obviously determined by dramatic and contextual considerations. For example, we find a number of derogatory allusions emanating from various sources of opposition, as, for example, from Ludovico (who as an ignoramus and typical 'Average Man' talks of 'der Erde-um-die Sonne-Sache' this Earth-round-the Sun business, or altern-atively, 'Zirkus', pantomime, in scene 9: 255. 22 and 253. 24 respectively). Other attempts to denigrate Galileo's findings come from Church sources at the Vatican (scene 6, Collegium Romanum); here a hint of eroticism and frivolity brings about a modification of the basic leitmotiv: 'die Venus steht schon ganz schief. Ich sehe nur noch ihren hablen Hintern . . .' (Venus is all askew. I can only see one half of her backside) (230. 31–2) or 'die Erde bewegt sich zu schnell' (the Earth's spinning round too fast) (230. 22–3). Later, in the crucial scene between Barberini and Galileo in which they are joined by the Cardinal Inquisitor (scene 7), the latter draws out the associated motiv of separation and distance, complaining about the loss of 'Abstand' (distance) between the higher and the lower orders inherent in Galileo's theories about 'Fixsterne' (fixed stars) (241. 32–8).

As evidence, however, of a much more deeply serious exploration of the implications of the *Grundmotiv*—and here we are especially aware of the extreme flexibility of Brecht's handling of the technique—we must consider the important scene between Galileo and the Little Monk, his disciple and scientific collaborator (scene 8). This transformation of the basic motiv of movement explores the drastic social implications of the revolutionary theories according to which all the celestial bodies now seem to be equal and no central focus of authority remains. For the poor peasants of the Campagna who have toiled all their lives in the expectation of heavenly reward this will render their lives quite meaningless. They have never questioned the hierarchical structure nor sought to penetrate behind it—more understandably than the frivolous monks in Rome whose intellectual laziness was encapsulated in the rhetorical question: 'muß der Mensch alles verstehen?' (Does mankind have to understand everything?) (232. 8–9.) The Little Monk now makes an eloquent plea for setting limits upon the nature of scientific enquiry in order to safeguard the social, political, and theological status quo, speaking of 'die Gefahren, die ein allzu hemmungsloses Forschen für die Menschheit in sich birgt' (the potential dangers for humanity in wholly unrestricted research) (243. 16–17). The image of a non-hierarchical arrangement of heavenly bodies, rolling freely through the heavens would strike at the heart of their beliefs: 'Was würden meine Leute sagen, wenn sie von mir erführen, daß sie sich auf einem kleinen Steinklumpen befinden, der sich unaufhörlich drehend im leeren Raum um ein anderes Gestirn bewegt, einer unter sehr vielen, ein ziemlich unbedeutender!' (What would my people say if I told them that they happen to be on a small knob of stone twisting endlessly through the void round a second-rate star, just one among myriads? (244. 15–19.) The argument for non-interference smacks, of course, strongly of the Marxist view of religion as the opiate of the people and is strongly opposed by Galileo, who uses the political implications of 'Bewegung' (motion) to convey the new form of thinking which will be required of ordinary people in a future, technologically based world: 'Aber wenn sie [*i.e. die Campagna-bauern*] nicht in Bewegung kommen und denken lernen, werden ihnen auch die schönsten Bewässerungsanlagen nichts nützen' (but unless they get moving and learn how to think, they will find even the finest irrigation systems won't help them) (246. 32–4). The Little Monk's rejection of the revolutionary implications of the new theories of movement shows the tremendous range of mood and of association which Brecht can evoke by means of leitmotiv patterns. How different is this rejection, for example, with its eloquent, elegiac—some might even say sentimental—holding fast to the known props and stays even of an unjust political and social order from the bigoted and thoughtless dismissal with which the new ideas are treated by the establishment clergy. And yet it is dramatically appropriate that this other side to Galileo's impatient, hustling forward in the name of progress should find expression too; it adds considerably to the richness of the drama's texture.

As so often with this complex of imagery the social, political, and theological implications are not very clearly distinguished and it seems to be Brecht's intention that they should be seen as interdependent. However, there is one memorable occasion (scene 3) when Sagredo, Galileo's assistant, 'catechizes' his master about the existence of God in the light of the new scientific findings and the implied dethronement of the idea of an all-powerful intelligence located centrally within a hierarchical cosmic order: 'Wo ist Gott?' (Where is God?), to which Galileo replies in the same vein as the 'heretic' Giordano Bruno: 'In uns oder nirgends' (within ourselves or nowhere) (210. 5), indicating a man-orientated universe which no longer offers external props such as had supported the human race over the centuries. Another slant on this man-based conception—but expressed in mocking fashion—comes from the masked Cardinal Barberini when he extracts the (negative) theological implications of the new shift away from external divine authority: 'Wie, Gott hat nicht sorgfältig genug Astronomie studiert, bevor er die Heilige Schrift verfaßte?' (I suppose God hadn't got far enough in his studies before he wrote the Bible, is that it?) (238. 30–1.) Time and again the motiv 'Himmel' is used as a short-hand reference to any external omnipotent Being, thus: 'sah, daß es kein

Himmel war' (saw that there was no heaven); or 'Himmel abgeschafft' (heaven done away with).

Brecht uses the leitmotiv imagery, however, not merely as a labelling device to identify major 'themes', nor even as a unifying binding force spreading horizontally across the work which, as Rainer Nägele has pointed out,[6] is almost carefully and intricately structured according to principles of parallelism and repetition (scenes 1–7 are balanced by scenes 9–15 with scene 8 as the 'axis' of the drama). Nor, I believe, does Nägele's theory that the 'analogy' set up between astronomy and social and political realities is historically grounded in medieval and scholastic traditions[7] provide more than an interesting suggestion of historical colouring. For what matters is the use to which Brecht puts this material and I shall try to demonstrate that the organization and development of the leitmotivs reflects closely the movement in thought and intention which in turn is closely linked to the character of Galileo himself, so that an interaction between the personal and the external levels—despite all Brecht's protestations to the contrary—can also be identified and clarified. It is above all in this area that the leitmotiv patterns assume the role of commentary and evaluation and help the reader or spectator to penetrate beneath the surface level of argument and disputation between the authorities and the free-thinking scientist. A first clear indication of this further elaboration of the network itself comes in scene 8, Nägele's 'axis' scene. Although it would seem to have no direct connetion with the network of movement, the motiv of the pearl whose beauty is produced by the introduction into the oyster shell of pathogenic substances—in this instance a grain of sand—can be regarded as an extension of the notion of comfort and stability afforded by the principle of non-movement of the Earth, i.e. the Ptolemaian picture of the universe and of the 'harmony of the spheres' which has served mankind for so many generations. Galileo's point is that such a view has all the attraction of an aesthetic construct which is stationary and complete in itself: in contemplating the seemingly hermetic beauty of the final product one is distracted from analysing the underlying dynamic, and sharply contrasting forces on which it depends. Brecht is indeed a firm opponent of Schiller's idea of 'schönes Spiel': art for him *must*

---

[6] Rainer Nägele, 'Zur Struktur von Brechts "Leben des Galilei" ', *Deutschunterricht*, 23 (1971), 86–99.   [7] Ibid. 88.

engage with these realities and pre-conditions for its production. In the case of the pearl closer investigation and identification of the process that has brought it about will reveal ugly and discordant elements: 'Indem sie [die Auster] in lebensgefährlicher Krankheit einen unerträglichen Fremdkörper, zum Beispiel ein Sandkorn, in eine Schleimkugel einschließt. Sie geht nahezu drauf bei dem Prozeß' (by a mortally dangerous disease which involves taking some unassimilable foreign body, like a grain of sand, and wrapping it in a slimy ball. The process all but kills it) (245. 11–14). The stationary, passive, purely contemplative approach to the 'order' of the world is thus identified with the principle of 'nicht-Bewegung' (non-motion) but the finely developed pearl image itself still carries an ambiguous flavour. Aesthetically pleasing phenomena exercise such a powerful and long-standing attraction on the human mind that already doubts are raised about the desirability of looking too closely at the foundations on which they are built. Well may Galileo exclaim: 'Tugenden sind nicht an Elend geknüpft' (virtues are not an offshoot of poverty) (245. 15–16) but it could be that the human psyche obstinately prefers things tht way and will continue to do so. This in turn sets problems for the author and instigator of 'Bewegung', Galileo himself, these problems relate to the field of ethics, however, rather than science, and it is precisely in this region of the sharp conflicts and oppositions that Galileo's own problematical position comes increasingly under scrutiny.

The pearl could be said to be a new motiv which develops out of, but is entirely distinct from, the basic *Grundmotiv* of motion and the absence of motion. It could, however, itself be regarded leitmotivic in that it recurs in the penultimate scene (Landhaus, scene 14) albeit in a modified form, when Galileo once more addresses the issue of the ingrained resistance of the vast majority of mankind towards the implications of a non-hierarchical world-view and links these conservative and superstitious attitudes with the (now short-hand) motiv of the pearl: 'Nun wird der Großteil der Bevölkerung von ihren Fürsten, Grundbesitzern und Geistlichen in einem perlmutternen Dunst von Aberglauben und alten Wörtern gehalten, welcher die Machinationen dieser Leute verdeckt' (now the bulk of the population is kept by its princes, landlords, and priests in a pearly haze of superstition and old saws which cloak what these people are up to) (283. 23–6). This highlights once more the contrast between appearance and reality which had been at the heart of the earlier presentation of the pearl. The motiv is repeated rhetorically shortly afterwards, as if to underline Galileo's recognition of the powerful force and attraction of 'das Ewig-Gestrige' (the eternal yester-year): 'Eine Menschheit, stolpernd in diesem tausend-jahrigen Perlmutterdunst von Aberglauben und alten Wörtern, zu unwissend, ihre eigenen Kräfte voll zu entfalten' (a human race which shambles around in a pearly haze of superstition and old saws, too ignorant to develop its own powers) (284. 6–10). By adding the word 'Dunst' (haze) to the already established pearl motiv Brecht is therefore able to extend its range and convey a clear negative 'Gestus'. It is perhaps appropriate to compare such motivic development with the way Wagner was able to extend and combine his motivic materials.

This exploration by means of leitmotiv of the theme of ingrained, reactionary tendencies in human behaviour is a matter which increasingly received Brecht's attention in his working of the material for *Galilei*; the pearl motiv, for example, first appears in the American version, that is at the point when Brecht's attention became focused on the issue of the scientist's personal and urgent responsibility for altering attitudes. As it turns out, Brecht's introduction of this new element—his well-documented response to the dropping of the atomic bomb, symbol of a science which now seemed to be running amok—has the effect of complicating his hero's dilemma to the extent where it is not wide of the mark to talk of elements of a tragic conflict. In so far as the pearl motiv highlights Galileo's clearly defined condemnation of his fellow-men for their time-honoured and old-fashioned attitudes, it simultaneously brings out the hypocrisy of his own position as a man whose human frailty prevents him from giving the kind of moral lead to these very benighted, traditionally minded souls. The strategic function of the leitmotiv is thus made clear and the fact that it reappears in 'short-hand' fashion near the end serves as a kind of 'Erinnerung' (reminiscence), as with the Wagnerian leitmotiv, a reference back in this case to the important scene in which Galileo had so easily and so eloquently opposed the views of the Little Monk before his recantation.

More directly linked to the *Grundmotiv* of movement are a series of leitmotivs relating to size and stature which start to push the matter of heroism ever more clearly into the forefront of our attention in the second half of the drama (i.e. scenes 8–15). In the first half the issue of relative *size* (for instance of heavenly bodies such as the 'Fixsterne', the Earth and the Sun) tends to be used to convey the idea of egalitarianism in contrast to the socially hierarchical and authoritarian view which has hitherto prevailed. Frequently, this view is linked to the motiv of 'Abstand' (distance) which has always been thought necessary between the great and the small, masters and servants. According to the Cardinal Inquisitor, the new scientific views propounded by Galileo and his followers place many astral bodies (e.g. 'Fixsterne') outside the Earth's sphere of influence altogether, thus subverting the notion of an Earth-dominated central focus in the cosmos: 'Nach diesen' [i.e. 'den Neueren'] ist sie [i.e. 'eine schöne Geräumigkeit'], wie wir hören, ganz unvorstellbar weit ausgedehnt, ist der Abstand der Erde von der Sonne, ein durchaus bedeutender Abstand, wie es uns immer geschienen hat, so verschwindend klein gegen den Abstand unserer armen Erde von den Fixsternen, die auf der alleräußersten Schale befestigt sind . . .' (apparently they—i.e. the innovators— feel that it is unimaginably far-flung and that the Earth's distance from the Sun—quite a respectable distance, we always found it—is so minute compared with its distance from the fixed stars on the outermost sphere) (241. 32–6).

The chess motiv—which originally, in the first version, appeared in scene 1 as well as scene 7—reflects the new spirit of social equality and mobility and the blurring of vast distinctions between great and small (as, for example, in the interchangeability of positions of King and rooks, known as 'rooking' or 'castelling'). Galileo observes the monks playing the old form of chess and complains of the 'Enge' (confinement) which puts the pieces into closer, more hierarchical relationships: 'Wie könnt ihr noch immer das alte Schach spielen? Eng, eng. Jetzt spielt man doch so, daß die größten Figuren über alle Felder gehen . . . Da hat man Raum und kann Pläne machen' (How can you go on playing old-style chess? Cramped, cramped. Nowadays the play is to let the chief pieces roam across the whole board. That way you have enough space and can plan ahead) (235. 30–4). Drawing here on authentic historical material, Brecht is able to extract appropriate symbolic meanings which subtly suggest the changing power structure as well as the stifling constriction of the old and much more sharply divided system.

In the second half of the drama this aspect of a revolutionary movement taking place in society and the relative power and strength of its individual members tends to be overshadowed by the issue, which, as I have suggested above, becomes central to Brecht's concerns—the question of leadership, example, and responsibility. It has been said[8] that this new question does not always link up smoothly with the other concerns of the drama and it will be interesting to see if that creates problems within the leitmotiv structure itself. The recantation scene (scene 13) brings this issue most fully to light by drawing out a completely new aspect of the question of 'great and small', which no longer refers to social relationships but instead to the moral standing of the scientist as a 'leader'. In the Danish and American versions the recantation itself had been followed by a quick exchange of sententiae between Galileo and the disillusioned Andrea: ANDREA: 'Unhappy is the land that breeds no hero'; GALILEO: 'Unhappy is the land that needs a hero'. Now, in the final version, an additional, succinct, and paradoxical formulation is achieved—as so often in this drama based on authentic sources—when Galileo produces a longish quotation from the *discorsi*. A number of diverse examples are brought together to illustrate the principle that in strength there is weakness, in weakness strength, as in the case of an oak tree: 'so halten sich die kleinen Pflanzen besser: eine zweihundert Ellen hohe Eiche könnte ihre Äste in voller Proportion mit einer kleinen Eiche nicht halten' (so small plants too stand up better: an oak tree two hundred ells high cannot sustain its branches in the same proportion as a small oak tree) (274. 37–9). How is this to be understood? Galileo, a man of the flesh, pursuing science as if it were meat and drink, observes that more is demanded of one who has pushed his subject so spectacularly beyond its original boundaries. A man who has achieved that kind of greatness may indeed be hopelessly inadequate morally when tested about these discoveries and beliefs. And yet another man who has achieved less will display greater fortitude and powers of resistance. But 'heroism' of that kind had never been part of Galileo's brief; indeed it clashes with his unpretentiousness, a quality which has engaged our sympathy throughout. The tree image is indeed one of which Brecht had long been fond: it links up with the fine early poem 'An

---

[8] Ronald Gray succinctly analyses the weakness and inconsistencies in Brecht's presentation which are the result of his major change of emphasis in response to the dropping of the Bomb, in *Brecht the Dramatist*, 113 ff.

den Baum Griehn', in which a similarly unpretentious, even puny specimen of tree manages to resist threats from vultures and storms.[9] It links too with the more abstractly expressed idea of 'die kleinste Größe' which, as we have seen, is at the heart of the *Badener Lehrstück* and according to which successful opposition to vicissitudes is achieved by surrendering personal, selfish claims in the interests of the community.[10]

The question which arises in *Galilei* is rather different: Galileo has, in fact, for much of the time 'made himself small' and by playing along with the authorities (palming them off with his telescope, for instance) rather than adopting a confrontational stance he has managed to give himself breathing-space. Even when at the Court of Florence he is forbidden by the Inquisition to carry on, he does so surreptitiously, observing sun-spots secretly. This is a policy of political expediency and as such it is practical and effective. But what is being asked of Galileo at the point when he is required to recant is altogether different: it is the considered opinion of his former friends and associates—and from what one knows of Brecht's views as expressed in the numerous prefaces to the drama, it is the severe perspective which we are meant to apply to the hero ourselves—that in recanting he is betraying his profession as scientist. It is not enough to pursue knowledge for its own ends and to the limits of one's abilities; one is also required to die for that knowledge. And from the supporting text one is also supposed to believe that the fact that Galileo's survival has made possible the continuation of his work on the *discorsi* is neither here nor there. Science being science this work would have been taken up eventually and continued by others. The important thing is that the great teacher must become a great martyr as well. This is what circumstances require.

What light on all this is shed by the leitmovis? From having successfully pursued a policy of 'kleinste Größe'—but only in the negative and practical sense—Galileo is called on to stand up and reveal his true qualities of strength, both intellectual and moral, at a crossroads in history—and fails. He is certainly inadequate in upbraiding the peasants for their passivity, while himself failing to engage head-on with the authorities. But are his disciples not guilty also of hypocrisy? Have they any right to demand that he should

---

[9] 'Morgendliche Rede an den Baum Griehn', 'Hauspostille', *GW* viii. 186–7.

[10] See discussion of this work above, p. 136.

succumb to the forces of the Inquisition? Especially when, like Andrea, they too are motivated by equally strong passions and desires to carry out research for its own sake. It is easy enough—so the leitmotiv patterns would seem to tell us—for the small and mediocre to survive, since *they* are not exposed to the test; it is the strong, here the intellectual leader, who is required to become a hero.

Galileo's summarizing statement of his dilemma in terms of the 'groß'/'klein' primary motiv network smacks very much of a tragic impasse: certainly the scientific examples suggest a generalizing principle to be at work in the natural world which has implications for the human world and which, specifically, in that context raises questions about heroism itself. It is not clear that such heroism as would have been required of Galileo is possible under the circumstances or even desirable. What we have is the tragic failure of the great man to live up to the expectations that society has of him. The section which Brecht added to the final version concerning the need for scientists to tailor their research to socially desirable objectives fits very poorly onto the existing structure of the action (the reference to a 'Hippocratic oath' shows little regard for the nature of scientific endeavour which, unfortunately, has to be open-ended if it is going to be of any value at all). But there is no gainsaying the fact that Brecht's hero is full of self-criticism, self-hatred, and bitterness for having betrayed his profession. That point can be accepted from the internal evidence: the human frailty which collides with the great work and the new vision of society is enough to suggest the tragic formula, tragic because it could not have been otherwise, given his own nature. Perhaps, after all, it is not surprising that the oak image is the one which, above all others, Heinrich von Kleist[11] used to summarize the tragic dilemma of *his* heroes and heroines.

Interestingly in the first version this paradoxical motiv was not used. However, Andrea did employ a rather diffuse motiv to suggest the 'fall' of a great man: 'Ich sehe, es ist, als ob ein Turm einstürzte, von ungeheurer Höhe und für unerschütterlich gehalten' (I understand: it's as if a tower of great height and which was thought to be indestructible were to collapse) (105. 16–17). In keeping with the different appraisal of the hero of this version—and

---

[11] See Donald Crosby, 'Heinrich von Kleist's Oak-Image', *German Quarterly*, 38 (1965), 14–19.

his 'guilt' in recanting is much diminished since it was more clearly tactical—not all of this vast tower-structure is destroyed: 12 upper storeys are lost, but 30 lower ones remain. 'Der Bau könnte dann weitergeführt werden' (the structure would be built up again). (105. 23–4). This is no tragic formulation. Brecht's fondness for drawing all the threads together in an 'integration point' remains, however, at this precise stage, and as we can see, an entirely new motiv, complex and paradoxical, replaces the earlier one.

As we have seen, the extent to which the leitmotiv patterns permeate this drama is considerable. The establishment of a network and the reiteration of motivs which can at one moment be elaborate, at another brief and succinct, provide the reader and spectator with important information about the major issues underlying the action. It is interesting to compare the role of these leitmotiv networks with those in *Die Heilige Johanna der Schlacht-höfe*. The 'movement' network, for instance, might be compared to the groups of leitmotivs in the earlier drama which aim to express a change of state: the see-saw, for instance, or the change of the masses from solid to liquid in Johanna's dream vision. In *Galilei* it could perhaps be said that the most persuasive and eloquent patterns are not concentrated so much around the dynamic principle of movement: rather it is the ambiguous pearl, representing an obstacle to enlightenment, and, above all, the climactic formulation of the endangered tree, that carry most authority, in the latter case highlighting through paradox the problematic nature of the strong individual. 'Revolutionary' statements relating to the masses are mainly conveyed through discursive means and it could be argued that these become unnecessarily tendentious by comparison. In short it would seem that, as with *Die Heilige Johanna*, leitmotivic utterance in *Galilei* carries more weight than other perspectival sources and reveals more about the work's inner meaning, although the emphasis in the two works has certainly altered, particularly as far as the individual is concerned.

An interesting feature of the later drama is the sense of a development in the presentation of leitmotivs. In the second half of *Galilei*, new motivs emerge from out of the existing network structure and acquire the status of summarizing statements, drawing the threads together, establishing the terms of reference clearly and in a way which is surely more effective than any prescriptive commentary from one source such as a chorus or a singer. In all this increasing weight is placed upon the character of Galileo himself, so that ultimately the various general issues established through the leitmotivs are viewed in terms of their implications for this one individual. Densely interlocking, economically deployed motivic patterns produce an intensity and concentration such as can be compared with their effect in other, more traditional dramatic contexts—which in this discussion Kleist and Wagner have served to exemplify.

8
Conclusion

We have now examined four works in which Brecht's technique of leitmotiv is displayed in a number of different ways. The nature of this virtuosity is particularly well highlighted by considering the point that all four dramas share a common core of basic motivs: first of these is the vertical pattern 'oben'/'unten' (above/below). In *Baal* this takes the form of 'Himmel'/'Erde' (sky, heaven/earth); in *Lehrstück* it is modified to 'sich erheben'/'stürzen' (rising/falling); in *Die Heilige Johanna der Schlachthöfe* it appears in basic, unmodified form (as well as in countless transformations); while in *Leben des Galilei* it occurs again in the form of 'Himmel'/'Erde'. A second basic motiv (*Grundmotiv*) which occurs across all four works is the semi-abstract notion of the relative insignificance of individual human beings when measured against larger-scale forces, be they cosmic, be they social; the antithesis 'klein'/'groß' (small/large) represents the most basic form taken by this particular motiv. While this abstract form is retained in *Das Badener Lehrstück vom Einverständnis*, in *Baal* the idea of *size* as such is not explicitly at the forefront, but it is implied, since the notion of self-surrender and loss of identity—a kind of transcendence—crystallizes around the motiv of 'schwimmen' (which is used similarly in the *Lehrstück*). In *Die Heilige Johanna der Schlachthöfe* obliteration of hierarchical divisions within the social system is focused on the motiv of 'Schnee' among a host of others (such as, for instance, the change from the solid to the liquid state, a *chiffre* to express the vision of a revolutionary mass). In *Leben des Galilei* we find references to the motiv both in its basic form 'klein'/ 'groß' as well as a rich vein of examples to illustrate the principle of relative size and power in the planetary network of motivs (the Sun and the Earth, the 'fixed stars', etc.) One could continue to chart and link up motiv-networks across the four works and would certainly find many other examples which connect the last three. *Baal*—probably as a result of its early position—stands rather apart from the others in this respect, though, as we have seen, significant motivic cross-patterns connect it up with the others too. The consistency of primary motivs across the four dramas is maintained despite the considerable fluctuations in Brecht's ideological and philosophical outlook in the period extending from *Baal* to *Leben des Galilei*.

Already, however, one can see how a brief review of common motivic patterns serves to highlight the diverse ways in which individual motivs repeated within the work may be treated from one drama to the next. The 'basic' form taken by an image or motiv is seldom the only one; the comparatively abstract forms of the antitheses 'oben'/'unten' and 'groß'/'klein' exist alongside variants which are more often than not more 'imagistic' and tangible, if not necessarily concrete. Particularly in view of their spatial implications, these would often seem to be ideally suited to a realization on stage. I find it helpful in these circumstances to refer to these more abstract forms as *Grundmotive*; in English they might be termed 'kernel images', since they provide a kind of originating seed from which many potential seedlings (or what Wolfgang Clemen calls 'clusters') may develop. Whether or not the author chooses to lay bare his *Grundmotive* seems to me incidental; they underlie most significant imagery in poetic drama and can generally be teased out (if there were any point in doing so, other than for purposes of demonstration).

It might be suggested that, because they can often be reduced to essentials in this way, it follows tht he is not using them in the ways described by Wagner and discussed above; that one motiv, in other words, is as good as the next and can be used more or less interchangeably across the whole *œuvre*. But the ability of *Grundmotive* to proliferate and diversify in response to contextual stimulus is, I believe, a powerful and irrefutable argument against this view. Our earlier analyses have shown Brecht's quite prodigious talents in this area in three of the four dramas selected (*Lehrstück*, predictably, because of its didactic function is the exception, and as such is a useful marker; the absence of proliferation from the grundmotivic base is underlined by the substitution of 'straight' repetition).

Baal affords an interesting insight into the difficult matter of hierarchical status of motivs. We have seen in it a uniquely rich lyrical texture and motivic proliferations from the 'Himmel'/'Erde' base which take us to the heart of the work's 'meaning'. But the many associated motivs, e.g. besmirching, 'Wolke', etc. do not appear to assume a marked hierarchical status within the work itself—apart, that is, from their status as offshoots, and therefore smaller units, emanating from the basic *Grundmotive*. When one looks for overarching structure—that is, a relationship among the subsidiary motivs (*Nebenmotive*) based on relative value or status which could serve as a 'perspective' upon the whole work—one is seeking in vain. Only the 'Prolog' with its 'Gestus' of detached irony provides anything like this, and it is, as we have seen, of limited relevance, and soon forgotten amidst the lyrical exuberance which is so reminiscent of the poetry of the *Hauspostille*.

In *Baal*, which hovers between the genres of lyric poem and drama, and where Brecht was able to give the fullest possible rein to the subconscious mainsprings of his creativity, the motivic networks serve no strategic function other than a self-referential one. They do not, that is, serve as perspectical devices upon the drama's 'action'; nor does it always matter too much where they are placed; but they do themselves constitute its core and express much of the 'meaning' that we glean from it. And, perhaps most importantly of all, they do knit the loosely constructed work together, giving it a powerful intensity. I think it follows from this that Wagner's strictures about leitmotiv are indeed not upheld at this point by Brecht and that if we are to use the term leitmotiv of *Baal* it must be understood as a secondary form, akin to Klotz's 'epic' variety which he associates with 'open' form (though I would want to dissociate myself from both those terms for reasons already explained). The motiv patterns in *Baal*, then, are both structurally and semantically crucial elements in its constitution; they are, so to speak, an end in themselves rather in the same way as a symbol unites signifier and signified.

The use of leitmotiv in *Die Heilige Johanna der Schlachthöfe* differs spectacularly from that deployed in both the other works just mentioned. An unusually high level of proliferation of motivic patterns from a *Grundmotiv* base occurs, nearly all of it demonstrably strategic, pointing *towards* the most important thematic issues lying beneath surface level rather than, as in *Baal*, overlapping with these. The parodistic intentions behind the work make for special problems in the working out of the hierarchical relationships set up among the many complex networks of motivs.

'Gestic' framing of certain motivs—a case in point would be Mauler's Atlas motiv—may contrast with 'straighter' perspectival presentations in the case of the numerous *Nebenmotive* that derive from the 'Bau' *Grundmotiv*, such as the base raw materials of which the building is composed. Value-ratings (here mostly negative) are a way in which signs of a perspectival stance can readily be detected. An important feature of this particular group of *Nebenmotive* is their generative function and their capacity to interact dynamically, so that they seem to be able to adapt to the particular circumstances of plot and character (Mauler's disillusionment leads, for instance, to a revaluation of the nature and meaning of 'Bau'). For such possibilities to be fulfilled the playwright has to ensure that the *Grundmotiv* itself is capable of this kind of development. If the 'Bau' motiv serves Brecht's purpose most adequately, the 'oben'/'unten' configuration is even more strikingly exploited. The particular set of *Nebenmotive* developed (prompted or inspired largely by the particular context) show remarkable potential for dynamic development and extension; thus, for instance, the development of the see-saw motiv itself generates the possibility for change and reversal of a presently entrenched position. The reader's or audience's appreciation of this point encourages an awareness of the underlying structure, acting in this respect similarly to Wagner's leitmotivs of 'Ahnung' (anticipation) and 'Erinnerung' (recollection).

It has been observed that the (parodistic) adoption of the Aristotelian model for this drama has the (probably unintentional) effect of unlocking all Brecht's inherent ability and sheer virtuosity at exploring the capacity of motiv patterns to serve dramatic ends— a device so well understood by Shakespeare, one of his most admired models. One important result of this deliberate adoption of the Aristotelian model is that it generates its own system of 'values' (this affects matters like audience response to shortcomings of the characters, which may be perceived as necessary rather than avoidable). The effect is to create a perspective whose relationship with the *Grundmotive* themselves has to be defined, so that value-rating suggested at the point of occurrence may have later to be reconsidered. As an example of this, one might consider the 'see-saw' extension to the 'oben'/'unten' *Grundmotiv*. When attempting to interpret the drama one would have to consider its optimistic implications alongside the more pessimistic indications about human nature—or more specifically the limits of human idealism—which emanate from the other 'perspectival' source. It must not be assumed from this that a final decision about such fundamental matters will necessarily be reached by this route alone. The analysis of leitmotivs is only one ingredient in the complex mix with which the critic is faced when attempting an interpretation. But it is an important and an all too often neglected one.

While possibly not displaying such an intricate medley of highly strategic motivs as does *Die Heilige Johanna der Schlachthöfe*, *Leben des Galilei* nevertheless presents many networks with similar characteristics. The hierarchical arrangement is less complex, however, in that there is no equivalent to the element of gestic disjunction through parody. This means, for instance, that the dazzling proliferation of motivs emanating from the *Grundmotiv* of planetary movement and spatial relationships stands unframed as a powerful statement of intellectual and social revolution (in this respect comparable, maybe, to the dream vision which Johanna has of the transfigured masses). But, in working towards a comprehensive view of the drama, other groups of motivs must still be examined alongside this. Most significant among these is the group deriving from the 'groß'/'klein' *Grundmotiv* which highlights both the means of effecting change through individuals and the problems relating to heroism; smaller units (which I have called *Nebenmotive*) such as the pearl, which expresses the notion of impedance to change in collective terms and identifies powerful obstacles in the way of recognizing the truth, also prove to be important pieces in the complex configuration. A notable feature which might appear to serve as an overarching frame is the high incidence of explicit statement, much of it proverbial or in the form of *sententiae*, which exists alongside the leitmotiv patterns. Galileo's extremely long final speech, added in the final version, makes crystal-clear his (and his creator's) strong sense of the need for responsibility in science in the wake of Hiroshima. But the very tendentiousness of this interpolation may be experienced as an intrusion and as being stylistically—and intellectually—at variance with the ambivalence and complex perspectives which emanate from the alternative perspectival sources presented by the motivic patterns.

It can be seen from both these examples that tensions can be set up both within motiv patterns themselves and between these sources of perspective and others in the work. Since in *Leben des Galilei* these tensions are also reflected within the main protagonist (one of the most contradictory, 'widerspruchsvoll', of all Brecht's character portrayals) and closely follow his fluctuating fortunes, one is aware of a polyperspectivism which is most eloquently brought to light by the motivic patterns. Without wishing to schematize these different applications too rigidly, I find it convenient to describe two contrasting applications as the 'horizontal' and the 'vertical' forms of leitmotiv. The first operates at the surface level of 'plot' or 'theme' and is reiterative in character (the ballad-singer's emphasis on rigid social hierarchy via the network of movement repeats a point already well established); the second is at the deeper level of progressively uncovering new ramifications within the thematic nexus (the pearl leitmotiv is a good example) and suggests to the reader or spectator a set of problems which have direct bearing on the individual hero's own struggle to have what is indubitably important new knowledge accepted (this had been elaborated by means of the 'movement network'): in short, the motiv highlights the difficulty experienced by the hero in bridging the gap between theory and practice, a problem to which Brecht himself appeared to have no one simple answer.

In attempting to identify more precisely the hierarchical status of the leitmotivs one notes Brecht's seemingly deliberate and certainly effective positioning of the different types. Motivs of the second (or 'vertical' type since they reach down into the deeper layers of meaning) prevail from the important pivotal scene 8 and gather momentum towards the end of the drama. One of these—the oak tree—inserted at the crucial turning-point of Galileo's recantation offers a profound commentary on these events—and has a prospective function as well—indeed it could be said to occupy the most important strategic place among all by virtue of its scope and relevance. Its key role within the hierarchy links it with Staiger's notion of the 'Zwischenbilanz', or 'summarizing statement'. Further, the motiv assumes the form of a *paradox*, which can also be regarded as a contradictory form of utterance of which Brecht was greatly fond, since it had the effect of surprising audiences out of their complacency. But whereas many of Brecht's paradoxes are meant to be read dialectically—that is, as contradictions which are a product of a particular society and which are ultimately surmountable—the paradox of the oak does not offer such an optimistic prospect of change. Along with other pieces of evidence which one could gather from other sources, it may tend to reinforce the interpreter's view of Galileo as a tragically blighted character who is placed in an impasse.

One final feature of Brecht's leitmotiv technique is worth noting in the two large-scale dramas, *Die Heilige Johanna der Schlacht-höfe* and *Leben des Galilei*. This is the tendency to 'ground' or integrate a motivic pattern within the fabric of the work itself. The 'Schlachthöfe', for example, form not only the setting but provide important motivic material as well, as can be seen from the animal group; Johanna actually makes three 'Descents' ('Gänge in die Tiefe') which provide a concrete equivalent to the pervasive motiv patterns of 'oben'/'unten' and 'Bewegung'. Galileo actually demonstrates his hypothesis about the planetary relationships by conducting an experiment. These integrating devices resemble the process of 'Vergegenwärtigung' (actualization) demanded by Wagner for the production of successful leitmotivs. It is often not hard to imagine the theatrical applications of these spatially defined leitmotivs. No more than Wagner, however, does Brecht always render his *Grundmotive* visual, and one would surely tire of the device if he did; but that does not prevent it from being both an effective and expressive tool which serves to knit the component parts together rather than to make them disjunctive.

It should be clear from these summarizing remarks based on analyses of only four of his dramas that Brecht's use of leitmotiv technique as an adjunct to drama must rank among the most impressive achievements of any German writer from any period. It should also be clear that this technique on which he relied so heavily more often than not works itself free from 'epic', 'gestic', or disjunctive forms of perspectival expression, becoming self-generating and fully integrated into the work's fabric. It is not clear why this should be, unless imagery was a natural form of expression for Brecht, as indeed the evidence of *Baal* and the *Hauspostille* might suggest and the patterns in *Lehrstück*, albeit austerely truncated, would seem to confirm. Brecht, on this showing, was essentially a writer whose imagination was fired by the symbolic possibilities of words. Our four examples certainly show much ingenuity on Brecht's part in the adaptation of the technique to meet the specific requirements of the texts. It may also be the case that this powerfully expressive device was able to fill the gaps left by 'epic' theatre in its more extreme forms: musical 'Gestus', theoretically such an important prop in Brecht's arsenal of perspectival devices in the disjunctive mode, proved in practice to be a difficult nut to crack, partly, perhaps, because Brecht was trying to squeeze too much out of the musical genre that ran against its particular grain, partly because he found himself unable to engage to this end the services of composers of the same calibre as himself. The fact remains that, despite Brecht's continued and extensive use of composers like Eisler and later Dessau, the works for which they composed music are frequently performed without it, and seemingly without detriment. Only *Die Dreigroschenoper* and *Mahagonny need* the support of Weill's musical scores.

In attempting as I have just done to identify a hierarchical structure among Brecht's motivs I should not wish to give the impression that my suggestions are anything more than tentative. Certainly, I do not wish to impose any rigidity upon the relationships between *Grundmotive* and *Nebenmotive*. Nor am I suggesting complete overlap or parity with Wagner's use of these terms. But I do find it significant that not only Wagner with his distinction between *Grundmotiv* and *Nebenmotiv* but also Brecht and Weill with their 'Grundgestus' are suggesting similar hierarchical relationships within the perspectival commentary. The terms as I have used them, however, indicate merely the scope and range of particular motivs and in no way imply a scheme of inherent values. Such a hierarchical arrangement, if it exists at all and if it is to be used as a means of building up or identifying one or more perspectival stances from the many component ingredients implied by the motivic patterns, can only be achieved in conjunction with other, equally compelling devices and strategies which the dramatist has at his disposal. The fact that such motivic patterns have attracted comparatively little individual attention and that their perspectival function has not yet been fully appreciated may not surprise us too much when we consider the amount of concentration and alertness they—like Richard Wagner's—demand. It is more puzzling, however, that they have not received more systematic analysis at the hands of theorists and that can only be explained, I believe, in terms of the peculiar path taken by the majority of theoretical works on drama in the twentieth century and to which I referred at the outset of this study. Wagner, retrospectively, stands alone in his detailed examination of the theory of the phenomenon. How paradoxical indeed to discover that Wagner's *theory* can shed so much light on Brecht's dramatic *practice*. This represents only one of the more curious paradoxes created by a literary criticism which has tended to overemphasize the rupture between modern and traditional forms. Another paradox is the fact that Wagner had recourse to the word drama as an inspiration for his new form of music drama; Brecht, conversely, sought assistance from the opera and tried to reclaim from music a role which it proved unable to carry out. Wagner would not appear as a kind of 'missing link' who is belatedly making important contributions to dramatic theory had such developments as have been described earlier not cut across the continuities and traditions which exist between nineteenth- and twentieth-century literature.

Finally, since Brecht's drama, despite all its considerable disjunctive apparatus, can be shown to demonstrate the perspectival role of leitmotivic imagery, then the fundamental significance of this technique for the drama form in general must be self-evident.

Select Bibliographies

1. General and Theoretical Works: Drama, Music Drama, Opera

ARNOLD, H. L., and BECK, T. (ed.) *Positionen des Dramas—Analysen und Theorie zur deutschen Gegenwartsliteratur* (Munich, 1977).

ASMUTH, B., *Einführung in die Dramenanalyse* (Stuttgart, 1980).

BERNATH, P., *Die Sentenz im Drama von Kleist, Büchner und Brecht* (Bonn, 1976).

BROWN, H. M., 'Der Chor im Drama des 19. Jahrhunderts und bei Heinrich von Kleist', *Jahrbuch der Heinrich-von-Kleist-Gesellschaft* (1981–2), 240–60.

BUJIC, B., *Music in European Thought: 1851–1912* (Cambridge, 1988).

BURDACH, K., 'Schillers Chordrama und die Geburt des tragischen Stils aus der Musik', in *Vorspiel: Gesammelte Schriften zur Geschichte des deutschen Geistes*, ii (Halle, 1926), 116–237.

CLEMEN, W., *Shakespeares Bilder: Ihre Entwicklung und ihre Funktion im dramatischen Werk* (Bonn, 1936) (English version: *The Development of Shakespeare's Imagery* (London, 1977)).

DÖBLIN, A., *Aufsätze zur Literatur* (Freiburg im Breisgau, 1963).

ELAM, K., *The Semiotics of Theatre and Drama* (London and New York, 1980).

ESSLIN, M., *The Field of Drama* (London, 1987).

FINK, G.-L., 'Volkslied und Verseinlage', in *Georg Büchner*, ed. W. Martens (Darmstadt, 1965), 443–87.

FREYTAG, G., *Die Technik des Dramas* (Darmstadt, 1965, reprint of 1922 13th edn.).

GRIMM, R., 'Pyramide und Karusell: Zum Strukturwandel im Drama', *Nach dem Naturalismus: Essays zur modernen Dramatik* (Kronberg, 1978), 13–27.

HAMBURGER, K., 'Das Verhältnis der dramatischen zur epischen Fiktion', *Die Logik der Dichtung* (2nd edn., Stuttgart, 1968).

JEFFERSON, A. (ed.), *Modern Literary Theory* (2nd edn., London, 1987).

KERMAN, J., *Opera as Drama* (New York, 1956).

KERR, A., 'Technik des realistischen Dramas', in *Das neue Drama* (Berlin, 1905), 295–309.

KESTEREN, VAN A., 'Der Stand der modernen Dramentheorie', *Moderne Dramentheorie* (Kronberg im Taunus, 1975), 41–58.

—— and SCHMID, H. (eds.), *The Semiotics of Drama: New Perspectives in the Theory of Drama and Theatre* (Amsterdam and Philadelphia, 1984).

KLOTZ, V., *Geschlossene und offene Form im Drama* (8th edn., Munich, 1976).

LINDENBERGER, H., *Opera, the Extravagant Art* (Ithaca, NY, and London, 1984).

NEUMAN, P.H., 'Einige Bemarkungen über Oper und Volkslied und die Idee der Einheit von Musik and Dichtung', *Jahrbuch der Jean-Paul-Gesellschaft*, 7 (1972), 103–23.

NOSKE, F. R., *The Signifier and the Signified: Studies in the Operas of Mozart and Verdi* (The Hague, 1977).

PAVIS, P., *Voix et images de la scène: Essais de sémiologie théâtrale* (Lille, 1982).

PETSCH, R., *Wesen und Form des Dramas* (Halle, 1945).

PFISTER, M., *Das Drama* (3rd edn., Munich, 1982) (*Theory and Analysis of Drama* (Cambridge, 1988)).

PÜTZ, P., *Die Zeit im Drama. Zur Technik dramatischer Spannung* (2nd edn., Göttingen, 1977)).

SEIFERT, W., *C. G. Körner: Ein Musikästhetiker der deutschen Klassik* (Regensburg, 1960).

SHAW, G. B., *The Complete Music Criticism*, ed. Dan H. Lawrence (3 vols., London, 1981).

STAIGER, E., *Grundbegriffe der Poetik* (6th edn. Zurich, 1963).

STRÄßNER, M., *Analytisches Drama* (Munich, 1980).

STRATMAN, G., review of M. Pfister, *Das Drama*, *Poetica*, 11 (1979), 263–9.

SZONDI, P., *Theorie des modernen Dramas* (4th edn., Frankfurt, 1967) (*The Theory of the Modern Drama*, ed. and trans. Michael Hays, foreword by Jochen Schulte-Sasse (Theory and History of Literature, 29; Minneapolis, 1987).

UBERSFELD, A., *Lire le théâtre* (Paris, 1977).

—— *Lire le théâtre 2* (Paris, 1981).

WIRTH, A., 'Vom Dialog zum Diskurs: Versuch einer Synthese der nachbrechtschen Theaterkonzepte', *Theater heute*, 1 (Jan. 1980), 16–19.

ZIMMER, R., *Dramatischer Dialog und außersprachlicher Kontext* (Göttingen, 1982).

2. Wagner, 'Gesamtkunstwerk' Leitmotiv

ABERBACH, A., *The Ideas of Richard Wagner* (Lanhem, Md., 1984).

ADORNO, T., *Versuch über Wagner* (Frankfurt-on-Main, 1974).

BORCHMEYER, D., 'Tristan, Tasso und die Kunst des "unendlichen Details". Zu Richard Wagners musikalischer Dramaturgie', *Jahrbuch der Bayerischen Staatsoper*, 3 (1979–80), 23–32.

—— *Das Theater Richard Wagners: Idee-Dichtung-Wirking* (Stuttgart, 1982).

BRANSCOMBE, P., 'Wagner as Poet', in Richard Wagner, *The Ring*, English trans. Andrew Porter (London, 1976), pp. xxix–xl.

BRINKMANN, R. (ed.), *Richard Wagner: Von der Oper zum Musikdrama* (Munich, 1978).

BULHOF, F., *Transpersonalismus und Synchronizität: Wiederholung als Strukturelement in Thomas Manns 'Zauberberg'* (Groningen, 1966).

BURBIDGE, P., and SUTTON, R. (eds.), *The Wagner Companion* (London, 1979).

CAIN, D., 'Wagner and Brecht as Major Theorists of Aesthetic Distance in the Theatre', diss. (Michigan, 1969) (Univ. Microfilms Intern., 1978).

CAMPBELL, T. M., 'Nietzsches "Die Geburt der Tragödie" and Richard Wagner', *Germanic Review*, 16 (1941), 185–200.

CICORA, M. A., 'From Metonymy to Metaphor: Wagner and Nietzsche on Language', *German Life and Letters*, 42 (1988), 16–31.

COOKE, D., *I Saw the World End: A Study of Wagner's* Ring (Oxford, 1979).

DAHLHAUS, C., 'Zur Geschichte der Leitmotivtechnik bei Wagner', in *Das Drama Richard Wagners als Kunstwerk*, ed. Dahlhaus (Studien zur Musikgeschichte des 19. Jahrhunderts, 23, Regensburg, 1979), 17–40.

—— *Richard Wagners Musikdramen* (Munich, 1988) (English version: *Richard Wagners Music Dramas*, trans. Mary Whittall (Cambridge, 1979)).

DEATHRIDGE, J., and DAHLHAUS, C., *The New Grove Wagner* (London, 1984).

DONINGTON, R., *Wagner's 'Ring' and its Symbols: The Music and the Myth* (2nd edn., London, 1969).

FURNESS, R., *Wagner and Literature* (Manchester, 1982).

GOERNER, R., 'Über die Trennung der Elemente', *Maske und Kothurn*, 29 (1983), 98–122.

GREGOR-DELLIN, M., 'Thomas Mann: Harmonieverschiebung und Leitmotiv', *Im Zeitalter Kafkas*, Essays (Munich, 1979), 37–47.

—— *Richard Wagner: His life, his Work, his Century* (London, 1983).

HISBRUNNER, T., 'Richtungsweisende Aspekte in Richard Wagners Musikdramen', *Universitas*, 40 (1985), 1029–38.

INGENHOFF, A., *Drama oder Epos? Richard Wagners Gattungstheorie des musikalischen Dramas* (Tübingen, 1987).

KOPPEN, E., *Dekadenter Wagnerismus: Studien zur europäischen Literatur des Fin de siècle* (Berlin and New York, 1973).

KUNZE, S., 'Richard Wagners Idee des Gesamtkunstwerks', *Beiträge zur Theorie der Künste im 19. Jahrhundert* (Frankfurt-on-Main, 1972), 196–229.

—— Über den Kunstcharakter des Wagnerischen Musikdramas', in *Richard Wagner, Von der Oper zum Musikdrama*, ed. S. Kunze (Berne and Munich, 1978), 9–24.

MANN, E. (ed.), *Thomas Mann, Wagner und unsere Zeit* (Frankfurt-on-Main, 1963) (English version: *Thomas Mann: Pro und contra Wagner*, trans. Allan Blunden with Introd. by Erich Heller (London, 1985)).

MAYER, H., *Richard Wagner* (Zurich, 1959).

MÜLLER, U., and WAPNEWSKI, P. (eds.), *Richard-Wagner-Handbuch* (Stuttgart, 1986).

NEWCOMB, A., 'The Birth of Music out of the Spirit of Drama: An Essay in Wagnerian Formal Analysis', *Nineteenth Century Music*, 5/1 (1982), 38–66.

NIETZSCHE, F., *Der Fall Wagner, Götzen-Dämmerung, Nietzsche contra Wagner* ed. with Postscript, P. Pütz (Munich, 1988).

PEACOCK, R., *Das Leitmotiv bei Thomas Mann* (Berne, 1934).

PFOTENHAUS, H., 'Richard Wagners Kunstmythologie und Friedrich Nietzsches Ästhetik', *Deutsche Literatur*, 7 (1982), 345–57.

RILEY, H. M., review of Richard Wagner's *Oper und Drama*, ed. K. Kropfinger (Stuttgart, 1984), *Colloquia Germanica*, 18 (1985), 174–7.

SCHADEWALDT, W., 'Richard Wagner und die Griechen', *Hellas und Hesperien*, (2nd edn., Zürich and Stuttgart, 1970), 341–405.

SHAW, G. B., *The Perfect Wagnerite: A Commentary on the Niblung's Ring* (New York, 1967) (reprint of 4th edn., London, 1928).

SILK, M. S., and STERN, J. P. (eds.), *Nietzsche's* Die Geburt der Tragödie (Cambridge, 1981).

STEIN, J. M., *Richard Wagner: The Synthesis of the Arts* (Detroit, 1960).

TAYLOR, R., *Wagner, His Life, Art and Thought* (London, 1979).

WAGNER, R., *Gesammelte Schriften und Dichtungen* (12 vols., Leipzig, 1871–1911; repr. Hildesheim, 1976).

—— *Skizzen und Entwürfe zur Ring-Dichtung*, ed. O. Strobel (Munich, 1930).

—— *Mein Leben* (Munich, 1963; Mainz, 1983).

—— *Oper und Drama*, ed. K. Kropfinger (Stuttgart, 1984).

WESTERNHAGEN, C. VON, *Wagner* (Zurich, 1968) (English trans. 1979).

ZUCKERMAN, E., 'Nietzsche and Music: "The Birth of Tragedy" and "Nietzsche contra Wagner" ', *Symposium*, 28 (1974), 17–32.

3. Brecht, 'Epic' Theatre

BENJAMIN, W., 'Was ist das epische Theater?' *Akzente*, 1 (1954), 263–70.

—— *Versuch über Brecht* (Frankfurt-on-Main, 1966).

BRANSCOMBE, P., 'Brecht, Weill and Mahagonny', *Musical Times* (Aug. 1961), 483–6.

BRECHT, B., *Gesammelte Werke* (Werkausgabe Edition Suhrkamp, 20 vols.; Frankfurt-on-Main, 1967).

—— *Größe kommentierte Berliner und Frankfurter Ausgabe* (30 vols.; Berlin and Frankfurt-on-Main, 1988 ff.).

DIETRICH, M., 'Episches Theater? Beitrag zur Dramaturgie des 20. Jahrhunderts', *Maske und Kothurn*, 2 (1956), 97–124 and 301–34.

DÜMLING, A., '*Laßt euch nicht verführen': Brecht und die Musik* (Munich, 1985).

EISLER, H., *Materialen zu einer Dialektik der Musik* (Leipzig, 1976).

ESSLIN, M., *Brecht: A Choice of Evils* (London, 1959).

EWEN, F., *Bertolt Brecht: His Life, his Art and his Times* (New York, 1967). (In German: *Bertolt Brecht: Sein Leben, sein Werk, seine Zeit* (Hamburg and Düsseldorf, 1970)).

FUEGI, J., *Chaos according to Plan* (Cambridge, 1987).

GRAY, R., *Brecht the Dramatist* (Cambridge, 1976).

GRIMM, R., *Bertolt Brecht und die Weltliteratur* (Nuremberg, 1961).

HINCK, W., *Die Dramaturgie des späten Brecht* (5th edn., Göttingen, 1971).

HINDERER, W., (ed.), *Brechts Dramen: Neue Interpretationen* (Stuttgart, 1984).

KESTING, M., 'Wagner/Meyerhold/Brecht oder die Erfindung des "epischen Theaters" ' *Brecht-Jahrbuch* (1977), 111–30.

—— *Das epische Theater* (7th edn., Stuttgart, 1978).

LUCCHESI, J., and SHULL, R., *Musik bei Brecht* (Frankfurt-on-Main, 1988).

MAYER, H., *Bertolt Brecht und die Tradition* (Pfullingen, 1961).

MITTENZWEI, J., 'Brechts Kampf gegen die kulinarische Musik', *Das Musikalische in der Literatur* (Halle, 1962).

MÜLLER-SEIDEL, W., 'Episches im Theater der deutschen Klassik', *Jahrbuch der deutschen Schillergesellschaft*, 20 (1976), 338–86.

NADAR, T. R., *The Music of Kurt Weill, Hanns Eisler and Paul Dessau in the Dramatic Works of Bertolt Brecht*, diss., 1974 (Ann Arbor, Mich., 1980).

NÄGELE, R., 'Zur Struktur von Brechts "Leben des Galilei" ', *Deutschunterricht*, 23 (1971), 86–99.

POHL, R., *Strukturelemente und Entwicklung von Pathosformen in der Dramensprache Bertold* [sic] *Brechts* (Bonn, 1969).

REXROTH, D., 'Paul Hindemith und Brechts "Lehrstück" ', *Hindemith Jahrbuch*, 12 (1983), 41–52.

RITTER, H. M., *Das gestische Prinzip bei Bertolt Brecht* (Cologne, 1986).

ROBERTS, D., 'Brecht and the Idea of a Scientific Theatre', *Brecht-Jahrbuch*, 13 (1984), 41–60.

SCHMIDT, D., *Baal und der junge Brecht* (Stuttgart, 1966).

—— *Baal: Drei Fassungen* (Frankfurt-on-Main, 1966).

—— *Baal: Der böse Baal der asoziale* (Frankfurt-on-Main, 1968).

SCHÖNE, A., 'Bertolt Brechts Theatertheorie und dramatische Dichtung', *Euphorion*, 52 (1958), 272–96.

SCHULZ, G., *Die Schillerbearbeitungen Bertolt Brechts* (Tübingen, 1972).

SCHUMACHER, E., *Bertolt Brecht: Die dramatischen Versuche 1918–1933* (Berlin, 1955; rev. edn., 1977).

SELIGER, H., *Das Amerikabild Bertolt Brechts* (Bonn, 1974).

SÖRING, J., 'Wagner und Brecht: Zur Bestimmung des Musiktheaters', *Richard Wagner 1883–1983*, ed. U. Müller (Stuttgart, 1984), 451–73.

SPEIRS, R., *Brecht's Early Plays* (London, 1982).

TABBERT-JONES, G., *Die Funktion der liedhaften Einlage in den frühen Stücken Brechts* (Frankfurt-on-Main, 1984).

VOIGTS, M., *Brechts Theaterkonzeptionen* (Munich, 1977).

WAGNER, P., 'Bertolt Brechts "Die Heilige Johanna der Schlachthöfe" ', *Jahrbuch der deutschen Schillergesellschaft*, 12 (1968), 493–519.

—— 'Zu Bertolt Brechts Theorie des epischen Theaters', *Zeitschrift für deutsche Philologie*, 89 (1970), 601–15.

WEILL, K., *Ausgewählte Schriften*, ed. D. Drew (Frankfurt-on-Main, 1975).

WEISSTEIN, U., 'From the Dramatic Novel to the Epic Theatre: A Study of the Contemporary Background of Brecht's Theory and Practice', *Germanic Review*, 38 (1963), 257–71.

—— 'Brecht und das Musiktheater: Die epische Oper als Ausdruck des europäischen Avantgardismus', *Kontroversen, alte und neue*, Akten des VII. Internationalen Germanisten-Kongresses (Göttingen, 1985), ix. 72–85.

WHITE, J. J., 'A Note on Brecht and Behaviourism', *Forum for Modern Language Studies*, 7 (1971), 249–58.

WITZKE, G., *Das epische Theater Wedekinds und Brechts*, diss., (Tübingen, 1972).

Index